FUNDAMENTALS OF
ENGLISH GRAMMAR

Third Edition

WORKBOOK

Volume B

 Longman

Betty Schrampfer Azar
with Stacy Hagen

Fundamentals of English Grammar, Third Edition
Workbook, Volume B

Azar Associates
Shelley Hartle, Editor
Susan Van Etten, Manager

Pearson Education, 10 Bank Street, White Plains, NY 10606

Vice president of instructional design: Allen Ascher
Editorial manager: Pam Fishman
Project manager: Margo Grant
Development editor: Janet Johnston
Vice president, director of design and production: Rhea Banker
Director of electronic production: Aliza Greenblatt
Executive managing editor: Linda Moser
Production manager: Ray Keating
Production editor: Robert Ruvo
Director of manufacturing: Patrice Fraccio
Senior manufacturing buyer: Edie Pullman
Cover design: Monika Popowitz
Illustrations: Don Martinetti
Text composition: Carlisle Communications, Ltd.
Text font: 10.5/12 Plantin

ISBN: 0-13-013653-0

Printed in the United States of America
5 6 7 8 9–CRK–10 09 08 07

Contents

PRACTICES

Chapter 10   THE PASSIVE

PRACTICES

Chapter 11   COUNT/NONCOUNT NOUNS AND ARTICLES

Chapter 12 ADJECTIVE CLAUSES

PRACTICES

Chapter 13 GERUNDS AND INFINITIVES

Chapter 14 NOUN CLAUSES

Appendix 1 PHRASAL VERBS

Preface

This ESL/EFL *Workbook* is a place for students to explore and practice English grammar on their own. It is a place where they can test and fine-tune their understandings of English structures and improve their abilities to use English meaningfully and correctly.

It is keyed to the explanatory grammar charts found in *Fundamentals of English Grammar, Third Edition,* a classroom teaching text for students of English as a second or foreign language, as well as in the accompanying *Chartbook,* a reference grammar with no exercises.

The *Workbook* is designed not only for students who desire the opportunity for independent study of English grammar but also as a resource for teachers who need exercise material for additional classwork, homework, testing, or individualized instruction.

The answers to ALL of the practices are given in the back of the book in an *Answer Key.* The *Answer Key* is on perforated pages so that it can be detached to construct a separate booklet. If teachers desire to use the *Workbook* as a classroom teaching text, the *Answer Key* can be removed at the beginning of the term.

A note on changes from the previous edition: The *Workbook* that accompanied the previous edition of *Fundamentals of English Grammar* had both self-study (answers given) and guided study (no answers given) practices. This *Workbook* has only self-study practices. The guided study practices that involved communicative, interactive, and/or task-based activities are now in the main teaching text, and other guided study practices from the previous edition have been adapted to a self-study format in this edition. A good portion of the material in this edition of the *FEG Workbook* is newly created.

CHAPTER *8*
Connecting Ideas

◇ **PRACTICE 1. Connecting ideas with AND. (Chart 8-1)**

Directions: Underline the words that are connected with **and**. Label these words as nouns, verbs, or adjectives.

           noun + noun +   noun

1. The farmer has a <u>cow</u>, a <u>goat</u>, and a black <u>horse</u>.

       adjective + adjective

2. Danny is a <u>bright</u> and <u>happy</u> child.

   verb   *+ verb*

3. I <u>picked</u> up the telephone and <u>dialed</u> Steve's number.

4. The cook washed the vegetables and put them in boiling water.

5. My feet were cold and wet.

6. Anita is responsible, considerate, and trustworthy.

7. The three largest land animals are the elephant, the rhinoceros, and the hippopotamus.

8. A hippopotamus rests in water during the day and feeds on land at night.

◇ **PRACTICE 2. Punctuating items connected with AND. (Chart 8-1)**

Directions: Add commas where necessary.

1. I opened the door and walked into the room.   *(no commas)*

2. I opened the door, walked into the room, and sat down at my desk.

3. Their flag is green and black.

4. Their flag is green black and yellow.

5. Tom ate a sandwich and drank a glass of juice.

6. Tom made a sandwich poured a glass of juice and sat down to eat his lunch.

7. Ms. Parker is intelligent friendly and kind.

8. Mr. Parker is grouchy and unhappy.

9. Did you bring copies of the annual report for Sue Dan Joe and Mary?

10. I always read the newspaper and watch the TV news in the morning.

11. Can you watch television listen to the radio and read the newspaper at the same time?

12. Doctors save lives and relieve suffering.

13. Doctors save lives relieve suffering and cure diseases.

14. The restaurant served a five-course dinner: soup fish entree salad and dessert.

15. I had fish and a salad for dinner last night.

16. An invitation should include your name address the date the time the purpose of the party and any special activities such as swimming or dancing.

◇ **PRACTICE 3. Punctuating sentences. (Chart 8-1)**

Directions: Each of these sentences contains two independent clauses. Find the subject (**s**) and verb (**v**) of each clause. Add a comma or a period. Capitalize as necessary.

1. Birds fly, and fish swim.
   (s over Birds, v over fly, s over fish, v over swim)

2. Birds fly. F̸ish swim.
   (s over Birds, v over fly, s over fish, v over swim)

3. Dogs bark lions roar.

4. Dogs bark and lions roar.

5. A week has seven days a year has 365 days.

6. A week has seven days and a year has 365 days.

7. Ahmed raised his hand and the teacher pointed at him.

8. Ahmed raised his hand the teacher pointed at him.

◇ PRACTICE 4. Punctuating sentences. (Chart 8-1)
Directions: Write "**C**" if the punctuation is correct. Write "**I**" if it is incorrect.

1. ___I___ Amy jogged along the road I rode my bicycle.

2. ___C___ Amy stopped after 20 minutes. I continued on for an hour.

3. _____ Trained dogs can lie down and perform other tricks on command.

4. _____ My mother trained our dog to get the newspaper, my father trained it to bark at strangers.

5. _____ The river rose, it flooded the towns in the valley.

6. _____ The river and streams rose. They flooded the towns and farms in the valley.

7. _____ Astrology is the study of the planets and their effect on our lives.

8. _____ Sharon reads her horoscope every day. She believes her life is shaped by the positions of the stars and planets.

9. _____ Sharon's children don't believe in astrology, they dismiss the information she gives them.

◇ PRACTICE 5. Using AND, BUT, and OR. (Chart 8-2)
Directions: Add commas where appropriate.

1. I talked to Amy for a long time**,** but she didn't listen.

2. I talked to Tom for a long time and asked him many questions. *(no change)*

3. Please call Jane or Ted.

4. Please call Jane and Ted.

5. Please call Jane Ted or Anna.

6. Please call Jane Ted and Anna.

7. I waved at my friend but she didn't see me.

8. I waved at my friend and she waved back.

9. I waved at my friend and smiled at her.

10. Was the test hard or easy?

11. My test was short and easy but Ali's test was hard.

◇ **PRACTICE 6. Using AND, BUT, OR, and SO. (Charts 8-1 → 8-3)**
Directions: Choose the correct completion.

1. I was tired, _____ I went to bed.
   A. but   B. or   C. so

2. I sat down on the sofa _____ opened the newspaper.
   A. but   B. and   C. so

3. The students were on time, _____ the teacher was late.
   A. but   B. or   C. so

4. I would like one pet. I'd like to have a dog _____ a cat.
   A. but   B. and   C. or

5. Our children are happy _____ healthy.
   A. but   B. and   C. or

6. I wanted a cup of tea, _____ I heated some water.
   A. but   B. and   C. so

7. The phone rang, _____ I didn't answer it.
   A. but   B. and   C. so

8. You can have an apple _____ an orange. Choose one.
   A. but   B. and   C. or

◇ **PRACTICE 7. Using AND, BUT, OR, and SO. (Charts 8-1 → 8-3)**
Directions: Add commas where appropriate. Some sentences need no commas.

1. I washed and dried the dishes. *(no change)*

2. I washed the dishes**,** and my son dried them.

3. I called their house but no one answered the phone.

4. He offered me an apple or a peach.

5. I bought some apples peaches and bananas.

6. I was hungry so I ate an apple.

7. Carlos was hungry and ate two apples.

8. My sister is generous and kind-hearted.

9. My daughter is affectionate shy independent and smart.

10. It started to rain so we went inside and watched television.

◇ **PRACTICE 8. Using AND, BUT, OR, and SO. (Chart 8-1 → 8-3)**
Directions: Add commas where appropriate. Some sentences need no commas.

1. Gina wants a job as an air traffic controller. Every air traffic controller worldwide uses English so it is important for Gina to become fluent in the language.

2. Gina has decided to take some intensive English courses at a private language institute but she isn't sure which one to attend. There are many schools available and they offer many different kinds of classes.

3. Gina has also heard of air traffic control schools that include English as part of their coursework but she needs to have a fairly high level of English to attend.

4. Gina needs to decide soon or the classes will be full. She's planning to visit her top three choices this summer and decide on the best one for her.

◇ **PRACTICE 9. Using AND, BUT, OR, and SO. (Charts 8-1 → 8-3)**
Directions: Add periods and capital letters as necessary.

1. There are over 100,000 kinds of flies they live throughout the world.
   → *There are over 100,000 kinds of flies.* **They live throughout the world.**

2. I like to get mail from my friends and family mail is important to me.

3. We are all connected by our humanity we need to help each other we can all live in peace.

4. There was a bad flood in Hong Kong the streets became raging streams luckily no one died in the flood.

5. People have used needles since prehistoric times the first buttons appeared almost two thousand years ago zippers are a relatively recent invention the zipper was invented in 1890.

NEEDLE   BUTTONS   ZIPPER

◇ **PRACTICE 10. Using AND, BUT, OR, and SO. (Charts 8-1 → 8-3)**
Directions: Add periods, commas, and capital letters as appropriate. Don't change any of the words or the order of the words.

1. James has a cold. H̸e needs to rest and drink plenty of fluids, so he should go to bed and drink water, fruit juices, or soda pop. H̸e needs to sleep a lot, so he shouldn't drink fluids with caffeine, such as tea or coffee.

2. My friend and I were tired so we went home early we wanted to stay until the end of the game but it got too late for us both of us had to get up early in the morning and go to our jobs.

3. The normal pulse for an adult is between 60 and 80 beats per minute but exercise nervousness excitement and a fever will all make a pulse beat faster the normal pulse for a child is around 80 to 90.

4. Many famous explorers throughout history set out on their hazardous journeys in search of gold silver jewels or other treasures but some explorers wanted only to discover information about their world.

5. Edward Fox was a park ranger for thirty-five years during that time, he was hit by lightning eight times the lightning never killed him but it severely burned his skin and damaged his hearing.

6. The Indian Ocean is bordered on four sides by the continents of Africa Asia Australia and Antarctica some of the important ports are Aden Bombay Calcutta and Rangoon.

7. The Indian Ocean has many fish and shellfish but it has less commercial fishing than the Atlantic or the Pacific the climate of the Indian Ocean is tropical so fish spoil quickly out of the water it is difficult and expensive for commercial fishing boats to keep fish fresh.

◇ **PRACTICE 11. Using auxiliary verbs after BUT and AND. (Chart 8-4)**
Directions: Practice using auxiliary verbs after ***but*** and ***and***.

1. Dan didn't study for the test, but Amy _____*did*_____ .

2. Alice doesn't come to class every day, but Julie _____ .

3. Jack went to the movie last night, but I _____ .

4. I don't live in the dorm, but Rob and Jim _____.

5. Rob lives in the dorm, and Jim _____ too.

6. I don't live in the dorm, and Carol _____ either.

7. My roommate was at home last night, but I _____.

8. Mr. Wong isn't here today, but Miss Choki _____.

9. Ted isn't here today, and Linda _____ either.

10. The teacher is listening to the tape, and the students _____ too.

11. Susan won't be at the meeting tonight, but I _____.

12. Susan isn't going to go to the meeting tonight, but I _____.

13. I'll be there, but she _____.

14. I'll be there, and Mike _____ too.

15. I can speak French, and my wife _____ too.

16. I haven't finished my work yet, but Erica _____.

17. I didn't finish my work last night, but Erica _____.

18. Jane would like a cup of coffee, and I _____ too.

19. I like rock music, and my roommate _____ too.

20. My son enjoys monster movies, but I _____.

21. Paul can't speak Spanish, and Larry _____ either.

22. My neighbor walks to work every morning, but I _____.

23. I am exhausted from the long trip, and my mother _____ too.

24. I don't have a dimple in my chin, but my brother _____.

25. I visited the museum yesterday, and my friend _____ too.

26. Water isn't solid, but ice _____.

27. Clouds aren't solid, and steam _____ either.

◇ PRACTICE 12. Auxiliary verbs after BUT and AND. (Chart 8-4)
Directions: Complete the sentences by using the word in *italics* and an appropriate auxiliary.

1. *Tom*   Jack has a mustache, and so _____does Tom_____.

Jack has a mustache, and _____Tom does_____ too.

2. *Brian*   Alex doesn't have a mustache, and neither _____.

Alex doesn't have a mustache, and _____ either.

3. *I*   Mary was at home last night, and so _____.

Mary was at home last night, and _____ too.

4. *Oregon*   California is on the West Coast, and so _____ .

California is on the West Coast, and _____ too.

5. *Jean*   I went to a movie last night, and so _____ .

I went to a movie last night, and _____ too.

6. *Jason*   I didn't study last night, and neither _____ .

I didn't study last night, and _____ either.

7. *Rick*   Jim can't speak Arabic, and neither _____ .

Jim can't speak Arabic, and _____ either.

8. *Laura*   I like to go to science fiction movies, and so _____ .

I like to go to science fiction movies, and _____ too.

9. *Alice*   I don't like horror movies, and neither _____ .

I don't like horror movies, and _____ either.

10. *porpoises*   Whales are mammals, and so _____ .

Whales are mammals, and _____ too.

BLUE WHALE

PORPOISE

11. *I*   Karen hasn't seen that movie yet, and neither _____ .

Karen hasn't seen that movie yet, and _____ either.

12. *my brother*   I have a car, and so _____ .

I have a car, and _____ too.

13. *Erin*   Rob won't join us for lunch, and neither _____ .

Rob won't join us for lunch, and _____ either.

◇ PRACTICE 13. Using TOO, SO, EITHER, or NEITHER after AND. (Chart 8-5)
Directions: Complete the sentences.

PART I. Complete the sentences with **an auxiliary** + TOO or EITHER.

1. I **can't cook**, and my roommate _____can't either_____ .

2. I **like** movies, and my wife _____ .

3. I **don't like** salty food, and my wife _____ .

4. Sugar **is** sweet, and honey _____ .

5. Rosa Gomez **wasn't** in class yesterday, and Mr. Nazari _____ .

6. Andy **didn't know** the answer to the question, and Tina _____ .

7. I **couldn't understand** the substitute teacher, and Yoko _____ .

8. Everyone in the room **laughed** at my foolish mistake, and I _____ .

9. Fish **can't walk**, and snakes _____ .

10. I **like** to fix things around the house, and Ted _____ .

11. I'**d rather stay** home this evening, and my husband _____ .

PART II. Complete the sentences with SO or NEITHER + **an auxiliary**.

12. Pasta **is** a famous Italian dish, and _____so is_____ pizza.

13. Anteaters **don't have** teeth, and _____neither do_____ most birds.

14. I **didn't go** to the bank, and _____ my husband.

15. Turtles **are** reptiles, and _____ snakes.

16. My sister **has** dark hair, and _____ I.

17. I'**m studying** English, and _____ Mr. Chu.

18. I'**m not** a native speaker of English, and _____ Mr. Chu.

19. Wood **burns,** and _____ paper.

20. Mountain climbing **is** dangerous, and _____ auto racing.

21. I'**ve never seen** a monkey in the wild, and _____ my children.

22. When we heard the hurricane warning, I **nailed** boards over my windows, and

    _____ all of my neighbors.

23. My brother and I studied chemistry together. I **didn't pass** the course, and

    _____ he.

◇ **PRACTICE 14. Adverb clauses with BECAUSE. (Chart 8-6)**
   Directions: Underline the adverb clauses. Find the subject (**S**) and verb (**V**) of each adverb clause.

1. Mr. Tanaka was late for work because [he] [missed] the bus.
                                              S   V

2. I closed the door because the room was cold.

3. Because I lost my umbrella, I got wet on the way home.

4. Joe didn't bring his book to class because he couldn't find it.

5. The teacher couldn't hear the question because the class was so noisy.

6. Because the ice cream was beginning to melt, I put it back in the freezer.

◇ **PRACTICE 15. Adverb clauses with BECAUSE. (Chart 8-6)**
   Directions: Add periods, commas, and capital letters as necessary.

1. I opened the window because the room was hot. We felt more comfortable then.

2. Because his coffee was cold, Jack didn't finish it. He left it on the table and walked away.

3. Because the weather was bad we canceled our trip into the city we stayed home and watched TV.

4. Debbie is a cheerleader she woke up in the morning with a sore throat because she had cheered loudly at the basketball game.

5. Francisco is an intelligent and ambitious young man because he hopes to get a good job later in life he is working hard to get a good education now.

◇ **PRACTICE 16. Adverb clauses with BECAUSE. (Chart 8-6)**
   Directions: Read each pair of phrases and circle the one that gives the reason (explains "why"). Then check the correct sentence.

1. *go on a diet*
   (lose weight)

   ✔ Eric went on a diet because he wanted to lose weight.

   ____ Because Eric went on a diet, he wanted to lose weight.

2. *didn't have money*
   couldn't buy food

   ____ The family couldn't buy food because they didn't have money.

   ____ Because the family couldn't buy food, they didn't have money.

3. *have several children*
   be very busy

   ____ Because our neighbors are very busy, they have several children.

   ____ Our neighbors are very busy because they have several children.

4. *go to bed*
   be tired

   ____ I am tired because I am going to bed.

   ____ Because I am tired, I am going to bed.

5. *be in great shape*
   exercise every day

   ____ Because Susan exercises every day, she is in great shape.

   ____ Susan exercises every day because she is in great shape.

6. *have a high fever*
   go to the doctor

   ____ Because Jennifer has a high fever, she is going to the doctor.

   ____ Jennifer has a high fever because she is going to the doctor.

◇ **PRACTICE 17. Adverb clauses with BECAUSE. (Chart 8-6)**

Directions: Complete the sentences with *so* or *because*. Add commas where appropriate. Capitalize as necessary.

1. a. He was hungry , so he ate a sandwich.

   b. Because he was hungry, he ate a sandwich.

   c. He ate a sandwich because he was hungry.

2. a. _____ my sister was tired she went to bed.

   b. My sister went to bed _____ she was tired.

   c. My sister was tired _____ she went to bed.

3. a. _____ human beings have opposable thumbs they can easily pick

   things up and hold them.

   b. Human beings have opposable thumbs _____ they can easily pick

   things up and hold them.

   c. Human beings can easily pick things up and hold them _____ they

   have opposable thumbs.

4. a. Schoolchildren can usually identify Italy easily on a world map _____ it is shaped like a boot.

   b. _____ Italy has the distinctive shape of a boot schoolchildren can usually identify it easily.

   c. Italy has the distinctive shape of a boot _____ schoolchildren can usually identify it easily on a map.

◇ **PRACTICE 18. Adverb clauses with EVEN THOUGH and ALTHOUGH. (Chart 8-6)**

Directions: Complete each sentence with the correct form of the verb in *italics*. Some verbs will be negative.

1. Even though I *(like)* _____like_____ fish, I don't eat it much.

2. Even though I *(like)* _____don't like_____ vegetables, I eat them every day.

3. Although my hairdresser *(be)* _____ expensive, I go to her once a week.

4. Even though the basketball game was over, the fans *(stay)* _____ in their seats cheering.

5. Although my clothes were wet from the rain, I *(change)* _____ them.

6. Even though Po studied for weeks, he *(pass)* _____ his exams.

7. Even though the soup was salty, everyone *(eat)* _____ it.

8. Although the roads *(be)* _____ icy, no one got in an accident.

◇ **PRACTICE 19. Using BECAUSE and EVEN THOUGH.** (Charts 8-6 and 8-7)
Directions: Choose the correct completion.

1. Even though I was hungry, I _____ a lot at dinner.
   A. ate   (B.) didn't eat

2. Because I was hungry, I _____ a lot at dinner.
   A. ate   B. didn't eat

3. Because I was cold, I _____ my coat.
   A. put on   B. didn't put on

4. Even though I was cold, I _____ my coat.
   A. put on   B. didn't put on

5. Even though Mike _____ sleepy, he stayed up to watch the end of the game on TV.
   A. was   B. wasn't

6. Because Linda _____ sleepy, she went to bed.
   A. was   B. wasn't

7. Because Kate ran too slowly, she _____ the race.
   A. won   B. didn't win

8. Even though Jessica ran fast, she _____ the race.
   A. won   B. didn't win

9. I _____ the test for my driver's license because I wasn't prepared.
   A. failed   B. didn't fail

10. I went to my daughter's school play because she _____ me to be there.
    A. wanted   B. didn't want

11. I bought a new suit for the business trip even though I _____ it.
    A. could afford   B. couldn't afford

12. Even though I had a broken leg, I _____ to the conference in New York.
    A. went   B. didn't go

◇ **PRACTICE 20. Adverb clauses with BECAUSE. (Chart 8-6)**
   Directions: Complete the sentences by using *even though* or *because*.

1. Yuko went to a dentist _____because_____ she had a toothache.

2. Colette didn't go to a dentist _____ she had a toothache.

3. Jennifer went to a dentist _____ she didn't have a toothache. She just wanted a checkup.

4. _____ Dan is fairly tall, he can't reach the ceiling.

5. _____ Matt is very tall, he can reach the ceiling.

6. _____ Tim isn't as tall as Matt, he can't reach the ceiling.

7. _____ Nick isn't tall, he can reach the ceiling by standing on a chair.

DAN   MATT   TIM   NICK

8. Louie didn't iron his shirt _____ it was wrinkled.

9. Eric ironed his shirt _____ it was wrinkled.

10. I would like to raise tropical fish _____ it's difficult to maintain a fish tank in good condition.

11. The baby shoved the pills into his mouth _____ they looked like candy. _____ he ingested several pills, he didn't get sick. Today many pill bottles have child-proof caps _____ children may think pills are candy and poison themselves.

◇ **PRACTICE 21. Using EVEN THOUGH/ALTHOUGH and BECAUSE.** (Charts 8-6 and 8-7)
Directions: Choose the best completion.

Example: I gave him the money because _____.
      A. I didn't have any
      B. he had a lot of money
      Ⓒ I owed it to him

1. Although _____, the hungry man ate every bit of it.
      A. an apple is both nutritious and delicious
      B. the cheese tasted good to him
      C. the bread was old and stale

2. The nurse didn't bring Mr. Hill a glass of water even though _____.
      A. she was very busy
      B. she forgot
      C. he asked her three times

3. When she heard the loud crash, Marge ran outside in the snow although _____.
      A. her mother ran out with her
      B. she wasn't wearing any shoes
      C. she ran as fast as she could

4. Even though his shoes were wet and muddy, Brian _____.
      A. took them off at the front door
      B. walked right into the house and across the carpet
      C. wore wool socks

5. Robert ate dinner with us at our home last night. Although _____, he left right after dinner.
   A. he washed the dishes
   B. there was a good movie at the local theater
   C. I expected him to stay and help with the dishes

6. Alex boarded the bus in front of his hotel. He was on his way to the art museum. Because he _____, he asked the bus driver to tell him where to get off.
   A. was late for work and didn't want his boss to get mad
   B. was carrying a heavy suitcase
   C. was a tourist and didn't know the city streets very well

7. Although _____, Eric got on the plane.
   A. he is married
   B. he is afraid of flying
   C. the flight attendant welcomed him aboard

8. Foxes can use their noses to find their dinners because _____.
   A. they have a keen sense of smell
   B. mice and other small rodents move very quickly
   C. they have keen vision

9. Cats can't see red even though _____.
   A. it's a bright color
   B. many animals are color-blind
   C. mice aren't red

10. When I attended my first business conference out of town, I felt very uncomfortable during the social events because _____.
   A. we were all having a good time
   B. I didn't know anyone there
   C. I am very knowledgeable in my field

11. Although _____, Sue drives to work every day in the middle of rush hour.
   A. her car is in good condition
   B. she isn't in a hurry
   C. traffic is always heavy

12. Everyone listened carefully to what the speaker was saying even though _____.
   A. they had printed copies of the speech in their hands
   B. she spoke loudly and clearly
   C. the speech was very interesting

13. Talil works in the city, but once a month he visits his mother, who lives in the country. He must rent a car for these trips because _____.
   A. he rides the local bus
   B. his mother doesn't drive
   C. he doesn't own a car

◇ PRACTICE 22. Error analysis. (Chapter 8)
Directions: Correct the sentences.

1. I don't drink coffee, and my roommate ~~isn't~~ doesn't either.

2. The flight was overbooked, I had to fly on another airline.

3. Many people use computers for e-mail the Internet and word processing.

4. The room was stuffy and hot but I didn't close the window.

5. The baby woke up crying. Because her diaper was wet.

6. Even my father works two jobs, he always has time to play soccer or baseball on weekends with his family.

7. I saw a bad accident and my sister too.

8. Oscar always pays his bills on time but his brother wasn't.

9. Because my mother is afraid of heights, I took her up to the observation deck at the top of the building.

10. Janey doesn't like to get up early and either Joe.

11. Although it was raining quite hard, but we decided to go for a bike ride.

12. My mother and my father. They immigrated to this country 30 years ago.

13. Even though Maya is very intelligent, her parents want to put her in an advanced program at school.

CHAPTER 9
Comparisons

◇ **PRACTICE 1. AS . . . AS. (Chart 9-1)**

Directions: Make comparisons using **as . . . as**.

1. Rita is very busy. Jason is very busy.

   → Rita is ____(just) as busy as Jason (is)_____ .

2. Rita is not very busy at all. Jason is very, very busy.

   → Rita isn't ____(nearly) as busy as Jason (is)_____ .

3. I was tired. Susan was very tired.

   → I was _____ .

4. Adam wasn't tired at all. Susan was very tired.

   → Adam wasn't _____ .

5. My apartment has two rooms. Po's apartment has two rooms.

   → My apartment is _____ .

6. My apartment has two rooms. Anna's apartment has six rooms.

   → My apartment is not _____ .

◇ **PRACTICE 2. AS . . . AS. (Chart 9-1)**

Directions: Using the given information and the words in parentheses, complete the comparisons using **as . . . as**. Use **not** with the verbs as necessary.

1. Dogs make more noise than cats do. *(be noisy)*

   → Cats ____aren't as noisy as____ dogs.

2. Both Anne and her sister Amanda are lazy. *(be lazy)*

   → Anne ____is as lazy as_____ her sister Amanda.

3. Adults have more strength than children. *(be strong)*

   → Children _____ adults.

4. Tom and Jerry are the same height. *(be tall)*

   → Tom _____ Jerry.

5. It's more comfortable to live at home than in a dormitory. *(be comfortable)*

   → Living in a dormitory _____ living at home.

6. A basketball is bigger than a soccer ball. *(be big)*

   → A soccer ball _____

   a basketball.

SOCCER BALL   BASKETBALL

7. The bride and the groom were equally

   nervous before the wedding. *(be nervous)*

   → The bride _____ the groom.

8. The air in a big city is more polluted than the air in the countryside. *(be fresh and clean)*

   → The air in a big city _____ the air in the countryside.

9. My sister wants to be a successful businesswoman. I don't have any plans for my future.

   (be ambitious)

   → I _____ my sister.

10. Some school subjects interest me, and others don't. *(be interesting)*

   → Some school subjects _____ others.

◇ PRACTICE 3. AS . . . AS. (Chart 9-1)

   Directions: Complete the sentences with one of the following:
   • just as . . . as
   • almost as . . . as/not quite as . . . as
   • not nearly as . . . as

   A   B   C   D

PART I.

1. Building B is ___not nearly as___ high as Building D.

2. Building A is _____ high as Building B.

3. Building C is _____ high as Building D.

4. Building A is _____ high as Building C.

PART II. Meeting time: 9:00 A.M. Compare the arrival times.

Arrival times:

David	9:01 A.M.
Julia	9:14 A.M.
Laura	9:15 A.M.
Paul	9:15 A.M.
James	9:25 A.M.

5. Paul was ___just as___ late as Laura.

6. David was _____ late as James.

7. Julia was _____ late as Laura and Paul.

8. Julia was _____ late as James.

PART III. Compare world temperatures.

Bangkok	92°F / 33°C
Cairo	85°F / 30°C
Madrid	90°F / 32°C
Moscow	68°F / 20°C
Tokyo	85°F / 30°C

9. Tokyo is _____ hot as Cairo.

10. Moscow is _____ hot as Bangkok.

11. Madrid is _____ hot as Bangkok.

PART IV. Compare world temperatures today and yesterday.

	Yesterday	*Today*
Bangkok	95°F / 35°C	92°F / 33°C
Cairo	95°F / 35°C	85°F / 30°C
Madrid	90°F / 32°C	90°F / 32°C
Moscow	70°F / 21°C	68°F / 20°C
Tokyo	81°F / 27°C	85°F / 30°C

12. Cairo was _____ hot as Bangkok yesterday.

13. It's _____ warm in Moscow today as yesterday.

14. Madrid is _____ hot today as yesterday.

15. It was _____ hot in Tokyo yesterday as in Bangkok.

16. It's _____ hot in Bangkok today as yesterday.

◇ **PRACTICE 4. AS . . . AS. (Chart 9-1)**
Directions: Choose the best sentence completion from the list.

> A. *as bad as she said it was*   ✓E. *as much as possible*
> B. *as easy as it looks*   F. *as often as I can*
> C. *as fast as I could*   G. *as often as I used to*
> D. *as good as they looked*   H. *as soon as possible*

1. I have a lot of homework. I will finish __E__ before I go to bed.

2. I'm sorry I'm late. I drove _____ .

3. I saw some chocolates at the candy store. They looked delicious, so I bought some. They tasted just _____ .

4. When I was in college, I went to at least two movies every week. Now I'm very busy with my job and family, so I don't go to movies _____ .

5. It took Julie years of lessons to be able to play the piano well. She makes it look easy, but we all know that playing a musical instrument isn't _____ .

6. I need to finish working on this report, so go ahead and start the meeting without me. I'll be there _____ .

7. Even though I'm very busy, I'm usually just sitting at my desk all day. I need more exercise, so I try to walk to and from work _____ .

8. My friend told me the movie was terrible, but I went anyway. My friend was right. The movie was just _____ .

◇ **PRACTICE 5. AS . . . AS. (Chart 9-1)**
Directions: Write your completions in the blanks.

PART I. Complete each expression with the correct phrase.

> as a bat   as ice   as a pillow
> as a bird   as a mouse   ✓as snow
> as a bone   as a picture   as a wink
> as pie

bat

1. very white: as white _____as snow_____ .

2. very cold: as cold _____ .

3. very pretty: as pretty _____ .

4. can't see anything: as blind _____ .

5. very dry: as dry _____ .

6. very soft: as soft _____ .

7. very quick: as quick _____ .

8. very quiet: as quiet _____ .

9. very free: as free _____ .

10. very easy: as easy _____ .

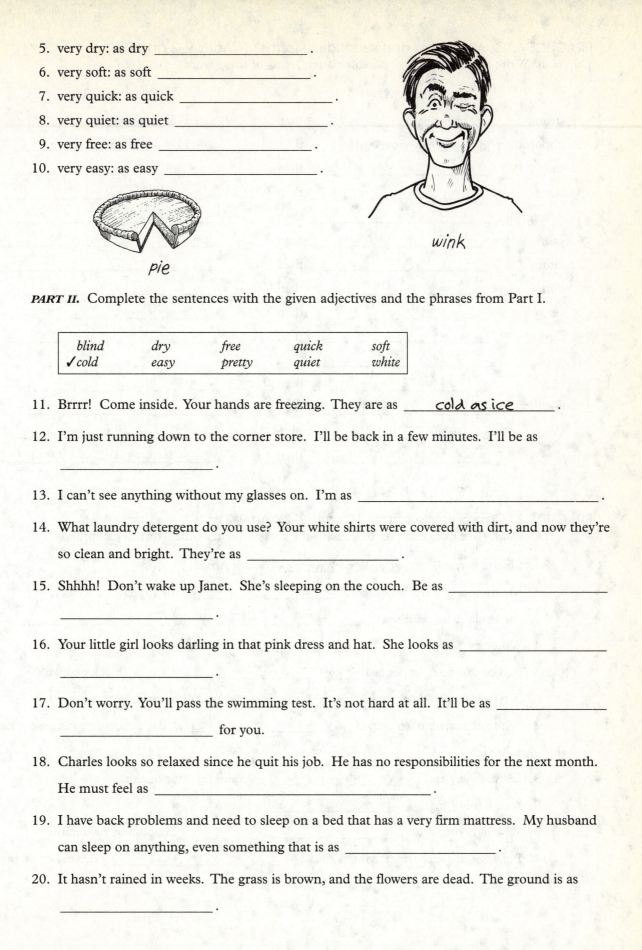

pie

wink

PART II. Complete the sentences with the given adjectives and the phrases from Part I.

blind	dry	free	quick	soft
✓cold	easy	pretty	quiet	white

11. Brrrr! Come inside. Your hands are freezing. They are as _____ cold as ice _____ .

12. I'm just running down to the corner store. I'll be back in a few minutes. I'll be as

_____ .

13. I can't see anything without my glasses on. I'm as _____ .

14. What laundry detergent do you use? Your white shirts were covered with dirt, and now they're

so clean and bright. They're as _____ .

15. Shhhh! Don't wake up Janet. She's sleeping on the couch. Be as _____

_____ .

16. Your little girl looks darling in that pink dress and hat. She looks as _____

_____ .

17. Don't worry. You'll pass the swimming test. It's not hard at all. It'll be as _____

_____ for you.

18. Charles looks so relaxed since he quit his job. He has no responsibilities for the next month.

He must feel as _____ .

19. I have back problems and need to sleep on a bed that has a very firm mattress. My husband

can sleep on anything, even something that is as _____ .

20. It hasn't rained in weeks. The grass is brown, and the flowers are dead. The ground is as

_____ .

◇ **PRACTICE 6. Comparative and superlative forms. (Charts 9-2 and 9-3)**
Directions: Write the comparative and superlative forms of these words.

	COMPARATIVE		SUPERLATIVE	
1. strong	_stronger_	than	_the strongest_	of all
2. important	_more important_	than	_the most important_	of all
3. soft	_____	than	_____	of all
4. lazy	_____	than	_____	of all
5. wonderful	_____	than	_____	of all
6. calm	_____	than	_____	of all
7. tame	_____	than	_____	of all
8. dim	_____	than	_____	of all
9. convenient	_____	than	_____	of all
10. clever	_____	than	_____	of all
11. good	_____	than	_____	of all
12. bad	_____	than	_____	of all
13. far	_____	than	_____	of all
14. slow	_____	than	_____	of all
15. slowly	_____	than	_____	of all

◇ **PRACTICE 7. Comparative forms. (Charts 9-2 and 9-3)**
Directions: Complete each sentence with the correct form of the word in parentheses.

1. Siberia is *(cold)* ____colder than____ South Africa.

2. My mother is a few years *(old)* _____ my father.

3. An airplane is *(expensive)* _____ a car.

4. Which is *(large)* _____ : Greenland or Iceland?

5. Red or cayenne pepper tastes *(hot)* _____ black pepper.

6. A typewriter is *(slow)* _____ a computer.

7. White chocolate is *(creamy)* _____ dark chocolate because it has

   more fat.

8. Is smoking *(bad)* _____ alcohol for your health?

9. A jaguar is *(fast)* _____ a lion.

10. Which is *(important)* _____ : happiness or wealth?

11. For long-distance trips, flying is *(quick)* _____ driving or taking

    a train.

12. Which is *(heavy)* _____ : a kilo of wood or a kilo of rocks?*

13. Driving in a car equipped with a seatbelt and an airbag is *(safe)* _____

driving in a car with just a seatbelt.

14. Calculus is *(difficult)* _____ arithmetic.

◇ **PRACTICE 8. Comparatives. (Charts 9-2 and 9-3)**

Directions: Complete the sentences with the correct comparative form *(more/-er)* of the given adjectives and adverbs.

careful	✓generous	soft
✓cold	lazy	softly
comfortable	pretty	slowly
friendly		

1. The average temperature in Moscow is ___colder___ than the average

temperature in Hong Kong.

2. Your father seems to give you plenty of money for living expenses. He is ___more___

___generous___ than mine.

3. Children seem to be able to appear out of nowhere. When I'm near a school, I always drive

_____ than I have to.

4. In my experience, old shoes are usually a lot _____ than

new shoes.

5. People in villages often seem to enjoy talking to strangers. They seem to be _____

_____ than people in large cities.

6. Babies don't like loud noises. Most people speak _____ than usual when

they're talking to a baby.

7. I like to sit on pillows. They are a lot _____ than a hardwood seat.

8. Sandy, when you drive to the airport today, you have to be _____

than you were the last time you went. You almost had an accident because you weren't paying

attention to your driving.

9. I like to grow flowers in my garden. They're a lot _____ than bushes.

10. I don't like to work hard, but my sister does. I'm a lot _____ than my sister.

_____

*This is a trick question. Answer: They weigh the same.

◇ PRACTICE 9. Comparatives and superlatives. (Charts 9-2 and 9-3)
Directions: Complete the sentences with **better, the best, worse,** or **the worst.**

1. I just finished a terrible book. It's _____the worst_____ book I've ever read.

2. The weather was bad yesterday, but it's terrible today. The weather is _____worse_____
   today than it was yesterday.

3. This cake is really good. It's _____ cake I've ever eaten.

4. My grades this term are great. They're much _____ than last term.

5. Being separated from my family in time of war is one of _____
   experiences I can imagine.

6. I broke my nose in a football game yesterday. Today it's very painful. For some reason, the
   pain is _____ today than it was yesterday.

7. The fire spread and burned down an entire city block. It was _____ fire
   we've ever had in our town.

8. I think my cold is almost over. I feel a lot _____ than I did yesterday.
   I can finally breathe again.

◇ PRACTICE 10. FARTHER and FURTHER. (Chart 9-3)
Directions: Choose the correct answer(s). Both answers may be correct.

1. The planet Earth is _____ from the sun than the planet Mercury is.
   (A.) farther   (B.) further

2. I have no _____ need of this equipment. I'm going to sell it.
   A. farther   (B.) further

3. I'm tired. I walked _____ than I should have.
   A. farther   B. further

4. A: Tell us more.
   B: I have no _____ comment.
      A. farther   B. further

5. I'll be available by phone if you have any _____ questions.
      A. farther   B. further

6. A: I heard that you and Tom are engaged to be married.
   B: Nothing could be _____ from the truth!
      A. farther   B. further

◇ PRACTICE 11. Adjectives vs. adverbs in the comparative. (Chart 9-3)

Directions: Complete each sentence with the comparative + the correct adjective or adverb. If it is an adjective, circle ADJ. If it is an adverb, circle ADV.

1. *slow*
   slowly

   I like to drive fast, but my brother William doesn't. As a rule, he drives
   _____more slowly_____ than I do.   ADJ (ADV)

2. *slow*
   slowly

   Alex is a _____slower_____ driver than I am.   (ADJ) ADV

3. *serious*
   seriously

   Some workers are _____ about their jobs than
   others.   ADJ ADV

4. *serious*
   seriously

   Some workers approach their jobs _____ than
   others.   ADJ ADV

5. *polite*
   politely

   Why is it that my children behave _____ at other
   people's houses than at home?   ADJ ADV

6. *polite*
   politely

   Why are they _____ at Mrs. Miranda's house than at
   home?   ADJ ADV

7. *careful*
   carefully

   I'm a cautious person when I express my opinions, but my sister will say anything
   to anyone. I'm much _____ when I speak to others than
   my sister is.   ADJ ADV

8. *careful*
   carefully

   I always speak _____ in public than my sister
   does.   ADJ ADV

9. *clear*
   clearly

   I can't understand Mark's father very well when he talks, but I can understand
   Mark. He speaks much _____ than his
   father.   ADJ ADV

10. *clear*
    clearly

    Mark is a much _____ speaker than his
    father.   ADJ ADV

◇ PRACTICE 12. Completing a comparative. (Chart 9-4)

Directions: Complete the comparisons with a pronoun and an appropriate auxiliary verb.

1. Bob arrived at ten. I arrived at eleven.

   → He arrived earlier than _____I did_____ .

2. Linda is a good painter. Steven is better.

   → He is a better painter than _____she is_____ .

3. Alex knows a lot of people. I don't know many people at all.

   → He knows a lot more people than _____ .

4. I won the race. Anna came in second.

   → I ran faster than _____ .

5. My parents were nervous about my motorcycle ride. I was just a little nervous.

   → They were a lot more nervous than _____ .

6. My aunt will stay with us for two weeks. My uncle has to return home to his job after a couple of days.

   → She will be here with us a lot longer than _____ .

7. Ms. Ross speaks clearly. Mr. Mudd mumbles.

   → She speaks a lot more clearly than _____ .

8. I've been here for two years. Sam has been here for two months.

   → I've been here a lot longer than _____ .

9. I had a good time at the picnic yesterday. Mary didn't enjoy it.

   → I had a lot more fun at the picnic than _____ .

10. I can reach the top shelf of the bookcase. Tim can only reach the shelf next to the top.

    → I can reach higher than _____ .

◇ PRACTICE 13. Completing comparisons with pronouns. (Chart 9-4)
Directions: Complete the comparisons both formal and informal pronouns: subject pronoun + verb OR object pronoun.

1. I have a brother. His name David. He's really tall. I'm just medium height.

   → He's taller than ____I am (formal)__ OR __me (informal)____ .

2. My brother is sixteen. I'm seventeen.

   → I'm older than _____ .

3. My sister is really pretty. I've never thought I was pretty.

   → She's a lot prettier than _____ .

4. I'm pretty smart, though. My sister isn't interested in school.

   → I'm smarter than _____ .

5. My mom tells me that I shouldn't compare myself to my sister. She says we are both individuals in our own right and have many fine qualities. My mom is wise. I don't think I'm wise yet.

   → My mom is much wiser than _____ .

6. My cousin Rita was born two days after I was.

   → She is two days younger than _____ .

◇ PRACTICE 14. VERY vs. A LOT / MUCH / FAR. (Chart 9-5)

Directions: Circle the correct answer or answers. More than one answer may be correct.

1. This watch is not _____ expensive.
   (A.) very   B. a lot   C. much   D. far

2. That watch is _____ more expensive than this one.
   A. very   (B.) a lot   (C.) much   (D.) far

3. My nephew is _____ polite.
   A. very   B. a lot   C. much   D. far

4. My nephew is _____ more polite than my niece.
   A. very   B. a lot   C. much   D. far

5. Ted is _____ taller than his brother.
   A. very   B. a lot   C. much   D. far

6. Ted is _____ tall.
   A. very   B. a lot   C. much   D. far

7. I think astronomy is _____ more interesting than geology.
   A. very   B. a lot   C. much   D. far

8. I think astronomy is _____ interesting.
   A. very   B. a lot   C. much   D. far

9. It took me a lot longer to get over my cold than it took you to get over your cold. My cold was _____ worse than yours.
   A. very   B. a lot   C. much   D. far

◇ PRACTICE 15. NOT AS . . . AS and LESS . . . THAN. (Chart 9-6)

Directions: All of the sentences contain **not as . . . as**. If possible, change them to sentences with the same meaning using **less . . . than**.

· 1. I don't live as close to my brother as I do to my sister.
   → *(no change possible using **less**)*

2. I don't visit my brother as often as I visit my sister.
   → *I visit my brother less often than I visit my sister.*

3. Sam isn't as nice as his brother.

4. Sam isn't as generous as his brother.

5. I'm not as eager to go to the circus as the children are.

6. A notebook isn't as expensive as a textbook.

7. Wood isn't as hard as metal.

8. Some people think that life in a city isn't as peaceful as life in a small town.

9. The moon isn't nearly as far away from the earth as the sun is.

10. I don't travel to Europe on business as frequently as I used to.

◇ **PRACTICE 16. Unclear comparisons. (Chart 9-7)**
Directions: Check the sentences that have unclear comparisons. Make the necessary corrections.

1. __✓__ Sam enjoys football more than his best friend ^does.

2. __ok__ Andy writes better financial reports than his boss.

3. _____ The coach helped Anna more than Nancy.

4. _____ Sara likes tennis more than her husband.

5. _____ Cathy leaves more generous tips at restaurants than her husband.

6. _____ Kelly eats more organic food than his roommate.

7. _____ Charles knows Judy better than Kevin.

◇ **PRACTICE 17. Using MORE with nouns. (Charts 9-3 and 9-8)**
Directions: Choose from the given words to complete the sentences with the comparative
(*more/-er*). If the word you use in the comparative is an adjective, circle ADJ. If it is an adverb,
circle ADV. If it is a noun, circle NOUN.

books	friends	✓newspapers
carefully	homework	pleasant
easily	loud	snow

1. My husband always wants to know everything that is going on in the world. He reads many

   ____more newspapers____ than I do. **ADJ   ADV   (NOUN)**

2. University students study hard. They have a lot _____ than high
   school students. **ADJ   ADV   NOUN**

3. There is far _____ in winter in Alaska than there is in Texas.
   ADJ   ADV   NOUN

4. I'm lonely. I wish I had _____ to go places with and spend time with.
   ADJ   ADV   NOUN

5. A warm, sunny day is _____ than a cold windy day.
   ADJ   ADV   NOUN

6. Rob picks up languages with little difficulty. For me, learning a second language is slow and

   difficult. I guess some people just learn languages a lot _____ than

   others. **ADJ   ADV   NOUN**

7. The New York City Public Library has many _____ than the public
   library in Sweetwater, Oregon. **ADJ   ADV   NOUN**

8. I have been driving _____ since my accident. **ADJ   ADV   NOUN**

9. Karen doesn't need a microphone when she speaks to the audience. She's the only person I

   know whose voice is _____ than mine. **ADJ   ADV   NOUN**

◇ **PRACTICE 18. Repeating a comparative. (Chart 9-9)**
Directions: Complete the sentences with words from the list. Repeat the comparative.

angry	expensive	cold	long
sleepy	friendly	fast	
big	✓good	loud	

1. His health is improving. He's getting ___better and better___.

2. They just had their sixth child. Their family is getting _____
   _____.

3. As we continued traveling north, the weather got _____.
   Eventually, everything we saw was frozen.

4. As the soccer game progressed, the crowd became _____.
   My ears started ringing!

5. I was really mad! I got _____ until my brother touched
   my arm and told me to calm down.

6. We were so glad we had arrived early at the ticket office. As we waited for it to open, the line
   got _____.

7. Textbooks are costly. They are getting _____
   every year.

8. We stayed up all night to work on our geology project. We became _____
   _____ as the night wore on, but we stayed awake and finally
   finished in time for class.

9. The people I met in my new job became _____ as
   we became better acquainted. Soon I began spending time with them after work.

10. When Joan was training for the marathon race, she was pretty slow in the beginning, but she
    got _____ as time went by. Eventually her time was so
    good that her coach thought she might have a chance to win.

◇ **PRACTICE 19. Double comparatives. (Chart 9-10)**
Directions: Complete the sentences with double comparatives.

1. I exercise every day. Exercise makes me strong. ___The more___ I exercise,
   ___the stronger___ I get.

2. If butter is soft, it is easy to spread on bread. __The_____ the butter is,

   __the_____ it is to spread on bread.

3. I know many things now that I wasn't aware of when I was younger. It seems that

   __the_____ I get, __the_____ I get.

4. I'm trying to make my life simpler. It makes me feel more relaxed.

   __The_____ my life, __the_____ I feel.

5. I spend a long time each day looking at a computer screen. My eyes get very tired.

   __The_____ I look at a computer screen, __the_____

   my eyes get.

6. When the wind blows hard, it whistles through the trees a lot. __The_____

   the wind blows, __the_____ it whistles through the trees.

◇ PRACTICE 20. Double comparatives. (Chart 9-10)
   Directions: Complete the sentences with double comparatives, using the ideas in parentheses.

   1. *(I became bored. He talked.)*
      I met a man at a party last night. I tried to be interested in what he was saying, but the

      ___more he talked, the more bored I became_____.

   2. *(You understand more. You are old.)*
      There are many advantages to being young, but the _____

      _____.

   3. *(I became confused. I thought about it.)*
      At first I thought I understood what she'd said, but the _____

      _____.

   4. *(The air is very polluted. The chances of developing respiratory diseases are great.)*
      Pollution poses many dangers. For example, the _____

      _____.

   5. *(Bill talked very fast. I became confused.)*
      Bill was trying to explain some complicated physics problems to help me prepare for an exam.

      He kept talking faster and faster. The _____

      _____.

   6. *(The fans clapped and cheered. The basketball team made more shots.)*
      The fans in the stadium were excited and noisy, and it seemed to make their team play better.

      The _____

      _____.

◇ **PRACTICE 21. Using superlatives. (Chart 9-11)**
Directions: Complete the sentences with the given ideas. Use the superlative. If you don't know the right answer, guess.

✓familiar	large eyes	long necks
intelligent	large ears	

1. Kangaroos are _____the most familiar_____ of all Australian grassland animals.

2. Giraffes have _____ of all animals.

3. African elephants have _____ of all animals.

4. Horses have _____ of all four-legged animals.

5. Bottle-nosed dolphins are _____ animals that live in

   water. Apes and monkeys are _____ animals that live on

   land (besides human beings).

◇ **PRACTICE 22. Using superlatives. (Chart 9-11)**
Directions: Make comparisons.

PART I. Complete the sentences with superlatives and the appropriate word: *in, of,* or *ever*.

1. Physics is *(difficult)* _____the most difficult_____ course I have _____ever_____ taken.

2. Isn't my hometown *(friendly)* _____the friendliest_____ place _____of_____ all the towns

   you have visited?

3. What is *(embarrassing)* _____the most embarrassing_____ experience you have had

   _____in_____ your life?

4. My friends say that my grandmother is *(wise)* _____ person they have

   _____ met.

5. My wife is *(good)* _____ cook _____ the world.

6. My three children all have artistic talent, but Jimmy is *(artistic)* _____

   _____ all.

7. My bedroom on the third floor is *(hot)* _____ room _____ the

   house.

8. July is *(warm)* _____ month _____ the year.

9. Min-Sok is one of *(bright)* _____ students I've _____ taught.

10. Which is *(high)* _____ mountain _____ the world, K2 or Mt. Everest?

11. My mother found Dr. John to be (knowledgeable) _____

doctor _____ all the doctors she has gone to.

12. What is (important) _____ thing you could do _____

your life?

PART II. Complete with **least** and the appropriate word: **in, of,** or **ever.**

13. Ed is not lazy, but he is certainly (ambitious) ___the least ambitious of___ all

the people I have worked with.

14. That painting didn't cost much. It is (expensive) _____

work of art we have _____ bought.

15. Antarctica is (populated) _____ continent _____

the world.

16. Kim seems addicted to the Internet. I think (amount) _____ of time

she has _____ spent on it is four hours.

◇ **PRACTICE 23. AS . . . AS, MORE/-ER, and MOST/-EST. (Charts 9-1 → 9-11)**
   Directions: Make comparisons.

   PART I. Compare the cost of the items in parentheses. Use the given expressions.

   1. (a pencil vs.* a telephone)

      _____A pencil_____ is less expensive than _____a telephone_____ .

   2. (a paper clip vs. a diamond ring)

      _____ is much more expensive than _____ .

   3. (a cup of coffee vs. a can of coffee beans)

      _____ is not as expensive as _____ .

   4. (radios vs. CD players vs. big screen TVs)

      _____ and _____ are both less expensive than

      _____ .

   5. (a compact car vs. a house)

      _____ is not nearly as expensive as _____ .

   6. (footballs vs. soccer balls vs. ping-pong balls vs. basketballs)

      _____ , _____ , and

      _____ are all more expensive than _____ .

_____

*vs. is an abbreviation for *versus*, which means "as opposed to, as compared to."

PART II. Compare the waterfalls by using the given expressions.

7. ____Angel Falls____ is much higher ____than Niagara Falls*____.

8. _____ is almost as high _____.

9. _____ is the highest _____.

10. _____ is not nearly as high _____.

11. _____ is not quite as high _____.

Waterfalls of the World

Niagara Falls	Giessbach Falls	Cuquenán Falls	Angel Falls
United States and Canada	Switzerland	Venezuela	Venezuela
53 meters	604 meters	610 meters	807 meters

PART III. Compare the weight of the items in parentheses. Use the given expressions.

12. *(air, iron)* ____Air____ is lighter ____than iron____.

13. *(iron, wood)* _____ is heavier _____.

14. *(water, iron, wood, air)* Of the four elements, _____ is the heaviest _____.

15. *(water, air)* _____ is not as heavy _____.

16. *(water, iron, wood, air)* Of the four elements, _____ is the lightest _____.

17. *(water, air)* _____ is not nearly as light _____.

18. *(water, iron, wood)* _____ and _____ are both heavier _____.

_____

*A singular verb is used after Angel Falls because it is the name of a place. Angel Falls is in Venezuela. Similarly, the United States takes a singular verb because it is the name of a place: *The United States is a big country.*

◇ **PRACTICE 24. Using NEVER with comparatives. (Chart 9-4)**
   Directions: Circle the letter of the sentence that is closest in meaning to the given sentence.

   1. I've never taken a harder test in this class.
      (a.) The test was hard.
      b. The test wasn't hard.

   2. I've never taken a hard test in this class.
      a. The tests in this class are hard.
      b. The tests in this class aren't hard.

   3. Professor Jones has never given a difficult test.
      a. The test was difficult.
      b. The test wasn't difficult.

   4. Professor Smith has never given a more difficult test.
      a. His tests are difficult.
      b. His tests aren't difficult.

   5. I've never heard of a worse economic situation in Leadville.
      a. Leadville has a bad economic situation.
      b. Leadville doesn't have a bad economic situation.

   6. I've never heard of a bad economic situation in Leadville.
      a. Leadville has bad economic situations.
      b. Leadville doesn't have bad economic situations.

   7. We've never stayed in a more comfortable hotel room.
      a. The room was comfortable.
      b. The room wasn't comfortable.

   8. We've never stayed in a comfortable room at that hotel.
      a. The rooms are comfortable.
      b. The rooms aren't comfortable.

◇ **PRACTICE 25. Using EVER and NEVER in comparisons. (Charts 9-4 and 9-11)**
   Directions: Complete the sentences with comparatives and superlatives.

   1. Pierre told a really *funny* story. It is _____the funniest_____ story I've ever heard

      (in my life). I've never heard a _____funnier_____ story (than that one).

   2. John felt very *sad* when he saw the child begging for money. In fact, he has never felt

      _____ (than he did then). That is _____ he has

      ever felt (in his life).

   3. Jan just finished a really *good* book. She thinks it was _____ book she has

      ever read. She says that she has never read a _____.

4. The villagers fought the rising flood all through the night. They were *exhausted* when the river finally crested. They have never had a _____ experience. That was _____ experience they have ever had.

5. When her daughter was born, Rachel felt extremely *happy*. In fact, she has never felt _____ (than she did then). That was _____ she has ever felt (in her life).

6. Oscar told a very *entertaining* story after dinner. In fact, he has never told a _____ _____ story. It is one of _____ stories I have ever heard in my life.

7. Mari studied very *hard* for her college entrance exams. In fact, she has never studied _____. That was _____ she has ever studied in her life.

8. The weather is really *hot* today! In fact, so far this year the weather has never been _____. This is _____ weather we've had so far this year.

◇ **PRACTICE 26. Review of comparatives and superlatives. (Charts 9-1 → 9-11)**
Directions: Complete the sentences. Use any appropriate form of the words in parentheses and add any other necessary words.

1. Sometimes I feel like all of my friends are *(intelligent)* __more intelligent than__ I am, and yet, sometimes they tell me that they think I am *(smart)* __the smartest__ person __in__ the class.

2. One of *(popular)* _____ holidays _____ Japan is New Year's.

3. A mouse is *(small)* _____ a rat.

4. Europe is first in agricultural production of potatoes. *(potatoes)* _____ are grown in Europe _____ on any other continent.

5. Mercury is *(close)* _____ planet to the sun. It moves around the sun *(fast)* _____ any other planet in the solar system.

6. In terms of area, *(large)* _____ state _____ the United States is Alaska, but it has one of *(small)* _____ populations _____ all the states.

7. Nothing is *(important)* _____ good health. Certainly, gaining wealth is much *(important)* _____ enjoying good health.

8. I need more facts. I can't make my decision until I get (information) _____

_____ .

9. Rebecca is a wonderful person. I don't think I've ever met a (kind) _____

and (generous) _____ person.

10. You can trust her. You will never meet a (honest) _____ person

_____ she is.

11. I'm leaving! This is (bad) _____ movie I've ever seen! I won't sit

through another second of it.

12. One of (safe) _____ places to be during a lightning storm is inside a car.

13. Small birds have a much (fast) _____ heartbeat _____ large birds.

14. Are your feet exactly the same size? Almost everyone's left foot is (big) _____

_____ their right foot.*

15. Both Bangkok and Venice are famous for their waterways, but Bangkok has (extensive)

_____ canals _____ Venice has.

◇ PRACTICE 27. Review of comparatives and superlatives. (Charts 9-1 → 9-11)

Directions: Complete the sentences. Use any appropriate form of the words in parentheses and
add any other necessary words.

1. I feel (safe) _____safer_____ in a plane _____than_____ I do in a car.

2. Jakarta is (large) _____ city _____ Indonesia.

3. Mountain climbing takes (strength) _____ walking on a

level path.

4. Cheese usually tastes (good) _____ at room temperature than it does just after

you take it out of the refrigerator.

5. The (short) _____ distance between two points is a straight line.

6. The (thin) _____ a lemon's rind is, the (juicy) _____

the lemon is.

7. Mr. Hochingnauong feels (comfortable) _____ speaking his

native language _____ he does speaking English.

---

*Grammar note: In formal English, a singular pronoun is used to refer to *everyone:*
Almost **everyone's** left foot is bigger than **his or her** right foot.
In everyday informal usage, a plural pronoun is frequently used:
Almost **everyone's** left foot is bigger than **their** right foot.

8. My friend has studied many languages. He thinks Japanese is *(difficult)* _____ _____ all the languages he has studied.

9. One of the *(bad)* _____ nuclear accidents _____ the world occurred at Chernobyl in 1986.

10. I think learning a second language is *(hard)* _____ learning chemistry or mathematics.

11. The *(low)* _____ temperature ever recorded in Alaska was minus 80°F (−27°C) in 1971.

12. Computers are complicated machines, but probably *(complex)* _____ _____ thing _____ the universe is the human brain.

13. I've seen a lot of funny movies over the years, but the one I saw last night was *(funny)* _____ all.

14. Riding a bicycle can be dangerous. *(people)* _____ were killed in bicycle accidents last year _____ have been killed in airplane accidents in the last four years.

15. Some people build their own boats from parts that they order from a manufacturer. They save money that way. It is *(expensive)* _____ to build your own boat _____ to buy a boat.

◇ **PRACTICE 28. LIKE, ALIKE. (Chart 9-12)**
Directions: Complete the sentences with *like* or *alike*.

1. My mother and my father rarely argue because they think ____alike____ .

2. The Browns designed their summer cabin to look ____like____ the inside of a boat.

3. Joe and John are twins, but they don't look _____ .

4. They dress _____ because they have the same taste in clothes.

5. This lamp doesn't look _____ the one I ordered.

6. Mike is 30, but he continually acts _____ a child.

7. Professor Miller's lectures are all _____ : repetitive and boring.

8. This coffee doesn't taste _____ the coffee we sampled at the store.

9. The clouds to the east look _____ rain clouds.

10. My grandmother and mother sound _____ on the phone.

◇ **PRACTICE 29. THE SAME AS, SIMILAR TO, DIFFERENT FROM.** (Chart 9-12)
   Directions: Complete the sentences with the correct preposition: **as, to,** or **from.**

1. My coat is different ___*from*___ yours.

2. Our apartment is similar ___*to*___ my cousin's.

3. The news report was the same ___*as*___ the report we heard on Channel Six last night.

4. How is the North Pole different _____ the South Pole?

5. Your jacket is exactly the same _____ mine.

6. I enjoyed reading your letters from China. My experiences in Beijing were similar _____ yours.

7. For many students, their grades in college are similar _____ their grades in high school.

8. The movie on our flight to London was the same _____ the movie on our flight to Paris.

9. Some herbal teas are somewhat similar _____ green tea.

10. Courtship and dating patterns in Europe are very different _____ those in many Middle Eastern and Asian countries.

11. Except for a few minor differences in grammar, spelling, and vocabulary, American English is the same _____ British English.

12. The English spoken in the United States is only slightly different _____ the English spoken in Britain, Canada, and Australia.

◇ **PRACTICE 30. LIKE, ALIKE, SIMILAR (TO), DIFFERENT (FROM).** (Chart 9-12)
   Directions: Make comparisons.

   PART I. Compare the figures. Use the words in parentheses.

   A   B   C   D

1. like _____*A is like D*_____ .
2. alike _____ .
3. similar (to) _____ and _____ .
4. different (from) _____ , _____ , and _____ .

PART II. Compare the figures. Use *the same (as)*, *similar (to)*, or *different (from)*.

A   B   C   D

5. All of the triangles are _____ each other.

6. A and D are _____ each other.

7. A and C are _____ .

8. A isn't _____ C.

9. B and C are _____ D.

◇ **PRACTICE 31. THE SAME, SIMILAR, DIFFERENT, LIKE, ALIKE.** (Chart 9-12)
   Directions: Complete the sentences with *the same*, *similar*, *different*, *like*, or *alike*.

1. Dana swims _____like_____ a fish. She never wants to come out of the water.

2. The lake doesn't have a ripple on it. It looks _____ glass.

3. There are six girls in our family, but none of us look _____ . Our brothers also look different.

4. A: Some people can tell we're sisters. Do you think we look _____ ?

   B: Somewhat. The color of your hair is not _____ , but your eyes are exactly

   _____ color. You also have _____ shaped face.

5. A: I'm sorry, but I believe you have my umbrella.

   B: Oh? Yes, I see. It looks almost exactly _____ mine, doesn't it?

6. A: How do you like the spaghetti sauce I made? I tried to make it exactly

   _____ yours.

   B: I can tell. Your sauce is very _____ the one I make, but I think it's missing one spice.

   A: Oh? What's that?

   B: That's a secret! But I'll tell if you promise to keep it a secret.

7. Some people think my sister and I are twins. We look _____ and talk

   _____ , but our personalities are quite _____ .

8. Homonyms are words that have _____ pronunciation but different spelling, such as "pair" and "pear" or "sea" and "see." For many people, "been" and "bean" are homonyms and have _____ pronunciation. For other people, however, "been" and "bean" are _____ words with different pronunciations. These people pronounce "been" like "bin" or "ben."

◇ PRACTICE 32. Error analysis. (Chapter 9)
Directions: Correct the errors.

1. My brother is older ~~from~~ than me.

2. A sea is more deeper than a lake.

3. A donkey isn't as big to a horse.

4. Ellen is happiest person I've ever met.

5. When I feel embarrassed, my face gets red and more red.

6. One of a largest animal in the world is the hippopotamus.

7. The traffic on the highway is more bad from than it was a few months ago.

8. Jack is the same old from Jerry.

9. Peas are similar from beans, but they have several differences.

10. Last winter was pretty mild. This winter is cold and rainy. It's much rain than last winter.

11. Mrs. Peters, the substitute teacher, is very friendly than the regular instructor.

12. Although alligators and crocodiles are similar, alligators are less big than crocodiles.

13. Mohammed and Tarek come from different countries, but they became friends easily because

    they speak a same language, Arabic.

14. Mothers of young children are busyier than mothers of teenagers.

15. We'd like to go sailing, but the wind is not as strong today that it was yesterday.

16. We asked for a non-smoking room, but the air and furniture in our hotel room smelled

    cigarette smoke.

CHAPTER 10
The Passive

◇ PRACTICE 1. Active vs. passive. (Chart 10-1)
　　Directions: Circle ACTIVE if the given sentence is active; circle PASSIVE if it is passive. <u>Underline</u> the verb.

　　1. (ACTIVE)　PASSIVE　　　Farmers <u>grow</u> rice.

　　2. ACTIVE　(PASSIVE)　　　Rice <u>is grown</u> by farmers.

　　3. ACTIVE　PASSIVE　　　Sara wrote the letter.

　　4. ACTIVE　PASSIVE　　　The letter was written by Sara.

　　5. ACTIVE　PASSIVE　　　The teacher explained the lesson.

　　6. ACTIVE　PASSIVE　　　The lesson was explained by the teacher.

　　7. ACTIVE　PASSIVE　　　Bridges are designed by engineers.

　　8. ACTIVE　PASSIVE　　　Engineers design bridges.

◇ PRACTICE 2. Active vs. passive. (Chart 10-1)
Directions: Change the active verbs in *italics* to passive.

　　1. Mr. Catt *delivers* our mail.　　Our mail _____is_____ ____delivered____ by Mr. Catt.

　　2. The children *have eaten* the cake.　　The cake _____ _____ by the children.

　　3. Linda *wrote* that letter.　　That letter _____ _____ by Linda.

　　4. The jeweler *is going to fix* my watch.　　My watch _____ _____ by the jeweler.

　　5. Ms. Bond *will teach* our class.　　Our class _____ _____ by Ms. Bond.

　　6. Anne *is going to bring* dinner.　　Dinner _____ _____ by Anne.

7. Our team *won* the final game.

The final game _____ _____ by our team.

8. Dr. Pitt *will treat* the patient.

The patient _____ _____ by Dr. Pitt.

9. Ms. Davis *has planted* several trees.

Several trees _____ _____ by Ms. Davis.

10. The police *catch* criminals.

Criminals _____ _____ by the police.

◇ **PRACTICE 3. Review of past participles. (Charts 2-6 and 2-7)**
Directions: Write the past participles of the verbs. The list contains both regular and irregular verbs.

Simple Form	Simple Past	Past Participle	Simple Form	Simple Past	Past Participle
1. bring	brought	*brought*	14. play	played	_____
2. build	built	_____	15. read	read*	_____
3. buy	bought	_____	16. save	saved	_____
4. eat	ate	_____	17. send	sent	_____
5. plan	planned	_____	18. speak	spoke	_____
6. give	gave	_____	19. spend	spent	_____
7. grow	grew	_____	20. take	took	_____
8. hit	hit	_____	21. teach	taught	_____
9. hurt	hurt	_____	22. go	went	_____
10. leave	left	_____	23. visit	visited	_____
11. lose	lost	_____	24. wear	wore	_____
12. make	made	_____	25. write	wrote	_____
13. find	found	_____	26. do	did	_____

◇ **PRACTICE 4. Passive form. (Charts 10-1, 10-2, and 10-5)**
Directions: Use the given form of *be (was, is, going to be, etc.)* and complete the sentences with the past participles of any verbs in the list in Practice 3.

1. *was*   There's no more candy. All the candy _____ *was eaten* _____ by the children.

2. *is*   Arabic _____ by the people of Syria and Iraq.

_____
*The simple past and past participle of *read* are pronounced "red," as the color red.

3. *are*   Books _____ by authors.

4. *was*   My friend _____ in an accident. He broke his nose.

5. *is going to be*   Bombay, India, _____ by thousands of tourists this year.

6. *has been*   *War and Peace* is a famous book. It _____ by millions of people.

7. *will be*   The championship game _____ in Milan next week.

8. *can be*   Everyone _____ to read. I'll teach you if you'd like.

9. *are going to be*   Our pictures _____ by a professional photographer at the wedding.

10. *have been*   Oranges _____ by farmers in Jordan since ancient times.

11. *is*   Special fire-resistant clothing _____ by firefighters.

12. *will be*   A new bridge across the White River _____ by the city government next year.

◇ **PRACTICE 5. Passive vs. active meaning. (Charts 10-1 and 10-2)**
Directions: Circle the letter of the sentence that has the same meaning as the given sentence.

1. My grandmother makes her own bread.

   (a.) This bread is made by my grandmother.

   b. Someone makes my grandmother's bread.

2. Bob was taken to the hospital by car.

   a. Bob drove to the hospital.

   b. Someone drove Bob to the hospital.

3. Suzanne has just been asked to her first dance.

   a. Suzanne has asked someone to the dance.

   b. Someone has asked Suzanne to the dance.

4. You will be informed of the test results.

   a. You will inform someone of the test results.

   b. Someone will inform you of the test results.

5. You are not allowed to enter.

   a. You do not allow people to enter.

   b. Someone says you cannot enter.

6. The child was saved after five minutes in the water.

    a. Someone saved the child.

    b. The child saved herself.

◇ **PRACTICE 6. Tense forms of the passive. (Charts 10-1 and 10-2)**
Directions: Complete the sentences with the passive form of the given verbs.

PART I. Use the SIMPLE PRESENT with:

✓collect	grow	understand
eat	pay	write

1. Taxes ___are collected___ by the government.

2. Books _____ by authors.

3. Rice _____ by farmers in Korea.

4. Small fish _____ by big fish.

5. I _____ for my work by my boss.

6. The meaning of a smile _____ by everyone.

PART II. Use the SIMPLE PAST with:

build	collect	destroy	write

7. Yesterday the students' papers ___were_____ by the teacher at the end of the test.

8. The Great Wall of China _____ by Chinese emperors more than 2500 years ago.

9. The book *War and Peace* _____ by Leo Tolstoy, a famous Russian novelist.

10. Several small buildings _____ by the earthquake in Los Angeles.

PART III. Use the PRESENT PERFECT with:

read	speak	visit	wear

11. The pyramids in Egypt ___have_____ by millions of tourists.

12. Spanish _____ by people in Latin America for nearly 600 years.

13. Mark Twain's books _____ by millions of people through the years.

14. Perfume _____ by both men and women since ancient times.

PART IV. Use ***will*** with:

discover	visit	save

15. New information about the universe ___will_____ by scientists in the twenty-first century.

16. Hawaii _____ by thousands of tourists this year.

17. Tigers _____ from extinction by people who care.

PART V. Use ***be going to*** with:

elect	hurt	offer

18. Your friend ___is going_____ by your unkind remark when she hears about it.

19. New computer courses _____ by the university next year.

20. A new leader _____ by the people in my country next month.

◇ PRACTICE 7. Passive to active. (Charts 10-1 and 10-2)
Directions: Change the passive sentences to active. Keep the same verb tense.

1. Taxes are collected by the government.
   → *The government collects taxes.*

2. Small fish are eaten by big fish.

3. The meaning of a smile is understood by everyone.

4. *War and Peace* was written by Leo Tolstoy.

5. The cat was chased by the dog.

6. ABC Corporation is going to be bought by XYZ Inc.

7. The pyramids in Egypt have been visited by millions of tourists.

8. New information about the universe will be discovered by scientists in the twenty-first century.

◇ PRACTICE 8. Passive to active. (Charts 5-2, 10-1, and 10-2)
Directions: Change the passive sentences to active. Keep the same tense. Some of the sentences are questions.

1. The letter was signed by Mr. Rice.
   → *Mr. Rice signed the letter.*

2. Was the letter signed by Mr. Foster?
   → *Did Mr. Foster sign the letter?*

3. The fax was sent by Ms. Owens.

4. Was the other fax sent by Mr. Chu?

5. Will Adam be met at the airport by Mr. Berg?

6. Have you been invited to the reception by Mrs. Jordan?

7. I have been invited to the reception by Mr. Lee.

8. Is the homework going to be collected by the teacher?

◇ **PRACTICE 9. Transitive vs. intransitive. (Chart 10-3)**

Directions: Circle TRANSITIVE if the verb takes an object; circle INTRANSITIVE if it does not. Underline the object of the verb.

1. (TRANSITIVE) INTRANSITIVE — Alex wrote <u>a letter</u>.

2. TRANSITIVE (INTRANSITIVE) — Alex waited for Amy. *(There is no object of the verb.)*

3. TRANSITIVE INTRANSITIVE — Rita lives in Mexico.

4. TRANSITIVE INTRANSITIVE — Sam walked to his office.

5. TRANSITIVE INTRANSITIVE — Kate caught the ball.

6. TRANSITIVE INTRANSITIVE — My plane arrived at six-thirty.

7. TRANSITIVE INTRANSITIVE — Emily is crying.

8. TRANSITIVE INTRANSITIVE — A falling tree hit my car.

9. TRANSITIVE INTRANSITIVE — I returned the book to the library yesterday.

10. TRANSITIVE INTRANSITIVE — A bolt of lightning appeared in the sky last night.

◇ **PRACTICE 10. Active and passive. (Charts 10-1 → 10-3)**

Directions: Underline the object of the verb if the given sentence has one. Then change the sentence to the passive. Some sentences cannot be changed to the passive.

ACTIVE	PASSIVE
1. A noise awakened <u>me</u>.	I was awakened by a noise.
2. It rained hard yesterday.	(no change)
3. Alice discovered the mistake.	
4. We stayed at a hotel last night.	

5. I slept only four hours last night. _____

6. Anita fixed the chair. _____

7. Did Susan agree with Prof. Hill? _____

8. Ann's cat died last week. _____

9. That book belongs to me. _____

10. The airplane arrived twenty minutes late. _____

11. The teacher announced a quiz. _____

12. I agree with Larry. _____

13. Do you agree with me? _____

14. Jack went to the doctor's office. _____

◇ PRACTICE 11. Review: identifying passives with transitive and intransitive verbs.
              (Charts 10-1 → 10-3)

Directions: Check the sentences that are passive.

1. _____ I came by plane.

2. ___✓___ I was invited to the party by Alex.

3. _____ Many people died during the earthquake.

4. _____ Many people were killed by collapsing buildings.

5. _____ The earthquake has killed many people.

6. _____ The game will be won by the Bulls.

7. _____ The Bulls will win the game.

8. _____ Gina's baby cried for more than an hour.

9. _____ Most of the fresh fruit at the market was bought by customers.

10. _____ Some customers bought boxes full of fresh fruit.

11. _____ Accidents always occur at that intersection.

◇ PRACTICE 12. The BY-phrase. (Chart 10-4)

Directions: <u>Underline</u> the passive verbs. Answer the questions. If you don't know the exact person or people who performed the action, write "unknown."

1. Soft duck feathers <u>are used</u> to make pillows.

   Who uses duck feathers to make pillows? _____unknown_____

2. The mail <u>was opened</u> by Shelley.

   Who opened the mail? _____Shelley_____

3. Eric Wong's new book will be translated into many languages.

   Who will translate Eric Wong's new book? _____

4. Rebecca's bicycle was stolen yesterday from in front of the library.

   Who stole Rebecca's bicycle? _____

5. Our wedding photos were taken by a professional photographer.

   Who took our wedding photos? _____

6. Malawi is a small country in southeastern Africa. A new highway is going to be built in Malawi next year.

   Who is going to build the new highway? _____

7. There are no more empty apartments in our building. The apartment next to ours has been rented by a young family with two small children.

   Who rented the apartment next to ours? _____

8. The apartment directly above ours was empty for two months, but now it has also been rented.

   Who rented the apartment directly above ours? _____

◇ PRACTICE 13. The BY-phrase. (Chart 10-4)
   Directions: Cross out the unnecessary *by*-phrases (those that do not give important information).

   1. We were helped right away at the appliance store ~~by someone~~.

   2. We were helped at the appliance store by a friendly and knowledgeable salesperson.

      (no change)

   3. Our mail was delivered early today by someone.

   4. My favorite lamp was broken by the children when they were playing ball in the house.

   5. Our house was built just last year by Baker Construction Company.

   6. Our neighbors' house was built ten years ago by someone who builds houses.

   7. The child will be operated on tomorrow by three specialists at Hope Hospital.

   8. The child will be operated on tomorrow by someone.

◇ PRACTICE 14. Active to passive. (Charts 10-1 → 10-4)
   Directions: Change the active sentences to passive. Use the *by*-phrase only if necessary.

   1. Someone has canceled the soccer game.
      → *The soccer game has been canceled.*

   2. The president has canceled the meeting.
      → *The meeting has been canceled by the president.*

   3. Someone serves beer and wine at that restaurant.

   4. Something confused me in class yesterday.

5. The teacher's directions confused me.

6. No one has washed the dishes yet.

7. Someone should wash them soon.

8. Did someone wash this sweater in hot water?

9. No one should wash wool sweaters in hot water.

10. Luis invited me to the party.

11. Has anyone invited you to the party?

◇ **PRACTICE 15. Review: active vs. passive. (Charts 10-1 → 10-4)**
Directions: Create sentences with the given words. Use the present tense. Some are passive. Some are not.

1. Sometimes keys / hide / under cars
   → *Sometimes keys are hidden under cars.*

2. Cats / hide / under cars
   → *Cats hide under cars.*

3. Students / teach / by teachers

4. Students / study / a lot

5. Cereal / often eat / at breakfast

6. Cats / eat / cat food

7. Mice / eat / by cats

8. Songs / sing / to children / by their mothers

9. Children / sing / songs / in school

10. Thai food / cook / in Thai restaurants

11. Chefs / cook / in restaurants

◇ **PRACTICE 16. Progressive tenses in passive. (Chart 10-5)**
Directions: <u>Underline</u> the progressive verb. Then complete each sentence with the correct passive form.

1. Some people <u>are considering</u> a new plan.

   → A new plan _____is being considered_____.

2. The grandparents are watching the children.

→ The children _____ by their grandparents.

3. Some painters are painting Mr. Rivera's apartment this week.

→ Mr. Rivera's apartment _____ this week.

4. We can't use the language lab today because someone is fixing the equipment.

→ We can't use the language lab today because the equipment _____

_____ .

5. We couldn't use the language lab yesterday because someone was fixing the equipment.

→ We couldn't use the language lab yesterday because the equipment _____

_____ .

6. Eric's cousins are meeting him at the airport this afternoon.

→ Eric _____ by his cousins at the airport this afternoon.

7. I watched while the movers were moving the furniture from my apartment to a truck.

→ I watched while the furniture _____ from my apartment to a

truck.

8. Everyone looked at the flag while they were singing the national anthem.

→ Everyone looked at the flag while the national anthem _____ .

9. Scientists are still discovering new species of plants and animals.

→ New species of plants and animals _____ .

◇ **PRACTICE 17. Passive forms of progressive verbs. (Chart 10-5)**
Directions: Complete the sentences with the given verbs. Use the present progressive or the past progressive. All the sentences are passive.

build	clean	fly	✓play	read	watch

1. A soccer game ____is being played____ in Wellstone Arena today.

2. The office ____was____ by the janitor when I got there early this
morning.

3. A new house _____ in our neighborhood right now.

4. The book _____ aloud to the children by the teacher in the first
grade class right now.

5. The protestors _____ by the police during the anti-war
demonstration.

6. The small plane _____ by the co-pilot when it crashed.

◇ **PRACTICE 18. Passive forms of progressive verbs. (Chart 10-5)**
   Directions: Circle the letter of the sentence with the same meaning as the given sentence.

   1. A mouse is being chased.
      a. A mouse is trying to catch something.
      (b.) Something is trying to catch a mouse.

   2. The soldiers are being trained.
      a. The soldiers are training someone.
      b. Someone is training the soldiers.

   3. The earthquake victims are being helped by the medics.
      a. The medics are receiving help.
      b. The victims are receiving help.

   4. The children were trying to find their parents after the school play.
      a. The children were looking for their parents.
      b. The parents were looking for their children.

   5. The airline passengers were being asked to wait while the plane was cleaned.
      a. The passengers made a request.
      b. Someone asked the passengers to wait.

◇ **PRACTICE 19. Review: active vs. passive. (Chart 10-1 → 10-5)**
   Directions: Write "C" if the sentence is correct. Write "I" if it is incorrect. Make any necessary corrections.

   1. __I__   It ~~was~~ happened many years ago.

   2. __C__   Rice is grown in California.

   3. _____   I was go to school yesterday.

   4. _____   Two firefighters have injured while they were fighting the fire.

   5. _____   Sara was accidentally broken the window.

   6. _____   Kara was eaten a snack when she got home from school.

   7. _____   Timmy was eating when the phone rang.

   8. _____   I am agree with you.

   9. _____   The little boy was fallen down while he was running in the park.

   10. _____   The swimmer was died from a shark attack.

   11. _____   The swimmer was killed by a shark.

   12. _____   I was slept for nine hours last night.

◇ PRACTICE 20. Passive modals. (Chart 10-6)

Directions: Change the sentences from active to passive. Include the *by*-phrase only if it contains important information.

1. Someone might cancel class.
   → *Class might be canceled.*

2. A doctor can prescribe medicine.

3. Mr. Hook must sign this report.

4. Someone may build a new post office on First Street.

5. People have to place stamps in the upper right-hand corner of an envelope.

6. Someone ought to paint that fence.

7. All of the students must do the assignment.

◇ PRACTICE 21. Passive modals. (Chart 10-6)

Directions: Complete the sentences by using the words in the list with the modals in parentheses. All of the completions are passive.

build	kill	✓ put off	teach	write
divide	know	sell	tear down	

1. Don't postpone things you need to do. Important work _____shouldn't be put off_____ until the last minute. *(should not)*

2. Your application letter _____ in ink, not pencil. *(must)*

3. Dogs _____ to do tricks. *(can)*

4. Mrs. Papadopolous didn't want her son to go to war because he _____
   _____ . *(could)*

5. My son's class is too big. It _____ into two classes.
   (ought to)

6. A: Hey, Tony. These bananas are getting too ripe. They _____
   today. Reduce the price. *(must)*
   B: Right away, Mr. Rice.

7. It takes time to correct an examination that is taken by ten thousand students nationwide.
   The test results _____ for at least four weeks. *(will not)*

8. The big bank building on Main Street was severely damaged in the earthquake. The structure
   is no longer safe. The building _____ . *(has to)* Then a
   new bank _____ in the same place. *(can)*

◇ **PRACTICE 22. Passive modals. (Chart 10-6)**
   Directions: Complete the sentences by changing the active modals to passive modals.

   1. This book *(have to return)* ___has to be returned___ to the library today.

   2. That book *(should return)* _____ tomorrow.

   3. This letter *(must send)* _____ today.

   4. This package *(could send)* _____ tomorrow.

   5. That package *(should send)* _____ by express mail.

   6. That box *(can put away)* _____ now.

   7. These boxes *(may throw away)* _____ soon.

   8. Those boxes *(might pick up)* _____ this afternoon.

   9. This room *(will clean up)* _____ soon.

◇ **PRACTICE 23. Summary: active vs. passive. (Charts 10-1 → 10-6)**
   Directions: Circle ACTIVE if the given sentence is active; circle PASSIVE if it is passive. Underline the verb.

   1. (ACTIVE) PASSIVE   People <u>have used</u> sundials since ancient times.

   2. ACTIVE (PASSIVE)   Sundials <u>have been used</u> for almost three thousand years.

   3. ACTIVE   PASSIVE   Sundials, clocks, and watches are used to tell time.

   4. ACTIVE   PASSIVE   Some watches show the date as well as the time.

   5. ACTIVE   PASSIVE   On digital watches, the time is shown by lighted numbers.

   6. ACTIVE   PASSIVE   The first watches were made in Europe six hundred years ago.

   7. ACTIVE   PASSIVE   The earliest watches were worn around a person's neck.

   8. ACTIVE   PASSIVE   Pocket watches became popular in the 1600s.

   9. ACTIVE   PASSIVE   Today most people wear wristwatches.

   10. ACTIVE   PASSIVE   Close to seventy million watches are sold in the United States each year.

   11. ACTIVE   PASSIVE   How many watches are made and sold throughout the world in one year?

12. ACTIVE   PASSIVE   Somewhere in the world, a watch is being sold at this very moment.

13. ACTIVE   PASSIVE   Many different styles of watches can be bought today.

14. ACTIVE   PASSIVE   Do you own a watch?

15. ACTIVE   PASSIVE   Where was it made?

◇ **PRACTICE 24. Summary: active vs. passive. (Charts 10-1 → 10-6)**
   Directions: Complete the sentences with the verbs in parentheses; use active or passive.

   1. I don't have my car today. It's in the garage. It *(repair)* _____is being_____

      ____repaired____ right now.

   2. Kate didn't have her car last week because it was in the garage. While it *(repair)*

      _____ , she took the bus to work.

   3. The mechanic *(repair)* _____ Tina's car last week.

   4. Glass *(make)* _____ from sand.

   5. You *(should carry, not)* _____ large sums of money with you.

   6. Large sums of money *(ought to keep)* _____ in a bank, don't
      you think?

   7. At our high school, the students' grades *(send)* _____ to their parents
      four times each year.

   8. I'm sorry, but the computer job is no longer available. A new computer programmer

      (hire, already) _____ .

   9. Household cleaning agents *(must use)* _____ with care. For

      example, mixing chlorine bleach with ammonium *(can produce)* _____

      toxic gases.

   10. What products *(manufacture)* _____ in your country?

   11. Aluminum* is a valuable metal that *(can use)* _____ again and again.

       Because this metal *(can recycle)* _____ , aluminum cans

       (should throw away, not) _____ .

   12. Endangered wildlife *(must protect)* _____ from extinction.

   13. People with the moral courage to fight against injustices *(can find)* _____

       in every corner of the world.

   _____

   Aluminum in American English = *aluminium* in British English.

◇ **PRACTICE 25. Summary: active vs. passive.** (Charts 10-1 → 10-6)
Directions: Complete the sentences with the verbs in parentheses; use active or passive.

1. Flowers (love) _____are loved_____ throughout the world. Their beauty (bring)
   _____brings_____ joy to people's lives. Flowers (use, often) _____
   _____ to decorate homes or tables in restaurants. Public gardens
   (can find) _____ in almost every country in the world.

2. Around 250,000 different kinds of flowers (exist) _____ in the world. The
   majority of these species (find) _____ only in the tropics. Nontropical
   areas (have) _____ many fewer kinds of flowering plants than tropical regions.

3. Flowers may spread from their native region to other similar regions. Sometimes seeds
   (carry) _____ by birds or animals. The wind also (carry) _____
   some seeds. In many cases throughout history, flowering plants (introduce) _____
   _____ into new areas by humans.

4. Flowers (appreciate) _____ mostly for their beauty, but they can
   also be a source of food. For example, honey (make) _____ from the
   nectar which (gather) _____ from flowers by bees. And some flower
   buds (eat) _____ as food; for example, broccoli and cauliflower are
   actually flower buds.

5. Some very expensive perfumes (make) _____ from the petals of flowers.
   Most perfumes today, however, (come, not) _____ from natural
   fragrances. Instead, they are synthetic; they (make) _____ from
   chemicals in a laboratory.

6. Some kinds of flowers (may plant) _____ in pots and (grow)
   _____ indoors. Most flowers, however, (survive) _____
   best outdoors in their usual environment.

◇ **PRACTICE 26. Using past participles as adjectives.** (Chart 10-7)
Directions: Complete the sentences with the correct prepositions.

PART I. Jack is . . .
1. married ___to___ Katie.
2. excited _____ vacation.
3. exhausted _____ work.
4. frightened _____ heights.
5. disappointed _____ his new car.

6. tired _____ rain.

7. pleased _____ his new boss.

8. involved _____ charity work.

9. worried _____ his elderly parents.

10. acquainted _____ a famous movie star.

PART II. Jack's friend is . . .

11. interested _____ sports.

12. done _____ final exams.

13. terrified _____ spiders.

14. related _____ a famous movie star.

15. opposed _____ private gun ownership.

16. pleased _____ his part-time job.

17. divorced _____ his wife.

PART III. Jack's house is . . .

18. made _____ wood.

19. located _____ the suburbs.

20. crowded _____ antique furniture.

21. prepared _____ emergencies.

◇ **PRACTICE 27. Using past participles as adjectives. (Chart 10-7)**
Directions: Each sentence has errors with the adjectives used as past participles. Correct the errors.

1. The little girl is ~~excite in~~ *excited about* her coming birthday party.

2. Mr. and Mrs. Rose devoted each other.

3. Could you please help me? I need directions. I lost.

4. The students are boring in their chemistry project.

5. The paper bags at this store is composed in recycled products.

6. Your friend needs a doctor. He hurt.

7. How well are you prepare the driver's license test?

8. Mary has been engaging with Paul for five years. Will they ever get married?

◇ **PRACTICE 28. -ED vs. -ING. (Chart 10-8)**

Directions: Complete the sentences with the appropriate **-ed** or **-ing** form of the words in parentheses.

Ben is reading a book. He really likes it. He can't put it down. He has to keep reading.

1. The book is really _____interesting_____ . *(interest)*

2. Ben is really _____ . *(interest)*

3. The story is _____ . *(excite)*

4. Ben is _____ about the story. *(excite)*

5. Ben is _____ by the characters in the book. *(fascinate)*

6. The people in the story are _____ . *(fascinate)*

7. Ben doesn't like to read books when he is _____ and
   _____ . *(bore, confuse)*

8. Ben didn't finish the last book he started because it was _____ and
   _____ . *(bore, confuse)*

9. What is the most _____ book you've read lately? *(interest)*

10. I just finished a _____ mystery story that had a very
    _____ ending. *(fascinate, surprise)*

◇ **PRACTICE 29. -ED vs. -ING. (Chart 10-8)**

Directions: Choose the correct adjective.

1. Don't bother to read that book. It's (*boring,*) *bored.*

2. The students are *interesting, interested* in learning more about the subject.

3. Ms. Green doesn't explain things well. The students are *confusing, confused.*

4. Have you heard the latest news? It's really *exciting, excited.*

5. I don't understand these directions. I'm *confusing, confused.*

6. I read an *interesting, interested* article in the newspaper this morning.

7. I heard some *surprising, surprised* news on the radio.

8. I'm *boring, bored.* Let's do something. How about going to a movie?

9. Mr. Sawyer bores me. I think he is a *boring, bored* person.

10. Mr. Ball fascinates me. I think he is a *fascinating, fascinated* person.

11. Most young children are *fascinating, fascinated* by animals.

12. Young children think that animals are *fascinating, fascinated.*

13. That was an *embarrassing, embarrassed* experience.

14. I read a *shocking, shocked* report yesterday on the number of children who die from starvation in the world every day. I was really *shocking, shocked.*

15. The children went to a circus. For them, the circus was *exciting, excited.* The *exciting, excited* children jumped up and down.

◇ **PRACTICE 30. -ED vs. -ING. (Chart 10-8)**
Directions: Choose the correct adjective.

1. The street signs in our city are *confused,* ⟨*confusing.*⟩

2. The drivers are *frustrated, frustrating.*

3. The professor's lecture on anatomy was *confused, confusing* for the students.

4. The student was very *embarrassed, embarrassing* by all the attention she got for her high test scores.

5. Sophie said it was *embarrassed, embarrassing* to have so many people congratulate her.

6. I am really *interested, interesting* in eighteenth-century art.

7. Eighteenth-century art is really *interested, interesting.*

8. What an *exhausted, exhausting* day! I am so *tired, tiring* from picking strawberries.

9. Some of the new horror movies are *frightened, frightening* because they are so realistic.

10. Young children shouldn't see them. They would become too *frightened, frightening.*

◇ **PRACTICE 31. -ED vs. -ING. (Chart 10-8)**
Directions: In each group, one sentence is incorrect. Write "I" beside the incorrect sentence.

1. a. _____ Science fascinates me.
   b. _____ Science is fascinating to me.
   c. __I__ Science is fascinated to me.

2. a. _____ The baby is exciting about her new toy.
   b. _____ The baby is excited about her new toy.
   c. _____ The new toy is exciting to the baby.

3. a. _____ The book is really interesting.
   b. _____ The book is really interested.
   c. _____ The book interests me.

4. a. _____ I am exhausting from working in the fields.
   b. _____ I am exhausted from working in the fields.
   c. _____ Working in the fields exhausts me.
   d. _____ Working in the fields is exhausting.

5. a. _____ Your grandmother is amazing to me.
   b. _____ Your grandmother amazes me.
   c. _____ Your grandmother is amazed to me.
   d. _____ I am amazed by your grandmother.

◇ **PRACTICE 32. GET + adjective and past participle. (Chart 10-9)**
Directions: Complete the sentences using words from the list.

arrested	dressed	invited	lost	stolen
bored	hungry	late	rich	wet
✓ sick	dizzy			

1. Just a few days before the Jensens were going to leave for a family reunion in Hawaii, everyone got _____sick_____ with the flu. They had to cancel their trip.

2. When Jane gave us directions to her house, I got _____ . So I asked her to explain again how to get there.

3. Some people are afraid of heights. They get _____ and have trouble keeping their balance.

4. I didn't like the movie last night. It wasn't interesting. I got _____ and wanted to leave early.

5. When's dinner? I'm getting _____ .

6. We should leave for the concert soon. It's getting _____ . We should leave in the next five minutes if we want to be on time.

7. I want to make a lot of money. Do you know a good way to get _____ quick?

8. Jake got _____ for stealing a car yesterday. He's in jail now.

9. I overslept this morning. When I finally woke up, I jumped out of bed, got _____ , picked up my books, and ran to class.

10. Anita got _____ when she stood near the pool of dolphins. They splashed her more than once.

11. Yes, I have an invitation to Joan and Paul's wedding. Don't worry. You'll get _____ to the wedding, too.

12. Tarik was afraid his important papers or his wife's jewelry might get _____ , so he had a wall safe installed in his home.

◇ **PRACTICE 33. GET + adjective and past participle. (Chart 10-9)**
   Directions: Complete the sentences with an appropriate form of ***get***.

1. Shake a leg! Step on it! _____Get_____ busy. There's no time to waste.

2. Tom and Sue _____got_____ married last month.

3. Let's stop working for a while. I _____am getting_____ tired.

4. I don't want _____to get_____ old, but I guess it happens to everybody.

5. I _____ interested in biology when I was in high school, so I decided to major
   in it in college.

6. My father started _____ bald when he was in his twenties. I'm in my twenties,
   and I'm starting _____ bald. It must be in the genes.

7. Brrr. It _____ cold in here. Maybe we should turn on the furnace.

8. When I was in the hospital, I got a card from my aunt and uncle. It said, "_____
   well soon."

9. When I went downtown yesterday, I _____ lost. I didn't remember to take my map
   of the city with me.

10. A: Why did you leave the party early?
    B: I _____ bored.

11. A: I _____ hungry. Let's eat soon.
    B: Okay.

12. A: What happened?
    B: I don't know. Suddenly I _____ dizzy, but I'm okay now.

13. A: Do you want to go for a walk?
    B: Well, I don't know. It _____ dark outside right now. Let's wait and
       go for a walk tomorrow.

14. I always _____ nervous when I have to give a speech.

15. A: Where's Bud? He was supposed to be home two hours ago. He always calls when he's
       late. I _____ worried. Maybe we should call the police.
    B: Relax. He'll be home soon.

16. A: Hurry up and _____ dressed. We have to leave in ten minutes.
    B: I'm almost ready.

17. A: I'm going on a diet.

    B: Oh?

    A: See? This shirt is too tight. I _____ fat.

18. A: Janice and I are thinking about _____ married in June.

    B: That's a nice month for a wedding.

◇ PRACTICE 34. BE USED/ACCUSTOMED TO. (Charts 2-11 and 10-10)
Directions: Choose the correct completion. More than one completion may be correct.

1. Frank has lived alone for twenty years. He _____ alone.
   A. used to live   (B.) is used to living   (C.) is accustomed to living

2. I _____ with my family, but now I live alone.
   (A.) used to live   B. am used to living   C. am accustomed to living

3. Rita rides her bike to work every day. She _____ her bike to work.
   A. used to ride   B. is used to riding   C. is accustomed to riding

4. Tom rode his bike to work for many years, but now he takes the bus. Tom _____ his bike to work.
   A. used to ride   B. is used to riding   C. is accustomed to riding

5. Carl showers every day. He _____ a shower every day.
   A. used to take   B. is used to taking   C. is accustomed to taking

6. Carl _____ a bath only once a week, but now he showers every day.
   A. used to take   B. is used to taking   C. is accustomed to taking

7. Ari _____ a small breakfast every day because he was always in a hurry.
   A. used to eat   B. is used to eating   C. is accustomed to eating

8. Maria _____ a large breakfast because she likes to take her time in the morning.
   A. used to eat   B. is used to eating   C. is accustomed to eating

◇ PRACTICE 35. USED TO vs. BE USED TO. (Chart 10-11)
Directions: Add an appropriate form of **be** if necessary. If no form of **be** is needed, write Ø in the blank.

1. Trains ___Ø___ used to be the main means of cross-continental travel. Today, most people take airplanes for long-distance travel.

2. Ms. Stanton's job requires her to travel extensively throughout the world. She ___is___ used to traveling by plane.

3. You and I are from different cultures. You _____ used to having fish for breakfast. I _____ used to having cheese and bread for breakfast.

4. People _____ used to throw away or burn their newspapers after reading them, but now many people recycle them.

5. Jeremy wakes up at 5:00 every morning for work. After a year of doing this, he _____ used to getting up early, even on weekends.

6. Mrs. Hansen _____ used to do all of the laundry and cooking for her family. Now the children are older and Mrs. Hansen has gone back to teaching, so the whole family shares these household chores.

7. Before modern dentistry, people _____ used to pull painful teeth.

8. Cindy swims only in swimming pools. She _____ used to swim in lakes and rivers, but now she finds them too cold.

◇ PRACTICE 36. USED TO vs. BE USED TO. (Chart 10-11)
Directions: Complete the sentences with *used to* or *be used to* and the correct form of the verb in parentheses.

1. Kate grew up on a farm. She (get) ____used to get____ up at dawn and go to bed as soon as the sun went down. Now she works in the city at an advertising agency and has different sleeping hours.

2. Hiroki's workweek is seven days long. He (work) _____ on Saturdays and Sundays.

3. Luis spends weekends with his family now. He (attend) _____ soccer games before he was married, but now he enjoys staying home with his young children.

4. Sally went back to school to become a computer programmer. She (work) _____ _____ as a typist, but now she has a job that she likes better.

5. Joan has taught kindergarten for eight years. She (teach) _____ small children and uses many creative techniques with them.

6. Before I went overseas, I had a very simple, uninteresting diet. After visiting many different countries, however, I (eat) _____ much spicier, tastier dishes now.

◇ PRACTICE 37. BE SUPPOSED TO. (Chart 10-12)
Directions: Create sentences with a similar meaning by using *be supposed to*.

1. Someone expected me to return this book to the library yesterday, but I didn't.
   → *I was supposed to return this book to the library.*

2. Our professor expects us to read Chapter 9 before class tomorrow.

3. Someone expected me to go to a party last night, but I stayed home.

4. The teacher expects us to do Exercise 10 for homework.

5. The weather bureau has predicted rain for tomorrow. According to the weather bureau, it . . . .

6. The directions on the pill bottle say, "Take one pill every six hours." According to the directions on the bottle, I . . . .

7. My mother expects me to dust the furniture and (to) vacuum the carpet.

◇ **PRACTICE 38. BE SUPPOSED TO. (Chart 10-12)**
Directions: Complete the sentences with *be supposed to* and any appropriate verb from the list.

take off	register	sweep	give
be	clean	cook	send

1. A: What are you doing home? You ___are supposed to be___ at work.
   B: I called in sick.

2. A: The floor is still dirty. You _____ it this morning before you left for school, weren't you?
   B: I know. I forgot.

3. Sarah's late paying her taxes. She _____ her check to the government last month.

4. When you eat in a restaurant, you _____ your order to the waitress or waiter.

5. I know you'd rather be playing tennis, but you _____ the house today. The house is dirty, and it's your turn.

6. A: Where _____ I _____ for my English class? I'm new here.
   B: Down the hall to your right.

7. Jack _____ dinner tonight, but he didn't get home until 9:00 P.M.

8. A: You're tracking mud all over the house.
   B: Sorry. We _____ our shoes at the door, aren't we?

◇ PRACTICE 39. Error analysis. (Chapter 10)
   Directions: Correct the errors.

1. The moving boxes ∧ᵂᵉʳᵉ packed by Pierre.

2. My uncle was died in the war.

3. Miami located in Florida.

4. I was very worried about my son.

5. Mr. Rivera interested in finding a new career.

6. Did you tell everyone the shocked news?

7. After ten years, I finally used to this wet and rainy climate.

8. The newspaper suppose to come every morning before eight.

9. The Millers have been marry with each other for 60 years.

10. I am use to drink coffee with cream, but now I drink it black.

11. What was happen at the party last night?

12. Several people almost get kill when the fireworks exploded over them.

13. A new parking garage being build for our office.

14. I have been living in England for several years, so I accustom driving on the left side of the road.

CHAPTER 11
Count/Noncount Nouns and Articles

◇ **PRACTICE 1. A vs. AN: singular count nouns. (Chart 11-1)**
Directions: Write *a* or *an* in the blanks.

1.	_a_	game	14.	_____	hour
2.	_an_	office	15.	_____	star
3.	_____	car	16.	_____	eye
4.	_____	friend	17.	_____	new car
5.	_____	mountain	18.	_____	old car
6.	_____	rock	19.	_____	used car
7.	_____	army	20.	_____	uncle
8.	_____	egg	21.	_____	house
9.	_____	island	22.	_____	honest mistake
10.	_____	ocean	23.	_____	hospital
11.	_____	umbrella	24.	_____	hand
12.	_____	university	25.	_____	ant
13.	_____	horse	26.	_____	neighbor

◇ **PRACTICE 2. Preview: count and noncount nouns. (Charts 11-2 → 11-5)**
Directions: Draw a line through the expressions of quantity that **cannot** be used to complete the sentences.

NONCOUNT NOUNS: *fruit, mail, traffic*
   COUNT NOUNS: *apples, letters, cars*

1. I ate _____ **fruit**.
   a. some
   b. several
   c. a little
   d. a few
   e. too many
   f. too much
   g. a lot of
   h. two

2. I ate _____ **apples**.
   a. some
   b. several
   c. a little
   d. a few
   e. too many
   f. too much
   g. a lot of
   h. two

3. I get _____ **mail** every day.
   a. a lot of
   b. some
   c. a little
   d. a few
   e. too much
   f. too many
   g. several
   h. three

4. I get _____ **letters** every day.
   a. a lot of
   b. some
   c. a little
   d. a few
   e. too much
   f. too many
   g. several
   h. three

5. There is _____ **traffic** in the street.
   a. several
   b. some
   c. too many
   d. a little
   e. a lot of
   f. a few
   g. too much
   h. five

6. There are _____ **cars** in the street.
   a. several
   b. some
   c. too many
   d. a little
   e. a lot of
   f. a few
   g. too much
   h. five

◇ **PRACTICE 3. Count and noncount nouns.** (Charts 11-2 → 11-4)
   Directions: Which of the words can follow **one** and which can follow **some**? Write the correct form of the noun in the blanks. If the noun does not have a singular form, write **Ø**.

	one . . .	some . . .
1. word	word	words
2. vocabulary	Ø	vocabulary
3. slang		
4. homework		
5. assignment		
6. grammar		
7. dress		
8. clothes		
9. clothing		
10. parent		
11. family		
12. knowledge		
13. information		
14. fact		
15. luck		
16. garbage		

◇ **PRACTICE 4. Count and noncount nouns. (Charts 11-2 → 11-4)**
Directions: Complete the sentences with the words below. Use the plural form as necessary.

✓apple trees	grass	machine	rice
✓bracelets	hardware	machinery	ring
✓bread	jewel	mountain	sandwich
✓corn	jewelry	pea	scenery
equipment	lake	plant	tool

1. I went to the grocery store and bought some ___bread, corn,___

___

2. I stood on a hill in the countryside and saw some ___apple trees,___

___

3. I went to a jewelry store and saw some ___bracelets,___

___

4. At the auto repair shop, I saw some ___

___

◇ **PRACTICE 5. Count and noncount nouns. (Charts 11-2 → 11-5)**
Directions: Fill in the blanks with *one*, *much*, or *many*.

1.	___one___	chair	14. ___	games
2.	___much___	furniture	15. ___	water
3.	___many___	vegetables	16. ___	parent
4.	___	clothing	17. ___	sand
5.	___	vegetable	18. ___	professors
6.	___	clothes	19. ___	dust
7.	___	fruit	20. ___	money
8.	___	facts	21. ___	stuff
9.	___	grammar	22. ___	thing
10.	___	word	23. ___	things
11.	___	idioms	24. ___	English
12.	___	vocabulary	25. ___	toast
13.	___	cars		

◇ **PRACTICE 6. Count and noncount nouns. (Charts 11-2 → 11-4)**

Directions: Complete the sentences with the correct form, singular or plural, of the given nouns. If a verb is needed, circle the correct one in the parentheses.

1. *snow*　　　In Alaska in the winter, there ((is,) are) a lot of ____snow____ on the ground.

2. *weather*　　There (is, are) a lot of cold _____ in Alaska.

3. *sunshine*　　_____ (is, are) a source of vitamin D.

4. *knowledge*　Prof. Nash has a lot of _____ about that subject.

5. *fun*　　　　We had a lot of _____ on the picnic.

6. *factory,**　Sometimes _____ cause _____ .
   pollution

7. *pride,*　　　Parents take _____ in the success of their _____ .
   child**

8. *people,*　　I admire _____ who use their _____ to the
   intelligence　fullest extent.

9. *peace*　　　There have been many conflicts and wars throughout the history of the world, but almost all people prefer _____ .

10. *hospitality*　Thank you for your _____ .

11. *beef*　　　The _____ we had for dinner last night (was, were) very good.

12. *fog*　　　　During the winter months along the coast, there (is, are) usually a lot of _____ in the morning.

*See Chart 6-1, p. 157, in the student book for variations in the pronunciation of words with a final **-s**.
**Some nouns have irregular plurals. See Chart 6-2, p. 158.

◇ PRACTICE 7. MANY vs. MUCH. (Chart 11-5)

Directions: Complete the sentences with **much** or **many** and the singular or plural form of the noun. If a verb is needed, circle the correct one in the parentheses.

1. *apple*   How _____many apples_____ did you buy?

2. *fruit*   How _____much fruit_____ did you buy?

3. *mail*   How _____ did you get yesterday?

4. *letter*   How _____ did you get yesterday?

5. *English*   Anna's husband doesn't know _____.

6. *slang*   Sometimes I can't understand my roommate because he uses too

                    _____.

7. *word*   How _____ *(is, are)* there in your dictionary?

8. *coffee*   Louise drinks too _____.

9. *sandwich*   Billy has a stomach ache. He ate too _____.

10. *sugar*   You shouldn't eat too _____.

11. *course*   How _____ are you taking this semester?

12. *homework*   How _____ do you have to do tonight?

13. *news*   There *(isn't, aren't)* _____ in the paper today.

14. *article*   How _____ *(is, are)* there on the front

                    page of today's paper?

15. *fun*   I didn't have _____ at the party. It was boring.

16. *star*   How _____ *(is, are)* there in the universe?

17. *sunshine*   There *(isn't, aren't)* _____ in Seattle in winter.

18. *pollution*   *(Is, Are)* there _____ in Miami?

19. *luck*   We didn't have _____ when we went fishing.

20. *kind*   There *(is, are)* _____ of flowers.

21. *violence*   I think there *(is, are)* too _____ on television.

22. *makeup*   I think that Mary wears too _____.

23. *car*   How _____ pass in front of this building in 30 seconds?

24. *traffic*   *(Is, Are)* there _____ in front of your apartment building?

◇ PRACTICE 8. HOW MANY and HOW MUCH. (Chart 11-5)
   Directions: Complete the questions with ***many*** or ***much***. Add final *-s/-es* if necessary to make a noun plural. (Some of the count nouns have irregular plural forms.) If a verb is needed, circle the correct one in the parentheses. If final *-s/-es* is not necessary, put a slash (/) in the blank.

1. How ____many____ letter __s__ (is, (are)) there in the English alphabet?*

2. How ____much____ mail __/__ did you get yesterday?

3. How ____many____ ~~man~~ men (has, (have)) a full beard at least once in their life?

4. How ____many____ famil~~y~~ _ies_ (is, (are)) there in your apartment building?

5. How _____ sentence _____ (is, are) there in this exercise?

6. How _____ chalk _____ (is, are) there in the classroom?

7. How _____ English _____ does Stefan know?

8. How _____ English **literature** _____ have you studied?

9. How _____ English **word** _____ do you know?

10. How _____ **gasoline** _____ does it take to fill the tank in your car?

   (British: How _____ **petrol** _____ does it take to fill the tank?)

11. How _____ **homework** _____ did the teacher assign?

12. How _____ **grandchild** _____ does Mrs. Cunningham have?

13. How _____ **page** _____ (is, are) there in this book?

14. How _____ **library** _____ (is, are) there in the United States?†

15. How _____ **glass** _____ of water do you drink every day?

16. How _____ **fun** _____ did you have at the amusement park?

17. How _____ **education** _____ does Ms. Martinez have?

18. How _____ **soap** _____ should I use in the dishwasher?

19. How _____ **island** _____ (is, are) there in Indonesia?**

20. How _____ **people** _____ will there be by the year 2050?††

21. How _____ **zero** _____ (is, are) there in a billion?***

---

   *Answer: twenty-six (26). There are twenty-six letters in the English alphabet.

   †Answer: approximately fifteen thousand (15,000).

   **Answer: more than thirteen thousand seven hundred (13,700).

   ††Answer: estimated at more than thirteen billion (13,000,000,000).

   ***Answer: nine (9).

◇ **PRACTICE 9. Review: count and noncount nouns.** (Charts 11-1 → 11-5)
Directions: Circle all the words that can be used with each given noun.

1. flower	(a)	an	some	much	many
2. flowers	a	an	(some)	much	(many)
3. coin	a	an	some	much	many
4. money	a	an	some	much	many
5. coins	a	an	some	much	many
6. salt	a	an	some	much	many
7. error	a	an	some	much	many
8. mistake	a	an	some	much	many
9. honest mistake	a	an	some	much	many
10. mistakes	a	an	some	much	many
11. dream	a	an	some	much	many
12. interesting dream	a	an	some	much	many
13. questions	a	an	some	much	many
14. soap	a	an	some	much	many
15. bar of soap	a	an	some	much	many
16. beauty	a	an	some	much	many
17. cup of tea	a	an	some	much	many
18. unsafe place	a	an	some	much	many
19. fruit	a	an	some	much	many
20. pieces of fruit	a	an	some	much	many

◇ **PRACTICE 10. A FEW vs. A LITTLE.** (Chart 11-5)
Directions: Complete the sentences with *a few* or *a little*. Add a final *-s* to the noun if necessary. Otherwise, write a slash (/) in the blank.

1. Let's listen to _____*a little*_____ **music** __/__ during dinner.

2. Let's sing _____*a few*_____ **song** _s_ around the campfire.

3. We all need _____ **help** _____ at times.

4. Ingrid is from Sweden, but she knows _____ **English** _____ .

5. I need _____ more **apple** _____ to make a pie.

6. I like _____ **honey** _____ in my coffee.

7. I have a problem. Could you give me _____ **advice** _____ ?

8. I need _____ **suggestion** _____ .

9. He asked _____ **question** _____ .

10. We talked to _____ **people** _____ on the plane.

11. Please give me _____ more **minute** _____ .

12. Ann opened the curtains to let in _____ **light** _____ from outdoors.

13. I have _____ **homework** _____ to do tonight.

14. Pedro already knew _____ English **grammar** _____ before he took this course.

15. I picked _____ **flower** _____ from my garden.

16. I've made _____ **progress** _____ in the last couple of weeks.

◇ **PRACTICE 11. Error analysis. (Charts 11-1 → 11-5)**
Directions: Correct the errors.

1. Kim has applied to ~~an~~ *a* university in England.

2. For Anita's wedding anniversary, her husband gave her a jewelry and a poetry he wrote.

3. The politician wanted specific suggestion for her speech on the economy.

4. Some of the homeworks for my English class was easy, but many of the assignment were unclear.

5. Diane has been to Rome several time recently. She always has wonderful time.

6. Many parents need advices about raising children.

7. The boys played together in the sands and dirts for hours.

8. A person doesn't need many equipment to play baseball: just ball and a bat.

9. Many happiness can come from enjoying the simple thing in life.

◇ **PRACTICE 12. Count and noncount nouns. (Charts 6-2 and 11-1 → 11-6)**
Directions: Add final *-s/-es* as necessary. Do not make any other changes. The number in parentheses at the end of each item is the number of nouns that need final *-s/-es*.

1. Plant*s* are the oldest living thing*s* on earth. (2) = [2 nouns need final *-s/-es*.]

2. Scientist divide living thing into two group: plant and animal. Generally speaking, plant stay in one place, but animal move around. (7)

3. Flower, grass, and tree grow every place where people live. Plant also grow in desert, in ocean, on mountaintop, and in polar region. (7)

4. Plant are useful to people. We eat them. We use them for clothing. We build house from them. Plant are also important to our health. We get many kind of beneficial drug from plant. In addition, plant provide beauty and enjoyment to all our lives. (7)

5. Crop are plant that people grow for food. Nature can ruin crop. Bad weather—such as too much rain or too little rain—can destroy field of corn or wheat. Natural disaster such as flood and storm have caused farmer many problem since people first began to grow their own food. (9)

6. Food is a necessity for all living thing. All animal and plant need to eat. Most plant take what they need through their root and their leaf. The majority of insect live solely on plant. Many bird have a diet of worm and insect. Reptile eat small animal, egg, and insect. (15)

◇ PRACTICE 13. Units of measure with noncount nouns. (Chart 11-7)
Directions: Use the words in the list to complete the sentences. Use the plural form if necessary. Some sentences have more than one possible completion.

bar	gallon	piece	sheet
bottle	glass	pound	spoonful
bowl	loaf	quart	tube
cup	kilo		

1. I drank a _____cup_____ of coffee.
2. I bought two _____pounds_____ of cheese.
3. I had a _____ of soup for lunch.
4. I drank a _____ of orange juice.
5. I had a _____ of toast and an egg for breakfast.
6. I put ten _____ of gas in my car.
7. I bought a _____ of milk at the supermarket.
8. I need a _____ of chalk.
9. I drank a _____ of beer.
10. I used two _____ of bread to make a sandwich.
11. There is a _____ of fruit on the table.
12. There are 200 _____ of lined paper in my notebook.

13. I bought one _____ of bread at the store.

14. I put a _____ of honey in my tea.

15. I need to buy a new _____ of toothpaste.

16. There is a _____ of soap in the bathroom.

17. Let me give you a _____ of advice.

18. I just learned an interesting _____ of information.

19. There were a dozen* _____ of mail in my mailbox today.

20. A three-piece suit is made up of three _____ of clothing: slacks, a jacket, and a vest.

◇ **PRACTICE 14. Units of measure with noncount nouns. (Chart 11-7)**

Directions: What units of measure are usually used with the following nouns? More than one unit of measure can be used with some of the nouns.

bag	bottle	box	can/tin**	jar

1. a ____jar____ of pickles.

2. a _____ of aspirin.

3. a _____ of laundry detergent

4. a _____ of instant coffee

5. a _____ of sardines

6. a _____ of sugar

7. a _____ of peanut butter

8. a _____ of soy sauce

9. a _____ of uncooked noodles

10. a _____ of refried beans

◇ **PRACTICE 15. MUCH vs. MANY. (Charts 11-5 → 11-7)**

Directions: Complete the questions with ***much*** or ***many***.

1. A: How ____many suitcases____ did you take with you on the plane to Tahiti?

   B: Three. (I took three suitcases on the plane to Tahiti.)

2. A: How ____much suntan oil____ did you take with you?

   B: A lot. (I took a lot of suntan oil with me.)

3. A: How _____ did you take?

   B: Two pairs. (I took two pairs of sandals.)

4. A: How _____ did you take?

   B: One tube. (I took one tube of toothpaste.)

_____

*A dozen = twelve. It is followed by a plural noun: *a dozen eggs*.

**a can = a tin in British English.

5. A: How _____ did you have?

   B: Twenty. (I had twenty kilos of luggage.)

6. A: How _____ did you pay in overweight baggage charges?

   B: A lot. (I paid of lot of money for overweight baggage.)

◇ PRACTICE 16. A/AN vs. SOME. (Chart 11-8)
Directions: Complete the sentences with *a/an* or *some*.

1. I wrote _____*a*_____ **letter**.

2. I got __*some*__ **mail**.

3. We bought _____ **equipment** for our camping trip.

4. You need _____ **tool** to cut wood.

5. I ate _____ **food**.

6. I had _____ **apple**.

7. I wore _____ old **clothing**.

8. I wore _____ old **shirt**.

9. Jim asked me for _____ **advice**.

10. I gave Jim _____ **suggestion**.

11. I read _____ interesting **story** in the paper.

12. The paper has _____ interesting **news** today.

13. I read _____ **poem** after dinner.

14. I read _____ **poetry** after dinner.

15. I know _____ **song** from India.

16. I know _____ Indian **music**.

17. I learned _____ new **word**.

18. I learned _____ new **slang**.

◇ PRACTICE 17. A vs. SOME. (Chart 11-8)
Directions: Write *a* or *some* in the blank before each singular noun. Then write a sentence with the plural form of the noun if possible.

Singular Objects	**Plural Objects**
1. I saw _____*a*_____ bird.	I saw some birds.
2. I ate __*some*__ corn.	Ø (none possible)
3. Would you like _____ tea?	
4. I picked _____ flower.	

5. I drank _____ water. _____

6. I fed grass to _____ horse. _____

7. Pat is wearing _____ jewelry. _____

8. I bought _____ honey. _____

9. Tom bought _____ new shirt. _____

10. I need _____ soap to wash the dishes. _____

◇ **PRACTICE 18. A/AN vs. THE: singular count nouns. (Chart 11-8)**
Directions: Complete the sentences with **a/an** or **the**.

1. A: _____A_____ dog makes a good pet.
   B: I agree.

2. A: Did you feed __the__ dog?
   B: Yes, I did.

3. My dorm room has _____ desk, _____ bed, _____ chest of drawers, and two chairs.

4. A: Jessica, where's the stapler?
   B: On _____ desk. If it's not there, look in _____ top drawer.

5. A: Sara, put your bike in _____ basement before dark.
   B: Okay, Dad.

6. Our apartment building has _____ basement. Sara keeps her bike there at night.

7. Almost every sentence has _____ subject and _____ verb.

8. Look at this sentence: *Jack lives in Miami.* What is _____ subject, and what is _____ verb?

9. A: I can't see you at four. I'll be in _____ meeting then. How about four-thirty?
   B: Fine.

10. A: What time does _____ meeting start Tuesday?
    B: Eight.

11. Jack's car ran out of gas. He had to walk _____ long distance to find _____ telephone and call his brother for help.

12. _____ distance from _____ sun to _____ earth is 93,000,000 miles.

13. A: Jake, _____ telephone is ringing. Can you get it?
    B: Sure.

14. A: Did you feed _____ cat?
    B: Yes. I fed him a couple of hours ago.

15. A: Does Jane have _____ cat?

    B: No, she has _____ dog. She doesn't like cats.

16. A: I wrote _____ poem. Would you like to read it?

    B: Sure. What's it about?

17. A: Was _____ lecture interesting?

    B: Yes. _____ speaker gave _____ interesting talk.

18. A: Where should we go for _____ cup of coffee after class?

    B: Let's go to _____ cafe around _____ corner from the First National Bank.

19. A: Where do you live?

    B: We live on _____ quiet street in the suburbs.

20. A: I'm hungry, and I'm tired of walking. How much farther is it to _____ restaurant?

    B: Just a couple of blocks. Let's cross _____ street here.

    A: Are you sure you know where you're going?

21. A: Did Bob find _____ job?

    B: Yes. He's working at _____ restaurant.

    A: Oh? Which one?

◇ **PRACTICE 19. Ø vs. THE. (Chart 11-8)**
   Directions: Write **Ø** or **the** in the blanks. Add capital letters as necessary.

1. A: ___Ø___ D dogs make good pets.

   B: I agree.

2. A: Did you feed __the__ dogs?

   B: Yes, I did.

3. A: ___Ø___ F fruit is good for you.

   B: I agree.

4. A: __The__ fruit in this bowl is ripe.

   B: Good. I think I'll have a piece.

5. John, where's _____ milk? Is it in _____ refrigerator or on _____ table?

6. _____ milk comes from cows and goats.

7. Tom usually has _____ wine with dinner.

8. Dinner's ready. Shall I pour _____ wine?

9. We usually have _____ meat for dinner.

10. _____ meat we had for dinner last night was tough.

11. A: Mom, please pass _____ potatoes.

    B: Here you are. Anything else? Want some more chicken, too?

12. _____ potatoes are _____ vegetables.

13. _____ frogs are _____ small animals without _____ tails that live on land or in

    water. _____ turtles also live on land or in water, but they have _____ tails and

    _____ hard shells.

14. A: Nicole, what are those animals doing in here!?

    B: We're playing. _____ frogs belong to Jason. _____ turtles are mine.

15. Do you like _____ weather in this city?

16. _____ copper is used in electrical wiring.

17. People used to use _____ candles for _____ light, but now they use _____

    electricity.

18. There are many kinds of _____ books. We use _____ textbooks and _____

    workbooks in school. We use _____ dictionaries and _____ encyclopedias for

    reference. For _____ entertainment, we read _____ novels and _____ poetry.

19. _____ books on this desk are mine.

◇ PRACTICE 20. Using THE for second mention. (Charts 11-6 → 11-8)
Directions: Use *a/an*, *some*, or *the* in the sentences. REMINDER: Use *the* when a noun is
mentioned for the second time.

1. I drank <u>some</u> coffee and <u>some</u> milk. <u>The</u> coffee was hot. <u>The</u> milk
   was cold.

2. I had _____ soup and _____ sandwich for lunch. _____ soup was too salty, but
   _____ sandwich was pretty good.

3. Yesterday I bought _____ clothes. I bought _____ suit, _____ shirt, and _____ tie. _____ suit is gray and comes with a vest. _____ shirt is pale blue, and _____ tie has black and gray stripes.

4. A: I saw _____ accident yesterday.

   B: Oh? Where?

   A: On Grand Avenue. _____ man in _____ Volkswagen drove through a stop sign and hit _____ bus.

   B: Was anyone hurt in _____ accident?

   A: I don't think so. _____ man who was driving _____ Volkswagen got out of his car and seemed to be okay. His car was only slightly damaged. No one in _____ bus was hurt.

5. Yesterday I saw _____ man and _____ woman. They were having _____ argument. _____ man was yelling at _____ woman, and _____ woman was shouting at _____ man. I don't know what _____ argument was about.

6. Yesterday while I was walking to work, I saw _____ birds in _____ tree. I also saw _____ cat under _____ tree. _____ birds didn't pay any attention to _____ cat, but _____ cat was watching _____ birds intently.

◇ **PRACTICE 21. Using THE for second mention. (Charts 11-6 → 11-8)**
Directions: Write **a/an, some,** or **the** in the blanks.

One day last month while I was driving through the countryside, I saw ____*a*____ man and
1

_____ truck next to _____ covered bridge. _____ bridge crossed _____ small
2　　　　　　　　　　3　　　　　　　　4　　　　　　　　　5

river. I stopped and asked _____ man, "What's the matter? Can I be of help?"
6

"Well," said _____ man, "my truck is about a half-inch* too tall. Or _____ top of
7　　　　　　　　　　　　　　　　　　　　　　　　　　　8

_____ bridge is a half-inch too short. Either way, my truck won't fit under _____
9　　　　　　　　　　　　　　　　　　　　　　　　　　　　　　　　　　　10

bridge."

"Hmmm. There must be _____ solution to this problem," I said.
11

"I don't know. I guess I'll have to turn around and take another route," he replied.

After a few moments of thought, I said, "Aha! I have _____ solution!"
12

"What is it?" asked the man.

"Let a little air out of your tires. Then _____ truck won't be too tall and you can cross
13

_____ bridge over _____ river."
14　　　　　　　15

"Hey, that's _____ great idea. Let's try it!" So _____ man let a little air out of
16　　　　　　　　　　　　　　　　　17

_____ tires and was able to cross _____ river and go on his way.
18　　　　　　　　　　　　　　19

_____
*One-half inch = 1.2 centimeters.

◇ **PRACTICE 22. Summary: A/AN vs. THE vs. Ø. (Chart 11-8)**
Directions: Complete the sentences with **a/an, the,** or **Ø**. Add capital letters as necessary.

1. A: What would you like for breakfast?

   B: ___An___ egg and some toast.

   A: How would you like ___the___ egg?

   B: Fried, sunny side up.

2. ___Ø___ eggs are nutritious.

3. It is _____ scientific fact: _____ steam rises when _____ water boils.

4. _____ gas is expensive nowadays.

5. _____ gas I got yesterday cost more than I've ever paid.

6. _____ newspapers are _____ important source of _____ information.

7. _____ sun is _____ star. We need _____ sun for _____ heat, _____ light, and _____ energy.

8. _____ ducks are my favorite farm animals.

9. _____ pizza originated in Italy. It is a pie with _____ cheese, _____ tomatoes, and other things on top. _____ "pizza" means "pie" in _____ Italian.

10. A: Hey, Nick. Pass _____ pizza. I want another piece.

    B: There are only two pieces left. You take _____ big piece, and I'll take _____ small one.

11. _____ gold is _____ excellent conductor of _____ electricity. It is used in many of the electrical circuits on _____ spaceship.

12. A: Where's Alice?

    B: She's in _____ kitchen making _____ sandwich.

13. A: Where'd _____ plumber go? _____ sink's still leaking!

    B: Relax. He went to shut off _____ water supply to _____ house. He'll fix _____ leak when he gets back.

14. A: Do you see _____ man who is standing next to Janet?

B: Yes. Who is he?

A: He's _____ president of this university.

15. A one-dollar bill has a picture of _____ president of the United States. It's a picture of George Washington.

16. A: What did you buy when you went shopping?

B: I bought _____ blouse and _____ jewelry.

A: What color is _____ blouse?

B: Red.

17. A: Where's my bookbag?

B: It's on _____ floor over there, in _____ corner next to _____ sofa.

18. We need to buy _____ furniture. I'd like to get _____ sofa and _____ easy chair.

19. _____ furniture is expensive these days.

20. _____ vegetarian doesn't eat _____ meat.

21. Only one of _____ continents in _____ world is uninhabited. Which one?

22. Last week, I took _____ easy exam. It was in my economics class. I had _____ right answers for all of _____ questions on _____ exam. My score was 100%.

23. Anyone who goes to _____ job interview should wear _____ nice clothes.

24. A mouse has _____ long, thin, almost hairless tail. _____ rats also have _____ long, skinny tails.

25. Years ago, people used _____ wood or _____ coal for _____ heat, but now most people use _____ gas, _____ oil, or _____ electricity.

26. I had _____ interesting experience yesterday. _____ man in _____ blue suit came into my office and handed me _____ bouquet of _____ flowers. I had never seen _____ man before in my life, but I thanked him for _____ flowers. Then he walked out _____ door.

27. A: What is your favorite food?

B: _____ ice cream—it's cold, sweet, and smooth.

28. We had _____ steamed rice, _____ fish, and _____ vegetables for lunch yesterday. _____ rice was cooked just right. _____ fish was very tasty. _____ vegetables were fresh.

29. Karen is _____ exceptionally talented person.

30. A: Where's _____ letter I wrote to Ted?

    B: It's gone. _____ strong wind blew it on _____ floor, and _____ dog tore it up. I threw _____ scraps in _____ wastebasket.

31. A: I'm looking for _____ tape player. Where is it?

    B: It's on one of _____ shelves next to my desk.

    A: Ah! There it is. Thanks.

    B: You're welcome.

    A: Hmmm. I don't think it works. Maybe _____ batteries are dead.

32. _____ chalk is _____ necessity in a classroom.

33. _____ efficient transportation system is _____ essential part of a healthy economy.

◇ **PRACTICE 23. Using THE or Ø with names. (Chart 11-9)**
   Directions: Complete the sentences with *the* or *Ø*.

1. Although Ingrid has been to Orly Airport several times, she has never visited ___Ø___ Paris.

2. ___The___ Atlantic Ocean is smaller than ___the___ Pacific.

3. _____ Dr. James was the youngest person at her university to get a Ph.D.

4. _____ Mt. Rainier in Washington State is in _____ Cascade Mountain Range.

5. _____ Nile is the longest river in _____ Africa.

6. Is _____ Toronto or _____ Montreal the largest city in Canada?

7. During her tour of Africa, Helen climbed _____ Mt. Kilimanjaro and visited several

   national parks in _____ Kenya.

8. _____ New Zealand is made up of two islands: North Island and South Island.

9. _____ Himalayas extend through several countries: _____ Pakistan, _____

   India, _____ Tibet, and _____ Nepal.

10. _____ President Davis was surprised to be elected to a fourth term.

11. _____ Ho Chi Minh City in _____ Vietnam was formerly called _____ Saigon.

12. _____ Andes Mountains in South America extend for 5000 miles.

Directions: Answer the questions. Choose from the list below. Use *the* if necessary. (Not all names on the list will be used.)

Africa	*Europe*	*Mont Blanc*	*Shanghai*
Alps	*Gobi Desert*	*Mt. Vesuvius*	*South America*
Amazon River	*Indian Ocean*	*Netherlands*	*Taipei*
Beijing	*Lagos*	*Nile River*	*Thames River*
Black Sea	*Lake Baikal*	*North America*	*Tibet*
Dead Sea	*Lake Tanganyika*	*Sahara Desert*	*United Arab Emirates*
Elbe River	*Lake Titicaca*	*Saudi Arabia*	*Urals*

GEOGRAPHY TRIVIA

Question	**Answer**
1. What is the lowest point on Earth?	the Dead Sea
2. What is the second-longest river in the world?	
3. What is the most populated city in China?	
4. What is the largest desert in the world?	
5. What river runs through London?	
6. On what continent is the Volga River?	
7. What mountains border France and Italy?	
8. What lake is in East Central Africa?	
9. On what continent is Mexico?	
10. What is the third-largest ocean in the world?	
11. What country is also known as Holland?	
12. What is the third-largest continent in the world?	
13. What country is located in the Himalayas?	
14. What mountains are part of the boundary between Europe and Asia?	
15. What is the capital of Nigeria?	
16. What country consists of seven kingdoms?	

◇ PRACTICE 25. Capitalization. (Chart 11-10)
   Directions: Add capital letters where necessary.

   1. I'm taking ƀ^Biology 101 this semester.

   2. I'm taking history, biology, english, and calculus this semester.

   3. Some lab classes meet on saturday.

   4. Marta lives on a busy street. Marta lives at 2358 olive street.

   5. We went to canada last summer. we went to montreal in july.

   6. My roommate likes vietnamese food, and i like thai food.

   7. The religion of saudi arabia is islam.

   8. Shelia works for the xerox corporation. it is a very large corporation.

   9. Pedro is from latin america.

10. My uncle lives in st. louis. I'm going to visit uncle bill next spring.

11. We went to a park. we went to waterfall park.

12. Are you going to the university of oregon or oregon state university?

13. Alice goes to a university in oregon.

14. The next assignment in literature class is to read *the adventures of tom sawyer.*

15. Many countries have holidays to celebrate the date they became independent. In france, they

call it "bastille day."

◇ PRACTICE 26. Capitalization. (Chart 11-10)
   Directions: Add capital letters where necessary.

   1. Do you know ɼ^Robert ɉ^Jones?

   2. Do you know my uncle? *(no change)*

   3. I like uncle joe and aunt sara.

   4. I'd like you to meet my aunt.

   5. susan w. miller is a professor.

   6. I am in prof. miller's class.

   7. The weather is cold in january.

   8. The weather is cold in winter.

   9. I have three classes on monday.

10. I would like to visit los angeles.

11. It's the largest city in california.

12. I like to visit large cities in foreign countries.

13. There are fifty states in the united states of america.

14. It used to take weeks or months to cross an ocean.

15. Today we can fly across the atlantic ocean in hours.

16. Mark lives on a busy street near the local high school.

17. Mark lives on market street near washington high school.

18. Our family stayed at a very comfortable hotel.

19. Our family stayed at the hilton hotel in bangkok.

20. Yoko is japanese, but she can also speak german.

◇ **PRACTICE 27. Error analysis. (Chapter 11)**
Directions: Correct the errors.

1. The mail carrier brought only one ~~mail~~ letter today.

2. Mr. Dale gave his class long history assignment for the weekend.

3. Tariq speaks several language, including Arabic and Spanish.

4. Dr. kim gives all her patients toothbrush and toothpaste at their dental appointments.

5. I usually have glass water with my lunch.

6. A helpful policeman gave us an information about the city.

7. This cookie recipe calls for two cup of nut.

8. Much vegetable are believed to have cancer-fighting ingredients.

9. Only applicants with the necessary experiences should apply for the computer position.

10. When Vicki likes a movie, she sees it several time.

11. A popular children's story is *Snow White And The Seven Dwarfs.*

12. Is it possible to stop all violences in the world?

CHAPTER 12
Adjective Clauses

◇ **PRACTICE 1. Using WHO in adjective clauses. (Charts 12-1 and 12-2)**
Directions: <u>Underline</u> the adjective clause in the long sentence. Then change the long sentence into two short sentences.*

1. *Long sentence:*   I thanked the man <u>who helped me move the refrigerator</u>.

   Short sentence 1: _____I thanked_____ the man.

   Short sentence 2: _____He helped_____ me move the refrigerator.

2. *Long sentence:*   A woman who was wearing a gray suit asked me for directions.

   Short sentence 1: _____ me for directions.

   Short sentence 2: _____ a gray suit.

3. *Long sentence:*   The woman who aided the rebels put her life in danger.

   Short sentence 1: _____ her life in danger.

   Short sentence 2: _____ the rebels.

4. *Long sentence:*   I saw a man who was wearing a blue coat.

   Short sentence 1: _____ a man.

   Short sentence 2: _____ a blue coat.

5. *Long sentence:*   The girl who broke the vase apologized to Mrs. Cook.

   Short sentence 1: _____ to Mrs. Cook.

   Short sentence 2: _____ the vase.

_____

*In grammar terminology, the "long sentence" is called a **complex sentence**, and the "short sentence" is called a **simple sentence**.
   • A complex sentence has an independent clause and one or more dependent clauses. For example:
     I thanked the man who helped me. = a complex sentence consisting of one independent clause (*I thanked the man*) and one dependent clause (*who helped me*).
   • A simple sentence has only an independent clause. For example:
     I thanked the man. = a simple sentence consisting of one independent clause.
     He helped me. = a simple sentence consisting of one independent clause.

◇ **PRACTICE 2. Using WHO in adjective clauses. (Chart 12-2)**

Directions: Combine the two short sentences into one long sentence using "short sentence 2" as an adjective clause. Use **who**. Underline the adjective clause.

1. *Short sentence 1:* The woman was polite.
   Short sentence 2: She answered the phone.
   Long sentence: The woman <u>who answered the phone</u> was polite.

2. *Short sentence 1:* The man has a good voice.
   Short sentence 2: He sang at the concert.

   Long sentence:

3. *Short sentence 1:* We enjoyed the actors.
   Short sentence 2: They played the leading roles.

   Long sentence:

4. *Short sentence 1:* The girl is hurt.
   Short sentence 2: She fell down the stairs.

   Long sentence:

5. *Short sentence 1:* I read about the soccer player.
   Short sentence 2: He was injured in the game yesterday.

   Long sentence:

◇ **PRACTICE 3. Using WHO and WHOM in adjective clauses. (Chart 12-2)**

Directions: Underline the adjective clause. Identify the subject and verb of the adjective clause. Then complete the change from one long sentence to two short sentences, and identify the subject and verb of the second short sentence.

1. *Long sentence:*   The people <u>who live next to me</u> are nice.
                                        S   V
   Short sentence 1: The people are nice.
   Short sentence 2: They live next to me.
                        S   V

2. *Long sentence:*   The people <u>whom Kate visited yesterday</u> were French.
                                        S   V
   Short sentence 1: The people were French.
   Short sentence 2: Kate visited them yesterday.
                        S   V

3. *Long sentence:*   The people whom I saw at the park were having a picnic.
   Short sentence 1: The people were having a picnic.

   Short sentence 2:

4. *Long sentence:*   The students who go to this school are friendly.
   Short sentence 1: The students are friendly.

   Short sentence 2:

5. *Long sentence:*   The woman whom you met last week lives in Mexico.
   Short sentence 1: The woman lives in Mexico.

   Short sentence 2:

◇ **PRACTICE 4. Using WHO and WHOM in adjective clauses. (Chart 12-2)**
   Directions: Change the two short sentences into one long sentence with an adjective clause.
   Use **who** or **whom**. <u>Underline</u> the adjective clause.

   1. *Short sentence 1:* The woman was polite.
      Short sentence 2: Jack met her.
      Long sentence: The woman <u>whom Jack met</u> was polite.

   2. *Short sentence 1:* I like the woman.
      Short sentence 2: She manages my uncle's store.
      Long sentence: I like the woman <u>who manages my uncle's store.</u>

   3. *Short sentence 1:* The singer was wonderful.
      Short sentence 2: We heard him at the concert.

      Long sentence:

   4. *Short sentence 1:* The people brought a small gift.
      Short sentence 2: They came to dinner.

      Long sentence:

   5. *Short sentence 1:* What is the name of the woman?
      Short sentence 2: Tom invited her to the dance.

      Long sentence:

◇ **PRACTICE 5. Using WHO and WHO(M) in adjective clauses. (Chart 12-2)**
   Directions: Complete the sentences with **who** or **who(m)**.*

   1. I know a man _____who_____ works at the post office.

   2. One of the people ____who(m)____ I watched at the race track lost a huge amount of money.

   3. My neighbor is a kind person _____ is always willing to help people in trouble.

   4. My mother is a woman _____ I admire tremendously.

   5. I thanked the man _____ helped me.

   6. The woman _____ I helped thanked me.

   7. The doctor _____ lives on my street is a surgeon.

   8. I talked to the people _____ were sitting next to me.

   _____

   *There are parentheses around the "m" in *who(m)* to show that, in everyday informal English, *who* may be used as an object
   pronoun instead of *whom*.

9. I saw the woman _____ was walking her dog.

10. Do you like the mechanic _____ fixed your car?

11. Mr. Polanski is a mechanic _____ you can trust.

12. There are many good people in the world _____ you can trust to be honest and honorable.

13. The children _____ live down the street in the yellow house are always polite.

14. The children _____ I watched at the park were feeding ducks in a pond.

15. My husband is a person _____ enjoys good food and good friends.

◇ PRACTICE 6. Using THAT or Ø in adjective clauses. (Chart 12-3)
Directions: Write **S** if *who* or *that* is the subject of the adjective clause. Write **O** if *who* or *that* is the object of the adjective clause. Cross out the words *who* or *that* where possible.

1. __O__ The secretary ~~that~~ I hired is very efficient.

2. __S__ The secretary **who** works in the office next door is interviewing for my old job.

3. _____ The students **who** worked together in study groups got the highest scores on the test.

4. _____ The students **who** the teacher helped did very well on the test.

5. _____ The man **that** lives next door is a famous scientist.

6. _____ The children **that** came to the party wore animal costumes.

7. _____ The teachers **who** went to the workshop felt encouraged to try new techniques.

8. _____ The teachers **that** I had for science were very well trained.

9. _____ The policeman **who** caught the thief had been watching him for days.

10. _____ The policeman **that** we met on the street told us about several interesting tourist spots.

◇ PRACTICE 7. Using THAT or Ø in adjective clauses. (Chart 12-3)
Directions: Cross out the word *that* if possible.

1. That man ~~that~~ I saw was wearing a black hat.

2. The people that visited us stayed too long. *(no change)*

3. The fruit that I bought today at the market is fresh.

4. My high school English teacher is a person that I will never forget.

5. The puppy that barked the loudest got the most attention in the pet store.

6. The girl that sits in front of Richard has long black hair that she wears in a ponytail.

7. The forest that lies below my house provides a home for deer and other wildlife.

8. The animals that live in our neighborhood behaved strangely before the earthquake.

◇ PRACTICE 8. Using WHO, WHO(M), THAT, or Ø in adjective clauses. (Chart 12-3)
Directions: In the box, write every possible pronoun that can be used to connect the adjective clause to the main clause: ***who, who(m),*** or ***that.*** Also, write ***Ø*** if the pronoun can be omitted.

1. The woman ⟦ who / that ⟧ sat next to me on the plane was very nice.

2. The woman ⟦ who(m) / that / Ø ⟧ I met on the plane was very nice.

3. Two people ⟦ ⟧ I didn't know walked into the classroom.

4. The people ⟦ ⟧ walked into the classroom were strangers.

5. My cousin's wife is the woman ⟦ ⟧ is talking to Mr. Horn.

6. I like the woman ⟦ ⟧ my brother and I visited.

◇ **PRACTICE 9. WHO and WHO(M) vs. WHICH. (Charts 12-2 → 12-4)**
Directions: Choose the correct answer.

1. The magazine _____ I read on the plane was interesting.
   A. who   B. who(m)   C. which ⓒ

2. The artist _____ drew my picture is very good.
   A. who   B. who(m)   C. which

3. I really enjoyed the experiences _____ I had on my trip to Nigeria.
   A. who   B. who(m)   C. which

4. Most of the games _____ we played as children no longer amuse us.
   A. who   B. who(m)   C. which

5. All of the people _____ I called yesterday can come to the meeting on Monday.
   A. who   B. who(m)   C. which

6. The teacher _____ was ill canceled her math class.
   A. who   B. who(m)   C. which

7. The flight _____ I took to Singapore was on time.
   A. who   B. who(m)   C. which

8. I read an article _____ discussed the current political crisis.
   A. who   B. who(m)   C. which

◇ **PRACTICE 10. Adjective clauses. (Charts 12-2 → 12-4)**
Directions: Complete the definitions with the given information. Use adjective clauses in the definitions.

> *S/he leaves society and lives completely alone.*
> *It has a hard shell and can live in water or on land.*
> ✓ *S/he designs buildings.*
> *It forms when water boils.*
> *S/he doesn't eat meat.*
> *It grows in hot climates and produces large bunches of yellow fruit.*
> *It cannot be understood or explained.*
> *It can be shaped and hardened to form many useful things.*

1. An architect is someone _____who/that designs buildings._____

2. A vegetarian is a person _____

3. Steam is a gas _____

4. A turtle is an animal _____

5. A hermit is a person _____

6. A banana tree is a plant _____

7. Plastic is a synthetic material _____

8. A mystery is something _____

◇ PRACTICE 11. WHICH and THAT. (Chart 12-4)
Directions: Write **S** if *which* or *that* is the subject of the adjective clause. Write **O** if *which* or *that* is the object of the adjective clause. Cross out the words *which* or *that* where possible.

1. __O__ The medicine ~~which~~ the doctor prescribed for me was very expensive.

2. __S__ The medicine **which** is on the shelf is no longer good.

3. _____ The computer **that** I bought recently has already crashed several times.

4. _____ The car **which** my husband drives is very reliable.

5. _____ The house **which** sits on top of the hill has won several architecture awards.

6. _____ The restaurant **that** offered low-cost dinners to senior citizens has recently closed.

7. _____ The baseball **which** all the players autographed will be donated to charity.

8. _____ The windstorm **that** is moving toward us is very powerful.

9. _____ The trees **that** shade our house are over 300 years old.

10. _____ The trees **that** we planted last year have doubled in size.

◇ PRACTICE 12. Using WHICH, THAT, and Ø in adjective clauses. (Chart 12-4)
Directions: Write the pronouns that can be used to connect the adjective clause to the main clause: *which* or *that*. Also write **Ø** if the pronoun can be omitted.

1. I really enjoyed the show | which / that / Ø | we saw last night.

2. Tim liked the show [ ] was playing at the Fox Theater.

3. The plane [ ] I took to Korea arrived on time.

4. The plane [ ] flew to the Gold Coast left on time.

5. The books ☐ Jane ordered came in the mail today.

6. Jane was glad to get the books ☐ came in the mail today.

◇ **PRACTICE 13. Error analysis: object pronouns in adjective clauses.** (Charts 12-3 and 12-4)
Directions: Cross out the incorrect pronouns in the adjective clauses.

1. I enjoy the relatives I visited ~~them~~ in Mexico City last year.

2. The coffee that I drank it was cold and tasteless.

3. The tennis shoes I was wearing them in the garden got wet and muddy.

4. My cousin Ahmed is a person I've known and loved him since he was born.

5. I have a great deal of respect for the wonderful woman I married her eleven years ago.

6. The dog which we have had him for several years is very gentle with young children.

◇ **PRACTICE 14. Pronoun usage in adjective clauses.** (Charts 12-2 → 12-4)
Directions: Choose the correct answers. NOTE: There is more than one correct answer for each sentence.

1. I liked the teacher _____ I had for chemistry in high school.
   Ⓐ whom   B. which   Ⓒ that   Ⓓ Ø

2. The university scientist _____ did research in the Amazon River basin found many previously unknown species of plants.
   A. who   B. whom   C. which   D. that   E. Ø

3. The children enjoyed the sandwiches _____ Mr. Rice made for them.
   A. who   B. whom   C. which   D. that   E. Ø

4. Have you ever read any books by the author _____ the teacher mentioned in class this morning?
   A. whom   B. which   C. that   D. Ø

5. The fans _____ crowded the ballpark roared their approval.
   A. who   B. whom   C. which   D. that   E. Ø

6. Have you been to the Clayton Art Gallery? It has a new exhibit _____ includes the work of several local artists.
   A. who   B. whom   C. which   D. that   E. Ø

7. The operation _____ the surgeon performed on my uncle was very dangerous.
   A. who   B. whom   C. which   D. that   E. Ø

8. Bricks are made of soil _____ has been placed in molds, pounded down, and dried.
   A. who   B. whom   C. which   D. that   E. Ø

9. The actors _____ we saw at Stratford performed out-of-doors.
   A. whom   B. which   C. that   D. Ø

10. Many of the games _____ children play teach them about the adult world.
    A. who   B. whom   C. which   D. that   E. Ø

11. When Jason arrived at the reunion, the first person _____ he encountered was Sally Sellers, one of his best friends when he was in high school.
    A. whom   B. which   C. that   D. Ø

12. Fire swept through an old apartment building in the center of town. I know some of the people _____ the firefighters rescued. The people lost all their possessions. They were grateful simply to be alive.
    A. whom   B. which   C. that   D. Ø

13. Most of the islands in the Pacific are the tops of volcanic mountains _____ rise from the floor of the ocean.
    A. who   B. whom   C. which   D. that   E. Ø

◇ **PRACTICE 15. Subject–verb agreement in adjective clauses. (Chart 12-5)**

Directions: In each sentence, choose the correct form of the verb in *italics*. Use the simple present. Underline the noun that determines whether the verb in the adjective clause is singular or plural.

1. The <u>students</u> who *is*, (*are*) in my class come from many countries.

2. The people who *is, are* standing in line to get into the theater are cold and wet.

3. Water is a chemical compound that *consists, consist* of oxygen and hydrogen.

4. There are two students in my class who *speaks, speak* Portuguese.

5. I met some people who *knows, know* my brother.

6. The student who *is, are* talking to the teacher is from Peru.

7. Do you know the people that *lives, live* in that house?

8. A carpenter is a person who *makes, make* things out of wood.

9. Sculptors are artists who *make, makes* things from clay or other materials.

◇ PRACTICE 16. Prepositions in adjective clauses. (Chart 12-6)

Directions: The adjective clauses in the following sentences need prepositions. Add the prepositions and give all the possible patterns for the adjective clause. Write Ø if nothing is needed.

1. The bus _____that_____ we were waiting _____for_____ was an hour late.

   The bus _____which_____ we were waiting _____for_____ was an hour late.

   The bus _____Ø_____ we were waiting _____for_____ was an hour late.

   The bus ___for which___ we were waiting _____Ø_____ was an hour late.

2. The music _____ I listened _____ was pleasant.

   The music _____ I listened _____ was pleasant.

   The music _____ I listened _____ was pleasant.

   The music _____ I listened _____ was pleasant.

3. Ecology is one of the subjects _____ I am very interested _____ .

   Ecology is one of the subjects _____ I am very interested _____ .

   Ecology is one of the subjects _____ I am very interested _____ .

   Ecology is one of the subjects _____ I am very interested _____ .

4. The man _____ Maria was arguing _____ was very angry.

   The man _____ Maria was arguing _____ was very angry.

   The man _____ Maria was arguing _____ was very angry.

   The man _____ Maria was arguing _____ was very angry.

◇ **PRACTICE 17. Prepositions in adjective clauses. (Chart 12-6 and Appendix 2)**

Directions: Complete the sentences with pronouns and prepositions as necessary. Give all possible patterns for the adjective clauses.

Example: The movie . . . we went . . . was good.
→ *The movie that we went to was good.*
The movie which we went to was good.
The movie Ø we went to was good.
The movie to which we went was good.

1. I enjoyed meeting the people . . . you introduced me . . . yesterday.
2. English grammar is a subject . . . I am quite familiar . . . .
3. The woman . . . Mr. Low told us . . . works for the government.
4. The people . . . I work . . . are very creative.
5. The train . . . you are waiting . . . is usually late.
6. The job . . . I am interested . . . requires several years of computer experience.

◇ **PRACTICE 18. Prepositions in adjective clauses. (Chart 12-6 and Appendix 2)**

Directions: Supply appropriate prepositions in the blanks. Write Ø if no preposition is necessary. Draw brackets around the adjective clause.

1. I enjoyed the CD [we listened ___to___ at Sara's apartment.]

2. I paid the shopkeeper for the glass cup [I accidentally broke ___Ø___ .]

3. The bus we were waiting _____ was only three minutes late.

4. Mrs. Chan is someone I always enjoy talking _____ about politics.

5. I showed my roommate the letter I had just written _____ .

6. One of the subjects I've been interested _____ for a long time is astronomy.

7. The people I talked _____ at the reception were interesting.

8. One of the places I want to visit _____ next year is Mexico City.

9. The book catalogue I was looking _____ had hundreds of interesting titles.

10. The book I wanted _____ wasn't available at the library.

11. I really enjoyed the music we were listening _____ at Jim's yesterday.

12. Botany is a subject I'm not familiar _____ .

13. The bags I was carrying _____ were really heavy.

14. My parents are people I can always rely _____ for support and help.

15. Taking out the garbage is one of the chores our fourteen-year-old is responsible _____ .

16. The newspaper I was reading _____ had the latest news about the election.

17. The furniture I bought _____ was expensive.

18. English grammar is one of the subjects _____ which I enjoy studying the most.

19. The friend I waved _____ didn't wave back. Maybe he just didn't see me.

20. The people _____ whom Alex was waiting were over an hour late.

◇ **PRACTICE 19. Adjective clauses with WHOSE. (Chart 12-7)**
Directions: <u>Underline</u> the adjective clause in each long sentence. Then change the long sentence into two short sentences.

1. *Long sentence:*   I know a man <u>whose daughter is a pilot.</u>

   Short sentence 1: _____ I know a man. _____

   Short sentence 2: _____ His daughter is a pilot. _____

2. *Long sentence:*   The woman whose husband is out of work found a job at Mel's Diner.

   Short sentence 1: _____

   Short sentence 2: _____

3. *Long sentence:*   The man whose wallet I found gave me a reward.

   Short sentence 1: _____

   Short sentence 2: _____

◇ **PRACTICE 20. Adjective clauses with WHOSE. (Chart 12-7)**
Directions: Follow these steps:
1. <u>Underline</u> the possessive pronoun.
2. Draw an arrow to the noun it refers to.
3. Replace the possessive pronoun with ***whose***.
4. Combine the two sentences into one.

1. The firefighters are very brave. <u>Their</u> department has won many awards.
   → *The firefighters whose department has won many awards are very brave.*

2. I talked to the boy. <u>His</u> kite was caught in a tree.
   → *I talked to the boy whose kite was caught in a tree.*

3. The family is staying in a motel. Their house burned down.

4. I watched a little girl. Her dog was chasing a ball in the park.

5. The reporter won an award. Her articles explained global warming.

6. I know a man. His daughter entered college at the age of fourteen.

7. We observed a language teacher. Her teaching methods included role-playing.

8. The teachers are very popular. Their methods include role-playing.

◇ **PRACTICE 21. Meaning of adjective clauses. (Charts 12-1 → 12-7)**
   Directions: Check all the sentences that are true.

1. The policeman who gave Henry a ticket seemed very nervous.

   a. __✓__ Henry received a ticket.

   b. _____ Henry seemed nervous.

   c. __✓__ The policeman seemed nervous.

2. A co-worker of mine whose wife is a pilot is afraid of flying.

   a. _____ My co-worker is a pilot.

   b. _____ My co-worker's wife is afraid of flying.

   c. _____ The pilot is a woman.

3. The man that delivers office supplies to our company bought a Ferrari.

   a. _____ Our company bought a Ferrari.

   b. _____ A man delivers office supplies.

   c. _____ A man bought a Ferrari.

4. The doctor who took care of my father had a heart attack recently.

   a. _____ My father had a heart attack.

   b. _____ The doctor treated a heart attack patient.

   c. _____ The doctor had a heart attack.

5. The forest fire which destroyed two homes in Woodville burned for two weeks across a wide area.

   a. _____ The forest fire burned for two weeks.

   b. _____ Two homes burned for two weeks.

   c. _____ The forest fire destroyed Woodville.

6. The salesman who sold my friend a used car was arrested for changing the mileage on cars.

   a. _____ My friend bought a car.

   b. _____ My friend was arrested.

   c. _____ The salesman changed the mileage on cars.

7. The waiter who took Julie's order is her best friend's cousin.

   a. _____ The waiter is Julie's cousin.

   b. _____ Julie's best friend is the waiter's cousin.

   c. _____ Julie's best friend is a waiter.

◇ PRACTICE 22. Adjective clauses. (Charts 12-1 → 12-7)

Directions: Use the given information to complete the sentences with adjective clauses. Omit the pronoun from the adjective clause if possible.

> *I share their views.*
> *Their children were doing poorly in her class.*
> *They disrupted the global climate and caused mass extinctions of animal life.*
> *Ted bought them for his wife on their anniversary.*
> *I slept on it at the hotel last night.*
> *They had backbones.*
> ✓*It is used to carry boats with goods and/or passengers.*

1. A waterway is a river or stream ___which/that is used to carry boats with goods___
   ___and/or passengers___ .

2. The second grade teacher talked to all the parents _____
   _____ .

3. The flowers _____
   wilted in the heat before he got home.

4. The candidates _____ will get my votes.

5. According to scientists, the first animals _____
   _____ were fish. They appeared on the
   earth about 500 million years ago.

6. Approximately 370 million years ago, seventy percent of Earth's
   marine species mysteriously vanished. Approximately 65 million
   years ago, the dinosaurs and two-thirds of all marine animal species
   became extinct. According to some scientific researchers, Earth was
   struck by speeding objects from space _____
   _____ .

◇ PRACTICE 23. Adjective clauses. (Charts 12-1 → 12-7)

Directions: Which of the following can be used in the blanks: ***who, who(m), which, that, whose***, or ***Ø***?

1. What do you say to people ___who/that___ ask you personal questions that you don't
   want to answer?

2. In my country, any person _____ is twenty-one years old or older can vote. I
   turned twenty-one last year. The person I voted for in the national election lost. I hope the
   next candidate for _____ I vote has better luck. I'd like to vote for a winning
   candidate.

3. Vegetarians are people _____ do not eat meat. True vegetarians do not eat flesh _____ comes from any living creature, including fish. Some vegetarians even exclude any food _____ is made from animal products, such as milk and eggs.

4. People _____ live in New York City are called New Yorkers.

5. Tina likes the present _____ I gave her for her birthday.

6. George Washington is the president _____ picture is on a one-dollar bill.

7. Have you seen the movie _____ is playing at the Fox Theater?

8. Do you know the woman _____ Michael is engaged to?

9. That's Tom Jenkins. He's the boy _____ parents live in Switzerland.

10. A thermometer is an instrument _____ measures temperature.

11. A high-strung person is someone _____ is always nervous.

12. The man _____ I told you about is standing over there.

◇ PRACTICE 24. Error analysis. (Chapter 12)
Directions: Correct the errors.

1. A movie that look ͜ interesting opens tomorrow.

2. My family lived in a house which it was built in 1900.

3. The little boy was lost who asked for directions.

4. I don't know people who their lives are carefree.

5. It is important to help people who has no money.

6. At the airport, I was waiting for friends which I hadn't seen them for a long time.

7. The woman live next door likes to relax by doing crossword puzzles every evening.

8. My teacher has two cats who their names are Ping and Pong.

9. A beautiful garden that separates my house from the street.

10. I asked the children who was sitting on the bench to help us.

11. The school that my children attend it is very good academically.

12. I enjoyed the songs which we sang them.

13. One of the places that I like to visit Central Park.

14. The movie we saw it last evening was very exciting.

15. I sent the parents who I hiked with their son a picture of us on Mt. Fuji.

16. Do you know the man who work in that office?

17. A mother who's daughter is in my class often brings cookies for the children.

18. The CD player who I bought can hold several CDs at once.

19. The bed which I sleep is very comfortable.

20. I would like to tell you about several problems which I have had them since I came here.

CHAPTER 13
Gerunds and Infinitives

◇ **PRACTICE 1. Verb + gerund. (Chart 13-1)**
Directions: Complete the sentences with the correct form of the verbs in parentheses.

1. Joan often talks about *(move)* _____moving_____ overseas.

2. The Browns sometimes discuss *(live)* _____ in a smaller town.

3. Christine enjoys *(take)* _____ care of her young niece.

4. Nathan keeps *(buy)* _____ lottery tickets, but he never wins.

5. My manager considered *(give)* _____ pay raises but decided not to.

6. I always put off *(do)* _____ my math homework.

7. The students finished *(review)* _____ for the test at 3:00 A.M.

8. Ann stopped *(run)* _____ and walked the rest of the way home.

9. Dana quit *(drive)* _____ after she had a serious car accident.

10. My dentist thinks about *(retire)* _____, but he enjoys his work too much.

11. Last week, Joan and David postponed *(get married)* _____ for the second time.

12. Do you mind *(work)* _____ another shift tonight?

◇ **PRACTICE 2. GO + gerund. (Chart 13-2)**
Directions: Complete the sentences with a form of *go* and one of the given words.

camp	fish	sail	sightsee	skydive
✓dance	hike	shop	ski	swim

1. I love to dance. Last night, my husband and I danced for hours.

    → Last night, my husband and I _____went dancing_____.

2. Later this afternoon, Ted is going to take a long walk in the woods.

    → Ted _____ later today.

3. Yesterday, Alice visited many stores and bought some clothes and makeup.

    → Yesterday, Alice _____.

4. Let's go to the beach and jump in the water.

→ Let's _____.

5. My grandfather takes his fishing pole to a farm pond every Sunday.

→ My grandfather _____ every Sunday.

6. When I visit a new city, I like to look around at the sights.

→ When I visit a new city, I like to _____.

7. I love to put up a small tent by a stream, make a fire, and listen to the sounds of the forest during the night.

→ I love to _____.

8. I want to take the sailboat out on the water this afternoon.

→ I want to _____ this afternoon.

9. Once a year, we take our skis to our favorite mountain resort and enjoy an exciting weekend.

→ Once a year, we _____ at our favorite mountain resort.

10. Last year on my birthday, my friends and I went up in an airplane, put on parachutes, and jumped out of the plane at a very high altitude.

→ Last year on my birthday, my friends and I

_____.

◇ **PRACTICE 3. Identifying gerunds and infinitives. (Charts 13-1 and 13-3)**
Directions: Underline the gerunds and infinitives in the sentences. Circle GER for gerunds. Circle INF for infinitives.

1. GER (INF) Ann promised to wait for me.
2. (GER) INF I kept walking even though I was tired.
3. GER INF Alex offered to help me.
4. GER INF Karen finished writing a letter and went to bed.
5. GER INF Don't forget to call me tomorrow.
6. GER INF David discussed quitting his job several times.
7. GER INF The police officers planned to work overtime during the conference.
8. GER INF Kevin would like to grow organic vegetables in his garden.

◇ **PRACTICE 4. Gerunds and infinitives. (Charts 13-1, 13-3, and 13-4)**
   Directions: Complete the sentences with the gerund or infinitive form of the verb.

   PART I. Complete the sentences with **work**.

   1. I agreed _____to work_____.

   2. I put off _____working_____.

   3. I would love _____.

   4. I thought about _____.

   5. I promised _____.

   6. I began _____.

   7. I decided _____.

   8. I offered _____.

   9. I quit _____.

   10. I refused _____.

   11. I stopped _____.

   12. I finished _____.

   PART II. Complete the sentences with **leave**.

   13. She expected _____.

   14. She wanted _____.

   15. She considered _____.

   16. She talked about _____.

   17. She postponed _____.

   18. She put off _____.

   19. She refused _____.

   20. She needed _____.

   21. She thought about _____.

   22. She hoped _____.

   PART III. Complete the sentences with **know**.

   23. They seemed _____.

   24. They expected _____.

   25. They would like _____.

   26. They don't mind _____.

   27. They would love _____.

   28. They want _____.

   29. They can't stand _____.

   30. They needed _____.

   31. They appeared _____.

   32. They hated _____.

◇ **PRACTICE 5. Verb + gerund vs. infinitive. (Charts 13-1 → 13-3)**
   Directions: Choose the correct completion.

   1. I would like _____ you and some of my other friends for dinner sometime.
      A. inviting   (B.) to invite

   2. I enjoyed _____ with my family at the lake last summer.
      A. being   B. to be

   3. Ron agreed _____ me move out of my apartment this weekend.
      A. helping   B. to help

   4. My parents can't afford _____ all of my college expenses.
      A. paying   B. to pay

   5. Liang-Siok, would you mind _____ this letter on your way home?
      A. mailing   B. to mail

   6. Do you expect _____ this course? If so, you'd better work harder.
      A. passing   B. to pass

7. Adam offered _____ for me tonight because I feel awful.
   A. working   B. to work

8. I refuse _____ your proposal. I've made up my mind.
   A. considering   B. to consider

9. I wish you would consider _____ my proposal. I know I can do the job.
   A. accepting   B. to accept

10. I don't think I'll ever finish _____ this report. It just goes on and on.
    A. reading   B. to read

11. I would enjoy _____ you in Cairo while you're studying there.
    A. visiting   B. to visit

12. The children seem _____ why they have to stay home tonight.
    A. understanding   B. to understand

13. Don't forget _____ all of the doors before you go to bed.
    A. locking   B. to lock

14. I'm really sorry. I didn't mean _____ your feelings.
    A. hurting   B. to hurt

15. Why do you keep _____ me the same question over and over again?
    A. asking   B. to ask

16. I've decided _____ for another job. I'll never be happy here.
    A. looking   B. to look

17. You need _____ harder if you want to get a promotion.
    A. trying   B. to try

18. Why do you pretend _____ his company? I know you don't like him.
    A. enjoying   B. to enjoy

19. Let's get together tonight. I want to talk about _____ a new business.
    A. opening   B. to open

20. I have a secret. Do you promise _____ no one?
    A. telling   B. to tell

21. The president plans _____ everyone a bonus at the end of the year.
    A. giving   B. to give

22. I have a good job, and I hope _____ myself all through school.
    A. supporting   B. to support

23. I can't wait _____ work today. I'm taking off on vacation tonight.
    A. finishing   B. to finish

24. My neighbor and I get up at six every morning and go _____ .
    A. jogging   B. to jog

◇ **PRACTICE 6. Verb + gerund or infinitive. (Charts 13-1 → 13-4)**
   Directions: Choose the correct answer(s). Both answers may be correct.

1. I want _____ the comedy special on TV tonight.
   A. watching   (B.) to watch

2. I'm a people-watcher. I like _____ people in public places.
   (A.) watching   (B.) to watch

3. I've already begun _____ ideas for my new novel.
   A. collecting   B. to collect

4. A group of Chinese scientists plan _____ their discovery at the conference next spring.
   A. presenting   B. to present

5. Whenever I wash my car, it starts _____ .
   A. raining   B. to rain

6. Angela and I continued _____ for several hours.
   A. talking   B. to talk

7. I love _____ on the beach during a storm.
   A. walking   B. to walk

8. I would love _____ a walk today.
   A. taking   B. to take

9. Are you sure you don't mind _____ Johnny for me while I go to the store?
   A. watching   B. to watch

10. Annie hates _____ in the rain.
    A. driving   B. to drive

11. My roommate can't stand _____ to really loud rock music.
    A. listening   B. to listen

12. I don't like _____ in front of other people.
    A. singing   B. to sing

13. Would you like _____ to the concert with us?
    A. going   B. to go

14. Charlie likes to go _____ when the weather is very windy.
    A. sailing   B. to sail

15. Most children can't wait _____ their presents on their birthday.
    A. opening   B. to open

◇ **PRACTICE 7. Verb + gerund or infinitive. (Charts 13-1, 13-3, and 13-4)**
    Directions: Complete the sentences with the infinitive or gerund form of the words in parentheses.

1. Cindy intends *(go)* _____**to go**_____ to graduate school next year.

2. Pierre can't afford *(buy)* _____ a new car.

3. Janice is thinking about *(look)* _____ for a new job.

4. I'm planning *(go)* _____ *(shop)* _____ tomorrow.

5. Would you mind *(pass)* _____ this note to Joanna? Thanks.

6. Tim expects *(go)* _____ *(fish)* _____ this weekend.

7. When Tommy broke his toy, he started *(cry)* _____ .

8. Oscar likes *(go)* _____ to professional conferences.

9. Would you like *(go)* _____ to Sharon's house next Saturday?

10. Mr. Blake appears *(have)* _____ a lot of money.

11. Eric agreed *(meet)* _____ us at the restaurant at seven.

12. Have you discussed *(change)* _____ your major with your academic advisor?

13. The Wilsons went *(camp)* _____ in Yellowstone National Park last summer.

14. What time do you expect *(arrive)* _____ in Denver?

15. Don't put off *(write)* _____ your composition until the last minute.

16. Ken had to quit *(jog)* _____ because he hurt his knee.

17. Don't forget *(call)* _____ the dentist's office this afternoon.

18. How do you expect *(pass)* _____ your courses if you don't study?

19. I haven't heard from Stacy in a long time. I keep *(hope)* _____ that I'll get a

    letter from her soon.

20. Shhh. I'm trying (concentrate) _____ . I'm doing a problem for my accounting class, and I can't afford (make) _____ any mistakes.

21. I'm sleepy. I'd like (go) _____ home and take a nap.

22. When are you going to start (do) _____ the research for your term paper?

23. Why did Marcia refuse (help) _____ us?

24. Khalid tries (learn) _____ at least 25 new words every day.

25. I considered (drive) _____ to Minneapolis. Finally I decided (fly) _____ .

26. Our teacher agreed (postpone) _____ the test until Friday.

27. I expect (be) _____ in class tomorrow.

28. I enjoy (teach) _____ .

29. Mr. Carter continued (read) _____ his book even though the children were making a lot of noise.

30. Would you like (go) _____ (dance) _____ tonight?

31. The Knickerbockers talked about (build) _____ a new house.

32. Children like (play) _____ make-believe games. Yesterday Tommy pretended (be) _____ a doctor, and Bobby pretended (be) _____ a patient.

33. My cousin offered (take) _____ me to the airport.

◇ **PRACTICE 8. Preposition + gerund. (Chart 13-5)**
Directions: Complete the sentences with the correct preposition and underline the gerund.

PART I. Liz . . .

1. is afraid ____of____ flying.

2. apologized _____ hurting her friend's feelings.

3. believes _____ helping others.

4. is good _____ listening to her friends' concerns.

5. is tired _____ working weekends.

6. is nervous _____ walking home from work late at night.

7. dreams _____ owning a farm with horses, cows, and sheep.

PART II. Leonard . . .

   8. is responsible _____ closing the restaurant where he works at night.

   9. thanked his father _____ lending him some money.

  10. plans _____ becoming an accountant.

  11. forgave his roommate _____ taking his car without asking.

  12. insists _____ eating only fresh fruits and vegetables.

  13. is looking forward _____ finishing school.

  14. stopped his best friend _____ making a bad decision.

  15. is worried _____ not having enough time for family and friends.

◇ **PRACTICE 9. Preposition + gerund. (Chart 13-5 and Appendix 2)**
    Directions: Complete the sentences. Use prepositions and gerunds.

   1. Bill interrupted me. He apologized __*for*__ that.

     → Bill apologized ____*for interrupting*____ me.

   2. I like to learn about other countries and cultures. I'm interested _____ that.

     → I'm interested _____ about other countries and cultures.

   3. I helped Ann. She thanked me _____ that.

     → Ann thanked me _____ her.

   4. Nadia wanted to walk to work. She insisted _____ that.

     → We offered Nadia a ride, but she insisted _____ to work.

   5. Nick lost my car keys. I forgave him _____ that.

     → I forgave Nick _____ my car keys when he borrowed my car.

   6. Sara wants to go out to eat just because she feels _____ it.

     → She feels _____ out to eat.

   7. I'm not a good artist. I try to draw faces, but I'm not very good _____ it.

     → I'm not good _____ faces.

   8. Mr. and Mrs. Reed have always saved for a rainy day. They believe _____ that.

     → Mr. and Mrs. Reed believe _____ for a rainy day.

   9. I may fall on my face and make a fool of myself. I'm worried _____ that.

     → I'm worried _____ on my face and _____ a fool

     of myself when I walk up the steps to receive my diploma.

10. The children are going to go to Disneyland. They're excited _____ that.

→ The children are excited _____ to Disneyland.

11. Their parents are going to Disneyland, too. They are looking forward _____ that.

→ Their parents are looking forward _____ there too.

12. Max doesn't like to stay in hotels because he is scared of heights. He is afraid _____ that.

→ Max is afraid _____ in hotels.

◇ PRACTICE 10. Review: gerund vs. infinitive. (Charts 13-1 → 13-5)
Directions: Complete the sentences with the gerund or infinitive form of the verb. Some verbs may require a preposition.

PART I. Use the verb *ask*.

1. Marie is thinking ____*about asking*____ the Petersons over for dinner.

2. Yoko intends ____*to ask*____ for a day off from work this week.

3. Mika insists _____ questions that have already been answered.

4. Chris is excited _____ the new girl in his class to the first school dance.

5. Tarik is new at school. He is nervous _____ anyone to the dance.

6. My father promised _____ the doctor for more information on his illness.

7. Mrs. Kim is responsible _____ parents to help in their children's classroom.

8. Jody would love _____ her former boyfriend to her wedding, but her fiance has said "no."

9. Jerry hates _____ for directions when he's lost.

10. Mansour is very independent and doesn't like _____ others for help with anything.

PART II. Use the verb *fix*.

11. Hiro agreed _____ the window after he broke it.

12. Hiro began _____ it, but he soon needed more parts.

13. Janet intends _____ her bicycle herself.

14. Janet learned how _____ her bicycle from her mother.

15. Her mother learned _____ bicycles from her father.

16. My parents talk _____ their sailboat before summer.

17. The little boy tried _____ his parent's leaky faucet.

18. His father attempted _____ his son's repairs, but couldn't.

19. A plumber promised _____ the faucet the next day.

20. The plumber finished _____ the faucet in ten minutes.

◇ PRACTICE 11. Review. (Charts 13-1 → 13-5)
Directions: Complete the sentences with verbs from the list. Use each verb only once.

adopt	cash	install	stay	use
be	go	lower	take	✓write

1. Ruth puts off _____*writing*_____ thank-you notes for gifts because she doesn't know what to say.

2. The city intends _____ a new traffic light at its most dangerous intersection.

3. I meant _____ my paycheck on the way home, but I forgot.

4. Would you mind _____ at the office late tonight so we can finish our budget review?

5. The bus drivers are on strike. They refuse _____ back to work until they get a new contract.

6. The Adamses want another child. They are discussing _____ a baby from another country.

7. Sue can't afford _____ a vacation this year because she didn't get a pay raise.

8. My mother is an old-fashioned cook. She doesn't believe _____ frozen or canned foods.

9. Little Daniel pretends _____ a monster whenever someone comes to the door.

10. Politicians always promise _____ taxes, but my taxes keep rising.

◇ PRACTICE 12. Review. (Charts 13-1 → 13-5)
Directions: Complete the sentences with the appropriate gerund or infinitive of the word in *italics*. (Some sentences can take either a gerund or an infinitive.) Some sentences require a preposition as well.

1. Matthew wanted to *go* to a different doctor for his back pain. He considered

    _____*going*_____ to a specialist.

2. Jim would rather walk than *drive* to work. Instead ____*of driving*____ , Jim walks along bike trails to his office.

3. I need to drive to the airport, but I don't want to *park* there. I'm not planning _____ there because it's too expensive.

4. I never *watch* commercials on TV. In fact, I can't stand _____ TV commercials, so I generally watch videotaped shows.

5. Joanne's hobby is *cooking*. She loves _____ gourmet meals for friends and relatives.

6. Here's some fresh bread I just *baked*. I enjoy _____ a variety of breads. They're so much better than store-bought.

7. Martina is nervous about *going* to the dentist for a filling. She has been afraid _____ _____ the dentist since she was a little girl.

8. Walter's dream is to *become* a doctor in a rural area. He has dreamed _____ _____ a doctor since he was hospitalized as a child.

9. Nathan *has* a chocolate milkshake every afternoon for a snack. He often feels like _____ two, but he doesn't.

10. Every morning, rain or shine, Debbie rises early and stretches. Then she goes outside and *runs* for 30 minutes. Every morning, Debbie goes _____ for half an hour.

11. Marta's neighbors *watered* her plants while she was out of town, and she thanked them with a bouquet of flowers when she returned. Marta thanked her neighbors _____ _____ her flowers while she was gone.

12. Sandy *spoke* harshly to her secretary one morning without meaning to. She immediately apologized _____ harshly.

13. Mark *washes* all his clothes in hot water. Although his roommates tell him hot water could damage some clothes, he doesn't listen. He insists _____ all his clothes in hot water.

14. The little girl didn't see the car rolling slowly toward her. No one was in it, and fortunately a neighbor jumped into the car and stopped it before it could *hit* her. The neighbor stopped the car _____ the girl.

15. When Rita came to work, her eyes *were* red and she appeared upset, but she said everything was OK. Later, she was laughing and looked more relaxed. Rita seemed _____ better.

16. If the construction company doesn't complete the highway repairs on time, it will have to pay a fine for every day it is late. Crews are working around the clock to *repair* the highway. They believe they will finish _____ it on time.

17. Richard's company is reorganizing. Some people will lose their jobs, and others will *get* new positions. Richard really likes this firm and hopes _____ a new position.

18. Christine grew up in a family of ten children. She enjoys her brothers and sisters, but doesn't want to *have* such a large family herself. She plans _____ a smaller family.

19. Noelle started her own company and hasn't had a vacation in three years. She doesn't feel she can *take* a vacation until the company is financially stable. She is looking forward _____ a vacation when the company is more financially secure.

20. Tang has been studying medicine abroad for two years and hasn't *seen* his family in all that time. He is going home next week and is very excited _____ his family.

◇ **PRACTICE 13. BY + gerund. (Chart 13-6)**
Directions: Describe what the people did by using *by* + a gerund.

1.   MARY: How did you comfort the child?
      SUE: I held him in my arms.

      → Sue comforted the child _____by holding_____ him in her arms.

2.   PAT: How did you improve your vocabulary?
      NADIA: I read a lot of books.

      → Nadia improved her vocabulary _____ a lot of books.

3.   KIRK: How did Grandma amuse the children?
      SALLY: She read them a story.

      → Grandma amused the children _____ them a story.

4.   MASAKO: How did you improve your English?
      PEDRO: I watched TV a lot.

      → Pedro improved his English _____ TV a lot.

5.   JEFFREY: How did you catch up with the bus?
      JIM: I ran as fast as I could.

      → Jim caught up with the bus _____ as fast as he could.

6.   MR. LEE: How did you earn your children's respect?
      MR. FOX: I treated them with respect at all times.

      → Mr. Smith earned his children's respect _____ them with respect at all times.

◇ **PRACTICE 14. BY + gerund. (Chart 13-6)**

Directions: Complete the sentences in Column A with **by** + an appropriate idea from Column B.

Example: I arrived on time
→ *I arrived on time by taking a taxi instead of a bus.*

Column A

1. I arrived on time
2. I put out the fire
3. Giraffes can reach the leaves at the tops of trees
4. I fixed the chair
5. Sylvia was able to buy an expensive stereo system
6. A hippopotamus can cross a river
7. I figured out how to cook the noodles
8. Pam finished her project on time
9. You can figure out how old a tree is

Column B

A. tighten the loose screws
B. count its rings
C. read the directions on the package
D. walk on the bottom of the riverbed
E. pour water on it
F. work all through the night
G. stretch their long necks
H. save her money for two years
✓I. take a taxi instead of a bus

CROSS-SECTION

20 RINGS
20 YEARS OLD

◇ **PRACTICE 15. BY vs. WITH. (Chart 13-6)**

Directions: Complete the sentences with **by** or **with**.

1. Alice greeted me _____with_____ a smile.

2. Ms. Williams goes to work every day _____by_____ bus.

3. I pounded the nail into the wood _____ a hammer.

4. Tom went to the next city _____ train.

5. I got in touch with Bill _____ phone.

6. Po eats _____ chopsticks.

7. I didn't notice that the envelope wasn't addressed to me. I opened it _____

   mistake.

8. I sent a message to Ann _____ fax.

9. Jack protected his eyes from the sun _____ his hand.

10. Janice put out the fire _____ a bucket of water.

11. I pay my bills _____ mail.

12. I solved the math problem _____ a calculator.

13. We traveled to Boston _____ car.

14. The rider kicked the sides of the horse _____ her heels.

15. Jim was extremely angry. He hit the wall _____ his fist.

16. At the beach, Julie wrote her name in the sand _____ her finger.

◇ **PRACTICE 16. Gerund as subject; IT + infinitive. (Chart 13-7)**

Directions: Complete the sentences by using *a gerund as the subject* or *it* + infinitive. Add the word *is* where appropriate. Use the verbs in the list.

complete	eat	live
drive	✓learn	swim

1. a. _____It is_____ easy for anyone _____to learn_____ how to cook an egg.

   b. _____Learning_____ how to cook an egg _____is_____ easy for anyone.

2. a. _____ nutritious food _____ important for your health.

   b. _____ important for your health _____ nutritious food.

3. a. _____ on the wrong side of the road _____ against the law.

   b. _____ against the law _____ on the wrong side of the road.

4. a. _____ fun for both children and adults _____ in the ocean.

   b. _____ in the ocean _____ fun for both children and adults.

5. a. _____ expensive _____ in a dormitory?

   b. _____ in a dormitory expensive?

6. a. _____ difficult _____ these sentences correctly?

   b. _____ these sentences correctly difficult?

◇ **PRACTICE 17. Purpose: TO vs. FOR. (Chart 13-8)**

Directions: Rewrite the sentences. Use *it ... for someone* + *an infinitive phrase.* Use the adjective in parentheses.

1. Shy people have a hard time meeting others at social events. *(difficult)*

   _____It is difficult for shy people to meet_____ others at social events.

2. Babies enjoy looking at black-and-white objects. *(interesting)*

   _____ at black-and-white objects.

3. In many cultures, young children sleep in the same room as their parents. *(customary)*

   In many cultures, _____ in the same

   room as their parents.

4. Airline pilots need to have good eyesight. *(necessary)*

   _____ good eyesight.

5. Many teenagers can't wake up early. *(hard)*

   _____ early.

6. Elderly people need to keep their minds active. *(important)*

   _____ their minds active.

7. People don't like listening to monotone speakers. *(boring)*

   _____ to monotone speakers.

8. Students need to have strategies to remember new information. *(necessary)*

   _____ strategies to remember new

   information.

9. Scientists will never know the origin of every disease in the world. *(impossible)*

   _____ the origin of every disease in

   the world.

10. Parents should teach their children by modeling good behavior. *(important)*

    _____ their children by modeling

    good behavior.

11. People are often more critical of others than of themselves. *(easy)*

    _____ more critical of others than of

    themselves.

12. Small children shouldn't cross a busy street without help *(dangerous)*

    _____ a busy street without help.

◇ **PRACTICE 18. Purpose: TO vs. FOR. (Chart 13-9)**
    Directions: Complete the sentences with **to** or **for**.

PART I. Yesterday, I called the doctor's office . . .

1. _____for_____ an appointment.
2. _____to_____ make an appointment.
3. _____ get a prescription.
4. _____ a prescription.
5. _____ ask a question.
6. _____ get some advice.
7. _____ some advice.

PART II. Yesterday, Chuck stayed after class . . .

8. _____ get help from the teacher.
9. _____ talk with the teacher.
10. _____ a talk with the teacher.
11. _____ extra help.
12. _____ finish a project.
13. _____ work with other students.
14. _____ a meeting with other students.
15. _____ help plan a class party.

◇ **PRACTICE 19. Purpose: TO vs. FOR. (Chart 13-9)**
    Directions: Complete the sentences with **to** or **for**.

1. We wear coats in the winter _____to_____ keep warm.
2. We wear coats in the winter _____for_____ warmth.
3. Mark contacted a lawyer _____ legal advice.
4. Mark contacted a lawyer _____ discuss a legal problem.
5. Sam went to the hospital _____ an operation.
6. I hired a cab _____ take me to the boat dock.
7. Frank went to the library _____ review for the test.
8. I play tennis twice a week _____ exercise and relaxation.
9. Jennifer used some medicine _____ cure an infection on her arm.
10. I lent Yvette money _____ her school expenses.
11. I went to my manager _____ permission to take the rest of the day off.

◇ **PRACTICE 20. (IN ORDER) TO. (Chart 13-9)**
    Directions: Combine the given phrases in *italics* to create sentences using **(in order) to**.

1. *watch the news + turn on the TV*

    After he got home from work, Jack _____turned on the TV (in order) to watch_____
    _____the news._____

2. *wash his clothes + go to the laundromat*

    Every weekend Martin _____
    _____

3. *run + get to class on time*

Every morning Jeannette _____

_____

4. *let in some fresh air + open the bedroom windows*

Every night I _____

5. *ask them for some money + write a letter to his parents*

Sometimes Pierre _____

6. *listen to a baseball game + have the radio on*

Some afternoons at work, my co-workers _____

_____

7. *study in peace and quiet + go to the library*

Some evenings, I _____

◇ **PRACTICE 21. TOO vs. ENOUGH. (Chart 13-10)**

Directions: Complete the sentences with the words in parentheses and **too** or **enough**.

1. I have a tight schedule tomorrow, so I can't go to the park.

   a. *(time)* I don't have ____enough time to go____ to the park.

   b. *(busy)* I'm ____too busy to go____ to the park.

2. I'm pretty short. I can't touch the ceiling.

   a. *(tall)* I'm not _____ to touch the ceiling.

   b. *(short)* I'm _____ to touch the ceiling.

3. Tom has been out of work for months. He can't pay any of his bills.

   a. *(money)* Tom doesn't have _____ to pay his bills.

   b. *(poor)* Tom is _____ to pay his bills.

4. This tea is very hot. I need to wait a while until I can drink it.

   a. *(hot)* This tea is _____ to drink.

   b. *(cool)* This tea isn't _____ to drink.

5. I feel sick. I don't want to eat anything.

   a. *(sick)* I feel _____ .

   b. *(well)* I don't feel _____ .

6. Susie is only six years old. She can't stay home by herself.

   a. *(old)* _____ .

   b. *(young)* _____ .

◇ **PRACTICE 22. TOO vs. ENOUGH. (Chart 13-10)**
   Directions: Complete the sentences with *too*, *enough*, or **Ø**.

1. I think this problem is _____Ø_____ important _____enough_____ to require our immediate
   attention.

2. Nora is not _____too_____ tired _____Ø_____ to finish the project before she goes home.

3. I can't take the citizenship test next week. I haven't had _____ time _____
   to study for it.

4. The sun is _____ bright _____ to look at directly.

5. You can do this math problem by yourself. You're _____ smart _____ to
   figure it out.

6. Our company is _____ successful _____ to start several new branches
   overseas.

7. My niece doesn't drive yet. She's _____ young _____ to get a driver's
   license.

8. Robert is an amazing runner. His coach thinks he is _____ good _____
   to begin training for an Olympic marathon.

9. Only one person volunteered to help us. We don't have _____ help _____
   to finish this task.

10. Look at the children watching the clowns. They can't sit still. They're _____
    excited _____ to stay in their chairs.

11. I would love to go hiking with you in the mountains, but I don't think I have _____
    energy or strength _____ to hike for two days.

12. The heat outside is terrible! It's _____ hot _____ to fry an egg on the
    sidewalk!

◇ **PRACTICE 23. Gerund vs. infinitive. (Chapter 13)**
   Directions: Underline the gerunds and infinitives.

1. Do you enjoy <u>being</u> alone sometimes, or do you prefer <u>to be</u> with other people all the time?

2. My son isn't old enough to stay home alone.

3. Jim offered to help me with my work.

4. I called my friend to thank her for the lovely gift.

5. Mary talked about going downtown tomorrow, but I'd like to stay home.

6. It is interesting to learn about earthquakes.

7. Approximately one million earthquakes occur around the world in a year's time. Six thousand can be felt by humans. Of those, one hundred and twenty are strong enough to cause serious damage to buildings, and twenty are violent enough to destroy a city.

8. It's important to recognize the power of nature. A recent earthquake destroyed a bridge in California. It took five years for humans to build the bridge. It took nature fifteen seconds to knock it down.

9. Predicting earthquakes is difficult. I read about one scientist who tries to predict earthquakes by reading the daily newspaper's lost-and-found ads for lost pets. He believes that animals can sense an earthquake before it comes. He thinks they then begin to act strangely. Dogs and cats respond to the threat by running away to a safer place. By counting the number of ads for lost pets, he expects to be able to predict when an earthquake will occur.

◇ PRACTICE 24. Gerund vs. infinitive. (Chapter 13)
Directions: Complete the sentences with the words in parentheses: gerund or infinitive.

1. *(study)* _____Studying_____ English is fun.

2. My boss makes a habit of *(jot)*★ _____ quick notes to her employees when they've done a good job.

3. From the earth, the sun and the moon appear *(be)* _____ almost the same size.

4. A: I don't like airplanes.

   B: Why? Are you afraid of *(fly)* _____?

   A: No, I'm afraid of *(crash)* _____.

5. A: Let's quit *(argue)* _____. We're getting nowhere. Let's just agree *(disagree)* _____ and still *(be)* _____ friends.

   B: Sounds good to me. And I apologize for *(raise)* _____ my voice. I didn't mean *(yell)* _____ at you.

   A: That's okay. I didn't intend *(get)* _____ angry at you either.

6. A: David, why did you want *(sneak)* _____ into the movie theater without *(pay)* _____?

   B: I don't know, Mom. My friends talked me into *(do)* _____ it, I guess.

_____
★*Jot* = write quickly and briefly.

A: That's not a very good reason. <u>You</u> are responsible for your actions, not your friends.

B: I know. I'm sorry.

A: How does this make you feel? Do you like yourself for *(try)* _____ *(sneak)* _____ into the theater?

B: No. It doesn't make me feel good about myself.

A: You're young. We all have lessons like this to learn as we grow up. Just remember: It's essential for you *(have)* _____ a good opinion of yourself. It's very important for all of us *(like)* _____ ourselves. When we do something wrong, we stop *(like)* _____ ourselves, and that doesn't feel good. Do you promise never *(do)* _____ anything like that again?

B: Yes. I promise! I'm really sorry, Mom.

7. People in the modern world are wasteful of natural resources. For example, every three months, people in North America throw away enough aluminum *(build)* _____ an entire airplane.

8. I am so busy! I have just enough time *(do)* _____ what I need *(do)* _____, but not enough time *(do)* _____ what I'd like *(do)* _____ .

9. A: What do you feel like *(do)* _____ this afternoon?

   B: I feel like *(go)* _____ *(shop)* _____ at the mall.

   A: I feel like *(go)* _____ to a used car lot and *(pretend)* _____ *(be)* _____ interested in *(buy)* _____ a car.

   B: You're kidding. Why would you want *(do)* _____ that?

   A: I like cars. Maybe we could even take one out for a test drive. You know I'm planning *(get)* _____ a car as soon as I can afford *(buy)* _____ one. I can't wait *(have)* _____ my own car. Maybe we'll find the car of my dreams at a used car lot. Come on. It sounds like fun.

   B: Nah. Not me. You go ahead. *(pretend)* _____ *(be)* _____ interested in *(buy)* _____ a used car isn't my idea of fun.

10. A: Have you called Amanda yet?

    B: No. I keep *(put)* _____ it off.

    A: Why?

    B: She's mad at me for *(forget)* _____ *(send)* _____ her a card on her birthday.

A: It's silly for her *(get)* _____ mad about something like that. Just call her

and say you are sorry about *(remember, not)* _____ to wish her a

happy birthday. She can't stay mad at you forever.

11. One of my good friends, Larry, has the bad habit of *(interrupt)* _____

others while they're talking.

12. In days of old, it was customary for a servant *(taste)* _____ the king's food

before the king ate *(make)* _____ sure it was not poisoned.

◇ PRACTICE 25. Error analysis. (Chapter 13)
Directions: Correct the errors.

1. I decided not ~~buying~~ a new car.
    ^{to buy}

2. The Johnsons are considering to sell their antique store.

3. Sam finally finished build his vacation home in the mountains.

4. My wife and I go to dancing at the community center every Saturday night.

5. Suddenly, it began to raining and the wind started to blew.

6. The baby is afraid be away from her mother for any length of time.

7. I am excited for start college this September.

8. You can send your application fax.

9. My country is too beautiful.

10. Is exciting a sports car to drive.

11. My grandparents enjoy to traveling across the country in a motor home.

12. Elena made this sweater with her hands.

13. Swimming it is one of the sports we can participate in at school.

14. That was very good, but I'm too full no eat any more.

15. My mother-in-law went to a tourist shop for buying a disposable camera.

16. Instead to get her degree in four years, Michelle decided traveling abroad first.

17. Swim with a group of people is more enjoyable than swim alone.

18. Is interesting meet new people.

19. Is hard me to stay up past 9:00.

20. The professor thanked his students do well on the test.

CHAPTER 14
Noun Clauses

◇ PRACTICE 1. Information questions and noun clauses. (Charts 5-2 and 14-2)

Directions: If the sentence contains a noun clause, underline it and circle NOUN CLAUSE. If the question word introduces a question, circle QUESTION. Add appropriate final punctuation: a period (.) or a question mark (?).

1. I don't know <u>where Jack bought his boots.</u> (NOUN CLAUSE) QUESTION

2. Where did Jack buy his boots? NOUN CLAUSE (QUESTION)

3. I don't understand why Ann left NOUN CLAUSE QUESTION

4. Why did Ann leave NOUN CLAUSE QUESTION

5. I don't know where your book is NOUN CLAUSE QUESTION

6. Where is your book NOUN CLAUSE QUESTION

7. When did Bob come NOUN CLAUSE QUESTION

8. I don't know when Bob came NOUN CLAUSE QUESTION

9. What does "calm" mean NOUN CLAUSE QUESTION

10. Tarik knows what "calm" means NOUN CLAUSE QUESTION

11. I don't know how long the earth has existed NOUN CLAUSE QUESTION

12. How long has the earth existed NOUN CLAUSE QUESTION

◇ PRACTICE 2. Noun clauses. (Chart 14-2)

Directions: Underline the noun clause in each sentence. Draw brackets around and identify the subject (**s**) and verb (**v**) of the noun clause.

1. I don't know <u>where [Patty] [went] last night</u>.

2. Do you know <u>where [Joe's parents] [live]</u>?*

---

*A question mark is used at the end of this noun clause because the main subject and verb of the sentence (*Do you know*) are a question. *Do you know* asks a question; *where Joe lives* is a noun clause.

3. I know where Joe lives.

4. Do you know what time the movie begins?

5. She explained where Brazil is.

6. I don't believe what Estefan said.

7. I don't know when the packages will arrive.

8. Please tell me how far it is to the post office.

9. I don't know who knocked on the door.

10. I wonder what happened at the party last night.

◇ **PRACTICE 3. Information questions and noun clauses. (Charts 5-2 and 14-2)**
Directions: Underline the noun clause. Change the underlined noun clause to a question.

1.   QUESTION: ___Why did Tim leave?___
     NOUN CLAUSE: I don't know <u>why Tim left</u>.

2.   QUESTION: ___Where___
     NOUN CLAUSE: I don't know <u>where he went</u>.

3.   QUESTION: _____
     NOUN CLAUSE: I don't know where he lives.

4.   QUESTION: _____
     NOUN CLAUSE: I don't know where he is now.

5.   QUESTION: _____
     NOUN CLAUSE: I don't know what time he will return.

6.   QUESTION: _____
     NOUN CLAUSE: I don't know how far it is to his house.

7.   QUESTION: _____
     NOUN CLAUSE: I don't know who lives next door to him.

8.   QUESTION: _____
     NOUN CLAUSE: I don't know what happened to him.

◇ **PRACTICE 4. Information questions and noun clauses. (Charts 5-2 and 14-2)**
Directions: Complete the question and noun clause forms of the given sentences.

1. Marcos left at 11:00.

When   ___did Marcos leave?___

Could you tell me   ___when Marcos left?___

2. He said good-bye.

What _____

I didn't hear _____

3. The post office is on Second Street.

Where _____

Could you please tell me _____

4. It's half-past six.

What time _____

Could you please tell me _____

5. David arrived two days ago.

When _____

I don't know _____

6. Anna is from Peru.

What country _____

I'd like to know _____

7. Kathy was absent because she was ill.

Why _____ absent?

Do you know _____ absent?

8. Pedro lives next door.

Who _____ next door?

Do you know _____ next door?

9. Eric invited Sonya to the party.

Who(m) _____ to the party?

Do you know _____ to the party?

10. The Bakers borrowed our camping equipment.

Who _____ our camping equipment?

Do you remember _____ our camping equipment?

11. The restrooms are located down the hall.

Where _____

Could you please tell me _____

◇ **PRACTICE 5. Noun clauses.** (Chart 14-2)
   Directions: Complete the sentences by changing the given questions to noun clauses.

1. *Who(m) did Helen talk to?* Do you know _____ who (m) Helen talked to? _____

2. *Who lives in that apartment?* Do you know _____

3. *What did he say?* Tell me _____

4. *What kind of car does Pat have?* I can't remember _____

5. *How old are their children?* I can't ever remember _____

6. *Why did you say that?* I don't understand _____

7. *Where can I catch the bus?* Could you please tell me _____

8. *Who did Sara talk to?* I don't know _____

9. *How long has Ted been living here?* Do you know _____

10. *What does this word mean?* Could you please tell me _____

◇ **PRACTICE 6. Information questions and noun clauses.** (Charts 5-2 and 14-2)
   Directions: Complete the sentences using the words in parentheses.

1. A: Why *(you, were)* _____ were you _____ late?
   B: What?
   A: I want to know why *(you, were)* _____ you were _____ late.

2. A: Where *(Tom, go)* _____ last night?
   B: I'm sorry. I didn't hear what *(you, say)* _____ .
   A: I want to know where *(Tom, go)* _____ last night.

3. A: What *(a bumblebee, is)* _____ ?
   B: Excuse me?
   A: I want to know what *(a bumblebee, is)* _____
      _____ .
   B: It's a big bee.

4. A: Whose car *(Oscar, borrow)* _____
      yesterday?
   B: I don't know whose car *(Oscar, borrow)* _____
      _____ yesterday.

5. A: Could you please tell me where *(Mr. Gow's office, is)* _____ ?
   B: I'm sorry. I didn't understand.
   A: Where *(Mr. Gow's office, is)* _____ ?
   B: Ah. Down the hall on the right.

6. A: Rachel left the hospital two weeks ago. When *(she, come)* _____

       back to work?

   B: I have no idea. I don't know when *(she, come)* _____ back to work.

   A: Why *(she, be)* _____ in the hospital?

   B: I don't know that either. I haven't heard. I'll ask Tom. Maybe he knows why *(she, be)*

       _____ in the hospital.

◇ **PRACTICE 7. Noun clauses with WHO, WHAT, WHOSE + BE. (Chart 14-3)**
Directions: Draw brackets around and identify the subject (**s**) and verb (**v**) of each noun clause.

1. I don't know who [that man] [is].

2. I don't know [who] [called].

3. I don't know who those people are.

4. I don't know who that person is.

5. I don't know who lives next door to me.

6. I don't know who my teacher will be next semester.

7. I don't know who will teach us next semester.

8. I don't know what a lizard is.

9. I don't know what happened in class yesterday.

10. I don't know whose hat this is.

11. I don't know whose hat is on the table.

◇ **PRACTICE 8. Noun clauses with WHO, WHAT, WHOSE + BE. (Chart 14-3)**
Directions: Add the word *is* to each sentence in the correct place. If nothing is needed, write a slash (/) in the blank.

1. I don't know who ____/____ that man ____is____ .

2. I don't know who ____is____ in that room ____/____ .

3. I don't know what _____ a crow _____ .

4. I don't know who _____ in the doctor's office _____ .

5. I don't know who _____ that person _____ .

6. I don't know what _____ our new address _____ .

7. I don't know what _____ on the carpet _____ .

8. I don't know what _____ the date _____ today.

9. I don't know what _____ day it _____ .

10. I don't know whose office _____ at the end of the hall _____ .

◇ **PRACTICE 9. Noun clauses with WHO, WHAT, WHOSE + BE. (Chart 14-3)**
Directions: Complete the sentences by changing the questions to noun clauses.

1. *Who is she?* I don't know _____

2. *Who are they?* I don't know _____

3. *Whose book is that?* I don't know _____

4. *Whose glasses are those?* Could you tell me _____

5. *What is a wrench?* Do you know _____

6. *Who is that woman?* I wonder _____

7. *What is a clause?* Don't you know _____

8. *What is in that drawer?* I don't know _____

9. *Who is in that room?* I don't know _____

10. *What is on TV tonight?* I wonder _____

11. *What is a carrot?* Do you know _____

12. *Who am I?* He doesn't know _____

◇ **PRACTICE 10. Noun clauses with WHO, WHAT, WHOSE + BE. (Chart 14-3)**
Directions: Complete the dialogues by changing the questions to noun clauses.

1. A: Whose car is that?

   B: I don't know ___*whose car that is*___ .

2. A: Whose car is in front of Sam's house?

   B: I don't know ___*whose car is in front of Sam's house*___ .

3. A: Who are the best students?

   B: Ask the teacher _____ .

4. A: What time is dinner?

   B: I'm not sure _____ .

5. A: Who's next in line?

   B: I don't know _____.

6. A: Whose purse is this?

   B: Ask the woman in black _____.

7. A: What are the main ideas of the story?

   B: Ask a student _____.

8. A: Whose shoes are those under the chair?

   B: I don't know _____.

9. A: What causes tornadoes?

   B: I'm not sure _____.

◇ PRACTICE 11. Noun clauses and yes/no questions. (Charts 5-2 and 14-4)
   Directions: Change each yes/no question to a noun clause.

1. YES/NO QUESTION: Is Tom coming?

   NOUN CLAUSE: I wonder ___*if (whether) Tom is coming*___.

2. YES/NO QUESTION: Has Jin finished medical school yet?

   NOUN CLAUSE: I don't know _____.

3. YES/NO QUESTION: Does Daniel have any time off soon?

   NOUN CLAUSE: I don't know _____.

4. YES/NO QUESTION: Is the flight on time?

   NOUN CLAUSE: Can you tell me _____?

5. YES/NO QUESTION: Is there enough gas in the car?

   NOUN CLAUSE: Do you know _____?

6. YES/NO QUESTION: Is Yuki married?

   NOUN CLAUSE: I can't remember _____.

7. YES/NO QUESTION: Are the Petersons going to move?

   NOUN CLAUSE: I wonder _____.

8. YES/NO QUESTION: Did Khaled change jobs?

   NOUN CLAUSE: I don't know _____.

◇ **PRACTICE 12. Noun clauses and yes/no questions. (Charts 5-2 and 14-4)**
   Directions: Complete the sentences using noun clauses. Use *if*.

1. A: Are you going to need help moving furniture to your new apartment?

   B: I don't know _____*if I'm going to need*_____ help. Thanks for asking. I'll let you know.

2. A: Is chicken okay for dinner tonight?

   B: I'm sorry. I couldn't hear you with the TV on.

   A: I want to know _____ okay for dinner tonight.

3. A: Does the new teaching position include health insurance?

   B: Oh, I'm sorry. Were you talking to me? I wasn't listening.

   A: Yes. I'd like to know _____ health insurance.

4. A: Will there be a movie on this flight?

   B: I'll ask the flight attendant. Excuse me, we're wondering _____

   _____ on this flight.

5. A: Does Greg have to come with us?

   B: Shhh. Don't ask _____ with us. Of course he does.

   He's your brother!

6. A: Do penguins ever get cold?

   B: That's an interesting question. I don't know _____

   cold.

7. A: Can I drive the car to the store, Dad?

   B: Are you serious? Of course not! Why do you ask _____ the car

   to the store? You haven't passed your driver's test.

8. A: Has Nasser already left the party?

   B: Sorry, it's so noisy here. I didn't catch that.

   A: I need to know _____ the party.

◇ **PRACTICE 13. Noun clauses. (Charts 5-2, 14-2, and 14-4)**
   Directions: Change the questions to noun clauses.

1. *Is Karen at home?* Do you know _____*if (whether) Karen is*_____ at home?

2. *Where did Karen go?* Do you know _____*where Karen went?*_____

3. *How is Pat feeling today?* I wonder _____ today.

4. *Is Pat feeling better today?* I wonder _____ better today.

5. *Does the bus stop here?* Do you know _____ here?

6. *Where does the bus stop?* I wonder _____

7. *Why is Elena absent today?* The teacher wants to know _____

   today.

8. *Is Elena going to be absent again tomorrow?* I wonder _____

   _____ again tomorrow.

9. *Should I buy that book?* I wonder _____ that book.

10. *Which book should I buy?* I wonder _____

11. *Are we going to have a test tomorrow?* Let's ask the teacher _____

    _____ a test tomorrow.

12. *Is there a Santa Claus?* The little boy wants to know _____ a Santa Claus.

◇ **PRACTICE 14. Noun clauses.** (Charts 14-2 and 14-4)

   Directions: Complete the sentences with the correct form of the verbs. Pay special attention to the use of final *-s/-es*.

1. Does it rain a lot here?

   Could you tell me if it _____ **rains** _____ a lot here?

2. How hot does it get in the summer?

   Could you tell me how hot it _____ in the summer?

3. What do people like to do here?

   Could you tell me what people _____ to do here?

4. Does Bus #10 run on holidays?

   Could you tell me if Bus #10 _____ on holidays?

5. Do the buses run on holidays?

   Could you tell me if the buses _____ on holidays?

6. How long does it take to get to the city?

   Could you tell me how long it _____ to get to the city?

7. What do people enjoy most about this area?

   Could you tell me what people _____ most about this area?

8. Does it seem like an expensive place to live?

   Could you tell me if it _____ like an expensive place to live?

◇ **PRACTICE 15. THAT-clauses.** (Charts 14-5 and 14-6)

Directions: Add the word ***that*** to the sentences at the appropriate places to mark the beginning of a noun clause.

1. I'm sorry ∧ you won't be here for Joe's party.
                that

2. I predict Jim and Sue will get married before the end of the year.

3. I'm surprised you sold your bicycle.

4. Are you certain Mr. McVay won't be here tomorrow?

5. Did you notice Marco shaved off his mustache?

6. John is pleased Claudio will be here for the meeting.

7. Anna was convinced I was angry with her, but I wasn't.

8. It's a fact the Nile River flows north.

9. A: Guido is delighted you can speak Italian.

   B: I'm surprised he can understand my Italian. It's not very good.

10. A: How do you know it's going to be nice tomorrow?

    B: I heard the weather report.

    A: So? The weather report is often wrong, you know. I'm still worried it'll rain on our picnic.

11. A: Mrs. Lane hopes we can go with her to the museum tomorrow.

    B: I don't think I can go. I'm supposed to babysit my little brother tomorrow.

    A: Oh, too bad. I wish you could join us.

12. A: Do you think technology benefits humankind?

    B: Of course. Everyone knows modern inventions make our lives better.

    A: I'm not sure that's true. For example, cars and buses provide faster transportation, but

    they pollute our air. Air pollution can cause lung disease and other illnesses.

◇ **PRACTICE 16. THAT-clauses.** (Charts 14-5 and 14-6)
   Directions: Complete the sentences with clauses from the list.

> *All people are equal.*
> *Flying in an airplane is safer than riding in a car.*
> *He always twirls his mustache when he's nervous.*
> *High school students in the United States don't study as hard as the students in my country do.*
> *A huge monster was chasing me.*
> *I should study tonight.*
> *I will get married someday.*
> ✓*I will have a peanut butter sandwich.*
> *John "Cat Man" Smith stole Mrs. Adams' jewelry.*
> *More than half of the people in the world go hungry every day.*
> *People are pretty much the same everywhere.*
> *Plastic trash kills thousands of marine animals every year.*

1. I'm hungry. I guess _____(that) I will have a peanut butter sandwich._____

2. I have a test tomorrow. I suppose _____, but I'd rather

   go to a movie.

3. Why are you afraid to fly in an airplane? Read this report. It proves _____

   _____

4. Right now I'm single. I can't predict my future exactly, but I assume _____

   _____

5. Last night I had a bad dream. In fact, it was a nightmare. I dreamed _____

   _____

6. The police are investigating the burglary. They don't have much evidence, but they suspect

_____

7. My cousin feels that people in the United States are unfriendly, but I disagree with him. I've discovered _____

8. I've learned many things about life in the United States since I came here. For example, I've learned _____

_____

9. I always know when Paul is nervous. Have you ever noticed _____

_____

10. I believe that it is wrong to judge another person on the basis of race, religion, or sex. I believe _____

11. World hunger is a serious problem. Do you realize _____

_____

12. Don't throw that plastic bag into the sea! Don't you know _____

_____

◇ **PRACTICE 17. THAT-clauses. (Charts 14-5 and 14-6)**
Directions: Write sentences with the given information. Combine one of the verbs in parentheses with a noun clause.

1. Smoking in public places should be prohibited. *(feel / don't feel)*
    → *I feel (don't feel) that smoking in public places should be prohibited.*

2. I'm living in this country. *(regret / don't regret)*

3. When will I die? *(would like to know / wouldn't like to know)*

4. There will be peace in the world soon. *(doubt / don't doubt)*

5. What was I like as a child? *(remember / can't remember)*

6. Why does the world exist? *(wonder / don't wonder)*

7. Someone may make unwise decisions about my future. *(am afraid / am not afraid)*

8. What do I want to do with my life? *(know / don't know)*

◇ **PRACTICE 18. THAT-clauses. (Chart 14-6)**
Directions: Write two sentences for each situation. Use the words in parentheses with a noun clause.

1. The Jensens celebrated the graduation of their granddaughter Alice from the university. After graduation, she was offered a good job in chemical research in a nearby town. *(be pleased)*
   → *The Jensens are pleased that their granddaughter graduated from the university. They are pleased that she was offered a good job.*

2. Po was asleep. Around one in the morning the smoke alarm in his apartment rang. He woke up and discovered that his apartment building was on fire. *(be lucky)*

3. Ming Soo didn't study for her math exam. Afterward, she thought she had failed, but got one of the highest grades in the class. Her teacher had known she would do well and praised her for earning such a high grade. *(be surprised)*

4. Karen lent her cousin Mark some money. She heard that he left town. He owed a lot of people money. She needs the money she gave her cousin. Her children need new shoes, but she can't afford to buy them. *(be sorry)*

◇ **PRACTICE 19. THAT-clauses. (Chart 14-7)**
Directions: Give the meaning of *so* by writing a *that*-clause.

1. A: Does Alice have a car?

   B: I don't think *so*. (= *I don't think* ___that Alice has a car___ .)

2. A: Is the library open on Sunday?

   B: I believe *so*. (= *I believe* _____ .)

3. A: Does Ann speak Spanish?

   B: I don't think *so*. (= *I don't think* _____ .)

4. A: Did Alex pass his French course?

   B: I think *so*. (= *I think* _____ .)

5. A: Is Mr. Kozari going to be at the meeting?

   B: I hope *so*. (= *I hope* _____ .)

6. A: Are the photos ready to be picked up at the photo shop?

   B: I believe *so*. (= *I believe* _____

   _____ .)

◇ **PRACTICE 20. Quoted speech. (Chart 14-8)**

Directions: All of the sentences contain quoted speech. Punctuate them by adding quotation marks (" . . ."), commas (,), periods (.), and question marks (?). Also use capital letters as necessary.

Example: My roommate said the door is open could you close it
→ *My roommate said,* "*T*he door is open. *C*ould you close it?"

1. Alex said do you smell smoke

2. Something is burning he said

3. He said do you smell smoke something is burning

4. Do you smell smoke he said something is burning

5. Rachel said the game starts at seven

6. The game starts at seven we should leave here at six she said

7. She said the game starts at seven we should leave here at six can you be ready to leave then

◇ **PRACTICE 21. Quoted speech. (Chart 14-8)**

Directions: All of the sentences contain quoted speech. Punctuate them by adding quotation marks (" . . ."), commas (,), periods (.), and question marks (?). Also use capital letters as necessary.

Example: Jack said please wait for me
→ *Jack said,* "*P*please wait for me."

1. Mrs. Hill said my children used to take the bus to school

2. She said we moved closer to the school

3. Now my children can walk to school Mrs. Hill said

4. Do you live near the school she asked

5. Yes, we live two blocks away I replied

6. How long have you lived here Mrs. Hill wanted to know

7. I said we've lived here for five years how long have you lived here

8. We've lived here for two years Mrs. Hill said how do you like living here

9. It's a nice community I said it's a good place to raise children

◇ **PRACTICE 22. Quoted speech. (Chart 14-8)**
Directions: Punctuate the quoted passage. Add quotation marks (" . . . "), commas (,), periods (.), and question marks (?). Also use capital letters as necessary.

"Why weren't you in class yesterday?" Mr. Garcia asked me.

I had to stay home and take care of my pet bird I said. He wasn't feeling well.

What? Did you miss class because of your pet bird Mr. Garcia demanded to know.

I replied yes, sir. That's correct. I couldn't leave him alone. He looked so miserable.

Now I've heard every excuse in the world Mr. Garcia said.

Then he threw his arms in the air and walked away.

◇ **PRACTICE 23. Quoted speech. (Chart 14-8)**
Directions: Punctuate the quoted passage. Add quotation marks (" . . . "), commas (,), periods (.), and question marks (?). Also use capital letters as necessary.

One day my friend Laura and I were sitting in her apartment. We were having a cup of tea together and talking about the terrible earthquake that had just occurred in Iran. Laura asked me, "Have you ever been in an earthquake?"

Yes, I have I replied.

Was it a big earthquake she asked.

I've been in several earthquakes, and they've all been small ones I answered. Have you ever been in an earthquake?

There was an earthquake in my village five years ago Laura said. I was in my house. Suddenly the ground started shaking. I grabbed my little brother and ran outside. Everything was moving. I was scared to death. And then suddenly it was over.

I'm glad you and your brother weren't hurt I said.

Yes, we were very lucky. Has everyone in the world felt an earthquake sometime in their lives Laura wondered. Do earthquakes occur everywhere on the earth?

Those are interesting questions I said but I don't know the answers.

◇ **PRACTICE 24. Reported speech: changing pronouns. (Chart 14-9)**
Directions: Complete the sentences with the correct pronouns.

1. Mr. Lee said, "I'm not happy with my new assistant."

   Mr. Lee said that ____he____ wasn't happy with ____his____ new assistant.

2. Tom said to his wife, "My parents invited us over for dinner next weekend."

   Tom said that _____ parents had invited _____ over for dinner next weekend.

3. The little girl said, "I don't want to wear my raincoat outside."

   The little girl said that _____ didn't want to wear _____ raincoat outside.

4. Jim said, "A policeman gave Anna and me tickets for jaywalking and told us to cross the street at the pedestrian crosswalk."

   Jim said that a policeman had given Anna and _____ tickets for jaywalking and told _____ to cross the street at the pedestrian crosswalk.

5. The Johnsons said to me, "We will send you an e-mail when we arrive in Nepal."

   The Johnsons said that _____ would send _____ an e-mail when _____ arrived in Nepal.

6. Jane said, "I want my daughter to feel good about herself."

   Jane said that _____ wanted _____ daughter to feel good about herself.

7. Mary and Jack said to me, "We are going to be out of town on the day of your party."

   Mary and Jack said that _____ were going to be out of town on the day of _____ party.

8. Bob said to us, "I will join you after I help my neighbors move some furniture."

   Bob told us that _____ would join _____ after _____ helped _____ neighbors move some furniture.

◇ **PRACTICE 25. Reported speech: changing verbs. (Chart 14-10)**
   Directions: Complete each sentence with the correct form of the verb.

1. Juan said, "I will meet you at the corner of 5th and Broadway."

   Formal: Juan said (that) he ___*would meet*___

   Informal: Juan said (that) he ___*will meet*___ ⟩ us at the corner of 5th and Broadway.

2. Maria said, "I'm going to be about 15 minutes late for work."

   Formal: Maria said she _____

   Informal: Maria said she _____ ⟩ about 15 minutes late for work.

3. Bob said, "My new car has a dent."

   Formal: Bob said his new car _____

   Informal: Bob said his new car _____ ⟩ a dent.

4. Phil said, "I need to borrow some money."

   Formal: Phil said he _____

   Informal: Phil said he _____ ⟩ to borrow some money.

5. Sandy said, "I have flown on an airplane only once."

Formal: Sandy said she _____

Informal: Sandy said she _____ on an airplane only once.

6. Sami and Jun said, "We are planning a surprise party for Naoko."

Formal: Sami and Jun said they _____

Informal: Sami and Jun said they _____ a surprise party for Naoko.

7. Naoko said, "I don't want any gifts for my birthday."

Formal: Naoko said she _____

Informal: Naoko said she _____ any gifts for her birthday.

8. Ms. Wall said, "I can babysit next weekend."

Formal: Ms. Wall said she _____

Informal: Ms. Wall said she _____ next weekend.

◇ **PRACTICE 26. Reported speech. (Charts 14-9 and 14-10)**

Directions: Complete the sentences. Write the opposite of the quoted speech. Use formal sequence of tenses.

1. A: I have a lot of time.

   B: Oh? I misunderstood you. I heard you say ___(that) you didn't have___ a lot of time.

2. A: I found my credit cards.

   B: I misunderstood you. I heard you say _____ your credit cards.

3. A: The Smiths canceled their party.

   B: I misunderstood you. I heard you say _____ their party.

4. A: It will rain tomorrow.

   B: I misunderstood you. I heard you say _____ tomorrow.

5. A: The Whites got a new dog.

   B: I misunderstood you. I heard you say _____ a new dog.

6. A: Mei exercises every day.

   B: I misunderstood you. I heard you say _____ every day.

7. A: My computer is working.

   B: I misunderstood you. I heard you say _____ .

8. A: Ali isn't coming on Friday.

   B: I misunderstood you. I heard you say _____ on Friday.

◇ PRACTICE 27. Reporting questions. (Charts 14-9 → 14-11)
   Directions: Change the quoted questions to reported questions. Use formal tense sequences.

1. Eric said to me, "How old are you?"

   → Eric asked me _____how old I was_____ .

2. Ms. Rush said to Mr. Long, "Are you going to be at the meeting?"

   → Ms. Rush asked Mr. Long _____if he was going to be_____ at the meeting.

3. Larry said to Ms. Ho, "Do you have time to help me?"

   → Larry asked Ms. Ho _____ time to help him.

4. Don said to Robert, "Did you change your mind about going to Reed College?"

   → Don asked Robert _____ mind about going to Reed College.

5. Igor said to me, "How long have you been a teacher?"

   → Igor asked me _____ a teacher.

6. I said to Tina, "Can you speak Swahili?"

   → I asked Tina _____ Swahili.

7. Kathy said to Mr. May, "Will you be in your office around three?"

   → Kathy asked Mr. May _____ around three.

8. The teacher said to Ms. Chang, "Why are you laughing?"

   → The teacher asked Ms. Chang _____ .

9. My uncle said to me, "Have you ever considered a career in business?"

   → My uncle asked me _____ a career in business.

◇ PRACTICE 28. Quoting questions. (Charts 14-8 → 14-11)
   Directions: Change the reported speech to quotations. Use quotation marks.

1. Eric asked me if I had ever gone skydiving.

   → Eric said, _____"Have you ever gone skydiving?"_____

2. Chris wanted to know if I would be at the meeting.

   → Chris said, _____

3. Kate wondered whether I was going to quit my job.

   → Kate said, _____

4. Anna asked her friend where his car was.

→ Anna said, _____

5. Brian asked me what I had done after class yesterday.

→ Brian said, _____

6. Luigi asked me if I knew Italian.

→ Luigi said, _____

7. Debra wanted to know if I could guess what she had in her pocket.

→ Debra asked, _____

8. My boss wanted to know why I wasn't working at my desk.

→ My boss angrily asked me, _____

◇ PRACTICE 29. Reporting questions. (Charts 14-9 → 14-11)
Directions: Look at the picture and complete the sentences with noun clauses. Use verbs that are appropriate for later reporting (rather than immediate reporting).

A new student, Mr. Sheko, joined an English class. The teacher asked the students to interview him. Later, Mr. Sheko told his friend about the interview.

1. They asked me ___where I was from.___

2. They asked me _____

3. They asked me _____

4. They asked me _____

5. They asked me _____

6. They asked me _____

7. They asked me _____

8. They asked me _____

9. They asked me _____

◇ **PRACTICE 30. Reported speech. (Charts 14-9 → 14-11)**
Directions: Complete the reported speech sentences. Use the formal sequence of tenses.

1. David said to me, "I'm going to call you on Friday."

   → David said (that) ___he was going to call me___

   on Friday.

2. John said to Ann, "I have to talk to you."

   → John told Ann _____

   to _____ .

3. Diane said to me, "I can meet you after work."

   → Diane said _____ after work.

4. Maria said to Bob, "I wrote you a note."

   → Maria told Bob _____

   a note.

5. I said to David, "I need your help to prepare for the exam."

   → I told David _____ help to

   prepare for the exam.

6. Anna asked Mike, "When will I see you again?"

   → Anna asked Mike when _____

   _____ again.

7. Mr. Fox said to me, "I'm going to meet Jack and you
   at the restaurant."

   → Mr. Fox said _____

   _____ Jack and _____ at the restaurant.

8. Laura said to George, "What are you doing?"

   → Laura asked George _____

   _____ .

9. A strange man looked at me and said, "I'm sure I've met you before."

   → A strange man looked at me and said _____

   before. I was sure I'd never seen him before in my entire life.

◇ **PRACTICE 31. SAY vs. TELL vs. ASK. (Chart 14-11)**
Directions: Complete the sentences with *said, told,* or *asked.*

I'M HUNGRY.

1. Ann ____told____ me that she was hungry.

2. Ann ____said____ that she was hungry.

3. Ann _____ me if I wanted to go out to lunch with her.

4. When the storm began, I _____ the children to come into the house.

5. When I talked to Mr. Grant, he _____ he would be at the meeting.

6. Ali _____ his friends that he had won a scholarship to college. His friends _____ they weren't surprised.

7. My supervisor _____ me if I could postpone my vacation. I _____ him what the reason was. He _____ that our sales department needed me for a project.

8. My neighbor and I had a disagreement. I _____ my neighbor that he was wrong. My neighbor _____ me that I was wrong.

FATIMA ISN'T GOING TO BE IN CLASS TODAY.

OH? IS FATIMA ALL RIGHT?

9. Fumiko _____ the teacher that Fatima wasn't going to be in class.

10. Ellen _____ if I could join her for a movie. I _____ I wasn't feeling well, but I _____ her what movie she was going to. The next day, Ellen _____ me she had enjoyed the movie.

◇ **PRACTICE 32. Reported speech. (Chapter 14)**
Directions: Complete the dialogues by changing the quoted speech to reported speech. Use *said, told, asked,* or *replied.* Practice using the formal sequence of tenses.

1. Bob said, "Where do you live?" Bob ___asked me where I lived.___

2. He said, "Do you live in the dorm?" He _____ in the dorm.

3. I said, "I have my own apartment." I _____ my own apartment.

4. He said, "I'm looking for a new apartment." He _____ for a new apartment.

5. He said, "I don't like living in the dorm." He _____ in the dorm.

6. I said, "Do you want to move in with me?" I _____

7. He said, "Where is your apartment?"

He _____

8. I said, "I live on Seventh Avenue."

I _____ on Seventh Avenue.

9. He said, "I can't move until the end of May."

He _____ until the end of May.

10. He said, "I will cancel my dorm contract at the end of May."

He _____ dorm contract at the end of May.

11. He said, "Is that okay?"

He _____

12. I said, "I'm looking forward to having you as a roommate."

I _____ as a roommate.

◇ **PRACTICE 33. Reported speech. (Chapter 14)**
Directions: Check **all** the sentences that are correct.

1. ____ The teacher asked are you finished?

 ✓ The teacher asked if I was finished.

 ____ The teacher asked if was I finished?

 ____ The teacher asked that I was finished?

 ✓ The teacher asked, "Are you finished?"

2. ____ Aki said he was finished.

 ____ Aki said that he was finished.

 ____ Aki replied that he was finished.

 ____ Aki answered that he was finished.

 ____ Aki said whether was he finished.

3. ____ Ann told Tom, she needed more time.

 ____ Ann told Tom she needed more time.

 ____ Ann told to Tom she needed more time.

 ____ Ann told she needed more time.

 ____ Ann said Tom she needed more time.

 ____ Ann said she needed more time.

4. ____ Donna answered that she was ready.

 ____ Donna answered was she ready.

 ____ Donna replied she was ready.

 ____ Donna answered, "I am ready."

 ____ Donna answered if she was ready.

5. ____ Mr. Wong wanted to know if Ted was coming.

 ____ Mr. Wong wanted to know is Ted coming?

 ____ Mr. Wong wondered if Ted was coming.

 ____ Mr. Wong wondered was Ted coming.

 ____ Mr. Wong wondered, "Is Ted coming?"

◇ **PRACTICE 34. Reported speech. (Chapter 14)**
Directions: Read the dialogues and complete the sentences. Use the formal sequence of tenses.

1. A: *Oh no! I forgot my briefcase! What am I going to do?*
 B: *I don't know.*

 → When Bill got on the bus, he realized ____(that) he had forgotten____ his briefcase.

2. A: *Where's your bicycle, Jimmy?*
   B: *I sold it to a friend of mine.*
   A: *You what?!*

   → Yesterday I asked my fourteen-year-old son _____ .
   He _____ it to a friend. I was flabbergasted.

3. A: *The bus is supposed to be here in three minutes. Hurry up! I'm afraid we'll miss it.*
   B: *I'm ready. Let's go.*

   → I told my friend to hurry because I was afraid _____ the bus.

4. A: *Can you swim?*
   B: *Yes.*
   A: *Thank heaven.*

   → When the canoe tipped over, I asked my friend _____ .

5. A: *Do you want to go downtown?*
   B: *I can't. I have to study.*

   → When I asked Kathy _____ to go downtown, she said
   _____ because she _____ .

6. A: *Ow! My finger really hurts! I'm sure I broke it.*
   B: *Let me see.*

   → When Nancy fell down, she was sure _____ her finger.

7. A: *Where's Jack? I'm surprised he isn't here.*
   B: *He went to Chicago to visit his sister.*

   → When I got to the party, I asked my friend where Jack _____ .
   I was surprised _____ there. My friend told me
   _____ to Chicago to visit his sister.

8. A: *Will you be home in time for dinner?*
   B: *I'll be home around 5:30.*

   → My wife asked me _____ home in time for dinner. I told her
   _____ home around 5:30.

9. A: *Have you ever been to Mexico?*
   B: *Yes, I have. Several times.*

   → I asked George _____ ever _____ to Mexico. He said
   _____ there several times.

10. A: *Where's my cane?*
    B: *I don't know. Do you need it?*
    A: *I want to walk to the mailbox.*
    B: *I'll find it for you.*

→ Grandfather asked me _____ . I told him
_____ . Then I asked him _____
it. He said _____ to the mailbox. I told him
_____ for him.

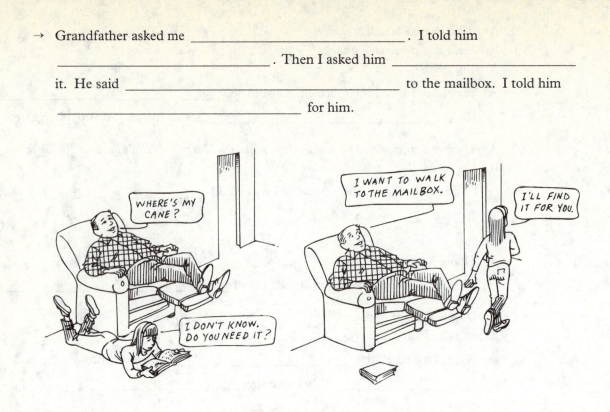

◇ **PRACTICE 35. Reported speech. (Charts 14-9 → 14-11)**

Directions: Write a report on the people in the pictures and what they say. Use the formal
sequence of tenses.

BEFORE SCHOOL IN THE MORNING

◇ **PRACTICE 36. Error analysis. (Chapter 14)**
   Directions: Correct the errors.

1. Excuse me. May I ask if how old are you?

2. I wonder did Rashed pick up something for dinner?

3. I'm unsure what does Lawrence do for a living.

4. Fernando said, "the best time for me to meet would be Thursday morning.

5. Eriko said to me was I coming to the graduation party. I say her that I wasn't.

6. I hope so that I will do well on my final exams.

7. Antonio asked his mother what does she want for her birthday?

8. I'm not sure if the price include sales tax.

9. My mother said to me that: "How many hours you spent on your homework?

10. Pedro asked is that okay? (*2 answers: direct and indirect speech*)

11. Mika told she would going to stay home today.

12. I'd like to know how do you do that.

13. My parents knew what did Sam and I do.

14. Beth said she had working hard all week but now had some time off.

15. Is a fact that life always changes.

APPENDIX 1
Phrasal Verbs

◇ PRACTICE 1. Phrasal verbs: separable. (Group A)
Directions: Complete each sentence with a correct particle from the list. Particles may be used more than once or not at all.

away	*in*	*on*	*up*
down	*off*	*out*	

1. I'd like to listen to some music. Would you please *turn* the radio _____*on*_____ ?

2. My husband *makes* _____ bedtime stories for our children.

3. My arms hurt, so I *put* the baby _____ for a minute. But he started crying right away, so I *picked* him _____ again.

4. A: We need a plumber to fix our leaky water faucet. You need to call one today.

   B: I will.

   A: Don't *put* it _____ .

   B: I won't. I'll call today. I promise.

5. A: Why are you wearing your new suit?

   B: I just *put* it _____ to see what it looks like.

   A: It looks fine. *Take* it _____ and hang it up before it gets wrinkled.

6. A: I found this notebook in the wastebasket. It's yours, isn't it?

   B: Yes. I *threw* it _____ . I don't need it anymore.

   A: Okay. I thought maybe it had fallen in the wastebasket accidentally.

7. A: I need Jan's address again.

   B: I gave you her address just yesterday.

   A: I'm afraid I've lost it. Tell me again, and I'll *write* it _____ .

   B: Just a minute. I have to *look* it _____ in my address book.

8. A: You'll never believe what happened in physics class today!

   B: What happened?

   A: We had a big test. When I first looked it over, I realized that I couldn't *figure*

   _____ any of the answers. Our teacher had *handed* _____ the wrong

   test! We hadn't covered that material yet.

9. A: You're all wet!

   B: I know. A passing truck went through a big puddle and splashed me.

   A: You'd better *take* those clothes _____ and *put* _____ something clean
   and dry before you go to work.

10. A: *Wake* _____ ! It's seven o'clock! Rise and shine!

    B: What are you doing!? *Turn* the light _____ and close the window curtain!

    A: My goodness but we're grumpy this morning. Come on. It's time to get up, dear. You
    don't want to be late.

◇ PRACTICE 2. Phrasal verbs: separable. (Group A)
Directions: Circle all the correct completions for each sentence.

1. Lisa took off   *her toys*   (*her socks*)   *her notebooks.*

2. Akiko turned off   (*the TV*)   *the butter*   (*the stove.*)

3. Jonas put on   *his new shoes*   *a fire*   *the dishes.*

4. Benjamin made up   *a story*   *a fairy tale*   *an excuse.*

5. Susanna threw out   *some air*   *some rotten food*   *an old shirt.*

6. Antonio put off   *a doctor's appointment*   *a meeting*   *a trip.*

7. Max figured out   *a puzzle*   *a math problem*   *a riddle.*

8. Kyong handed in   *some candy*   *a report*   *some late homework.*

9. The secretary wrote down   *a message*   *a pencil*   *a phone number.*

10. The mail carrier put down   *a box*   *the mail truck*   *a sack of mail.*

11. I took off   *my coat*   *my bicycle*   *my wedding ring.*

12. Mustafa turned off   *the light*   *the computer*   *the car engine.*

◇ **PRACTICE 3. Phrasal verbs: nonseparable. (Group B)**
   Directions: Complete each sentence with a correct particle from the list. Particles may be used more than once.

from	*into*	*on*	*over*
in	*off*	*out of*	

1. A: Why are your pants so dirty?

   B: I lost my balance when I got ____out of____ the car, and I fell in the mud.

2. A: I was so embarrassed in class today.

   B: What happened?

   A: The teacher called _____ me, and I didn't know the answer.

3. A: The bus is coming. When do I pay?

   B: Don't pay when you get on. Pay the driver when you get _____.

4. A: You look great! I thought you had the flu.

   B: I did, but I got _____ it very quickly.

5. A: Why haven't we gotten a reply to our letter to the telephone company?

   B: I don't know. I'll look _____ it.

6. A: Guess who I ran _____ today?

   B: Who?

   A: Melanie Nelson, from high school. She's married now and has seven children.

7. A: Mommy, where do butterflies come _____?

   B: Well, first they are caterpillars. Then, when the caterpillars become large, they turn into butterflies.

8. A: Hurry! Get _____ the car. We've got to be at the train station in ten minutes.

   B: OK. I'm ready. Let's go.

9. A: I went downtown by mistake today.

   B: How on earth did that happen?

   A: I got _____ the wrong bus. It didn't stop until we were in the city.

◇ **PRACTICE 4. Phrasal verbs: nonseparable. (Group B)**
Directions: Complete each sentence in Column A with the correct phrase from Column B.

Example: Annette speaks both French and English because she comes . . .
   → *Annette speaks both French and English because she comes from Quebec.*

Column A

1. Annette speaks both French and English because she comes . . .

2. When Sylvia lost her job, it took her several weeks to get . . .

3. Our office will need several days to look . . .

4. When a plane lands, the first-class passengers get . . .

5. While I was walking in the mall, I ran . . .

6. When he left the hotel, David got . . .

7. Mrs. Riley, our math teacher, often calls . . .

Column B

A. into your request for medical records.

✓B. from Quebec.

C. over the shock.

D. in a taxi and went to the airport.

E. on unprepared students.

F. into several friends from high school.

G. off first.

◇ **PRACTICE 5. Phrasal verbs: separable. (Group C)**
Directions: Complete each sentence with a correct particle from the list. Particles may be used more than once.

away	*down*	*on*	*up*
back	*off*	*out*	

1. You still owe me the money I lent you. When are you going to *pay* me ___**back**___?

2. *Turn* _____ the radio! It's too loud! I can't hear myself think.

3. Debra *put* _____ the fire in the wastebasket with a fire extinguisher.

4. After I wash and dry the dishes, I *put* them _____. I put them in the cupboard where they belong.

5. Before you buy shoes, you should *try* them _____ to see if they fit.

6. I can't hear the TV. Could you please *turn* it _____? No, don't shut it _____! I wanted you to make it louder, not turn it off. I want to hear the news.

7. A: That's mine! *Give* it _____!

   B: No, it's not. It's mine!

   C: Now children, don't fight.

8. A: I don't hear anyone on the other end of the phone.

   B: Just *hang* _____ . It's probably a wrong number.

9. A: I hear that Tom *asked* you _____ for next Saturday night.

   B: Yes, he did. He *called* me _____ a couple of hours ago and invited me to the symphony concert.

   A: The concert's been *called* _____ because the musicians are on strike. Didn't you hear about it?

   B: No, I didn't. I'd better *call* Tom _____ and ask him what he wants to do instead.

10. I don't mind if you look at these maps, but please *put* them _____ in the drawer when you're finished.

◇ PRACTICE 6. Phrasal verbs: separable. (Groups A, B, C)
Directions: Complete the sentences with a given particle where possible. If not possible, write "X."

1. *out* a. Paulo asked _____out_____ one of his classmates.

   b. Paulo asked one of his classmates _____out_____ .

2. *on* a. The teacher called _____on_____ Ted for the answer.

   b. The teacher called Ted _____X_____ for the answer.

3. *into* a. The police are looking _____ the murder, but need help from the public to solve it.

   b. The police are looking the murder _____ , but need help from the public to solve it.

4. *into* a. Khalifa ran _____ his cousin at the store.

   b. Khalifa ran his cousin _____ at the store.

5. *up* a. Claire turned _____ the ringer on the phone.

   b. Claire turned the ringer on the phone _____ .

6. *away* a. Dr. Benson threw _____ a valuable coin by mistake.

   b. Dr. Benson threw a valuable coin _____ by mistake.

7. *down* a. Yumi's baby cries whenever she puts him _____ .

   b. Yumi's baby cries whenever she puts _____ him.

8. *up* a. Would you please wake _____ me in one hour?

   b. Would you please wake me _____ in one hour?

9. *away*   a. You can leave the dishes. I'll put them _____ later.

   b. You can leave the dishes. I'll put _____ them later.

10. *up*   a. When Joan feels lonely, she calls _____ a friend and talks for a while.

    b. When Joan feels lonely, she calls a friend _____ and talks for a while.

11. *off*   a. The hill was so steep that I had to get _____ my bicycle and walk.

    b. The hill was so steep that I had to get my bicycle _____ and walk.

12. *from*   a. This fruit is very fresh. It came _____ my garden.

    b. This fruit is very fresh. It came my garden _____ .

◇ PRACTICE 7. Phrasal verbs: separable. (Group D)

Directions: Complete each sentence with a correct particle from the list. Particles may be used more than once or not at all.

around	down	in	out	up
back	from	off	over	

1. When I finish writing on one side of the paper, I *turn* it ____over____ and write on the back.

2. When the teacher finds a mistake in our writing, she *points* it _____ so we can correct it.

3. When I write words in this practice, I am *filling* _____ the blanks.

4. When I discover new information, I *find* something _____ .

5. When I need to see information from my computer on paper, I *print* it _____ .

6. When buildings are old and dangerous, we *tear* them _____ .

7. When I turn and go in the opposite direction, I *turn* _____ .

8. When I remove a piece of paper from a spiral notebook, I *tear* the paper _____ of my notebook.

9. When I write something that I don't want anybody else to see, I tear the paper into tiny pieces. I *tear* _____ the paper.

10. When I write information on an application form, I *fill* the form _____ .

11. When I make a mistake in something I write, I erase the mistake if I'm using a pencil. If I'm using a pen, I *cross* the mistake _____ by drawing a line through it.

12. When my teacup is empty, I *fill* it _____ again if I'm still thirsty.

13. When I check my homework carefully before I give it to the teacher, I *look* it _____ .

◇ **PRACTICE 8. Phrasal verbs: separable and nonseparable. (Groups A, B, C, D)**
    Directions: Complete the sentences with the particles in *italics*. The particles may be used more than once or not at all.

1. *out, away, back, down, off, on*

    Carol . . .

    a. put _____off_____ her vacation because she was sick.

    b. put _____ her boots to go out in the rain.

    c. put the phone _____ when she saw a spider crawling toward her.

    d. put her things _____ in her suitcase after the customs officer checked them.

    e. put _____ the stovetop fire with a small fire extinguisher.

    f. put _____ all the groceries she bought before she started dinner.

2. *out, in, up*

    James . . .

    a. handed _____ his financial report before the due date.

    b. handed _____ cigars when his son was born.

3. *into, off, on, up, over, out of*

    Linda . . .

    a. got _____ the flu in three days and felt wonderful.

    b. got _____ the bus and walked home.

    c. got _____ the bus and sat down behind the driver.

    d. got _____ a taxi to go to the airport.

    e. got _____ the taxi, paid the driver, and left a nice tip.

4. *in, down, up, out*

    a. This book has a few pages missing. The baby tore them _____ .

    b. Before I throw my credit card receipts away, I tear them _____ . I don't want anyone to read them.

    c. The building across the street will be torn _____ to make room for a parking garage.

5. *over, into, up*

    a. The neighbors asked the sheriff to look _____ a crime in their neighborhood.

    b. The sheriff looked _____ a suspect's address on the computer.

    c. The sheriff took the suspect's I.D., looked it _____ , and decided it was fake.

6. *off, down, up, back*

    a. I called Rita _____ several times, but got no answer. I'm a little worried.

    b. The meeting was called _____ because the chairperson was sick.

    c. Jack called and left a message. I'll call him _____ after dinner.

7. *over, up, in, off, back*

    a. My ears are ringing! Please turn _____ the music.

    b. It's cold, and I'm tired. Let's turn _____ and go home.

    c. Could I turn _____ the TV? I can't hear the news.

    d. Joe, the meat needs to be cooked on the other side. Would you turn it _____,
       please?

8. *in, out, up*

    a. I forgot to fill _____ a couple of blanks on the test.
       I hope I passed.

    b. Can I take this application home and fill it _____?
       I don't have much time now.

    c. Jack carries a thermos bottle to work. He fills _____
       his cup when he gets thirsty.

◇ **PRACTICE 9. Phrasal verbs: separable. (Group E)**
Directions: Complete each sentence with a correct particle from the list. Particles may be used more than once or not at all.

away	back	off	on	out	over	up

1. It's pretty chilly in here. You might want to leave your jacket ____on____ .

2. Mrs. Jefferson became a widow at a young age. She had to bring _____ six children
   by herself.

3. Give us a few hours. We'll work this problem _____ and let you know our solution.

4. Those are trick birthday candles. Every time you blow them _____ , they light
   again.

5. My roommate gives homeless people his old clothes. He tries to help them _____
   as often as possible.

6. A: Robert has taken Diane _____ several times. They go to restaurants and
      movies, but he doesn't seem serious about her.

   B: I know. Diane keeps trying to talk _____ their future, but he isn't interested in
      doing that.

7. A: It's hard to understand our company's policies. All the senior managers are getting large bonuses while the company is laying _____ people in every department.

   B: I know. I need to think _____ whether I want to continue with this job.

8. A: What is your store's return policy?

   B: You can bring clothes _____ within two weeks, and you need your receipt.

9. A: Are you going to meet with your supervisor this morning?

   B: Yes. I'm going to try to bring _____ the idea of a raise.

10. A: What time are you coming home?

    B: Around midnight.

    A: OK. I'll leave some lights _____ .

11. A: We did something that will cheer you _____ .

    B: What's that?

    A: We cleaned _____ your yard and garden while you were in the hospital. You'll see as soon as we get there.

    B: Thanks! What a wonderful surprise.

◇ PRACTICE 10. Phrasal verbs: separable. (Group E)
Directions: Complete the sentences with a phrasal verb from the list.

blow out	cheer up	give away	take back	think over
bring up	clean up	✓lay off	take out	work out

1. Michael is worried. His company is planning to ___lay___ 20% of its workforce ___off___ , and he doesn't have much seniority.

2. If you decide these shoes won't work for you, you can _____ them _____ within seven days.

3. That was so nice of you to water my plants while I was gone. I'd like to _____ you _____ to dinner to thank you.

4. There are ten candles on this cake, Jenny. Can you _____ them all _____ ?

5. Pauline has many clothes in her closet that she doesn't wear. Why doesn't she _____ them _____ ?

6. I have some news that will _____ you _____. We're getting two weeks additional vacation!

7. Let's set aside some time this weekend and finally _____ this place _____. This apartment is a mess.

8. The Smiths had a lot of arguments during the first year of their marriage, but I think they've finally _____ their differences _____. They seem pretty happy now.

9. Buying this house is a huge decision. We really need more time to _____ it _____ .

10. You'd better not _____ the subject of politics _____ with Ron. He becomes very upset when someone disagrees with his point of view.

◇ PRACTICE 11. Phrasal verbs: intransitive. (Group F)
Directions: Complete each sentence with a correct particle from the list. The particles may be used more than once or not al all.

back	in	off	out	to
down	of	on	over	up

1. The plane shook a little when it *took* _____off_____ . It made me nervous.

2. Emily's parents are upset because she *goes* _____ with friends every night and doesn't seem to have enough time for her studies.

3. Ken *grew* _____ in a small town and isn't used to the fast pace of the city.

4. I'm afraid we can't hear you in the back of the room. Could you please *speak* _____ ?

5. The computer teacher was so confusing. I didn't learn a thing! I think I'll just *start* _____ with a new teacher next term.

6. I'm exhausted. All week long I've been *getting* _____ between 4:00 and 5:00 A.M. for work.

7. A: Professor Wilson, do you have a minute?
   B: Sure. *Come* _____ and *sit* _____ .

8. A: I don't feel like cooking tonight.
   B: Me neither. Let's *eat* _____ .

9. A: Sorry I'm late. The bus *broke* _____ on the highway, and we had to wait for another.

   B: No problem. The meeting just started.

10. A: Mrs. Taylor is in the hospital again.

    B: What happened?

    A: She *fell* _____ and broke her hip.

11. A: The children are all *dressed* _____. They look so nice.

    B: Yes. They're having their school pictures taken today.

12. A: I'm really excited about Victoria and Nathan's wedding next month. They're such a great couple.

    B: I'm afraid I have bad news. They *broke* _____ two days ago.

13. A: Ever since I *gave* _____ smoking, I want to eat all the time.

    B: Try chewing gum. It helped me when I quit.

14. A: Look who just *showed* _____.

    B: Rover, what are you doing here? Dogs were not invited to this party!

15. A: Our new house will be finished April 1.

    B: We can help you *move* _____ _____ your old apartment.

    A: That would be wonderful.

16. A: Where's Julia?

    B: At the doctor's. She *broke* _____ in a rash last night, and she doesn't know what it is.

17. A: Don't stop now. Finish the story for us. Please!

    B: Okay, children. I'll *go* _____ if you promise to listen quietly.

18. A: Buddy, if you get all ready for bed, you can *stay* _____ and watch your favorite cartoon.

    B: O.K., Mom.

19. A: How was your dental appointment?

    B: I tried to *sit* _____ and relax. Even though it didn't hurt, I was nervous the whole time.

20. A: I feel very dizzy. I think I *stood* _____ too fast.

    B: Keep your head down and rest for a minute.

21. A: Someone keeps calling and *hanging* _____.

    B: Call the phone company. They have a way for you to find out who it is.

◇ PRACTICE 12. Phrasal verbs: intransitive. (Group F)

Directions: Complete each sentence with a correct particle from the list. Particles may be used more than once.

of	out	up

1. *Lazy Leo . . .*

   a. broke ___up___ with his girlfriend because she didn't want to wash his clothes.

   b. stayed _____ all night and didn't come home until morning.

   c. showed _____ late for class without his homework.

   d. goes _____ with friends to parties on school nights.

   e. eats _____ at restaurants because he doesn't like to cook.

   f. moved _____ _____ his apartment without telling the manager.

2. *Serious Sally . . .*

   a. goes to bed very early. She never stays _____ past 9:00.

   b. gets _____ at 5:00 every morning.

   c. speaks _____ in class when no one will answer.

   d. dresses _____ for school.

   e. never gives _____ when she gets frustrated.

   f. grew _____ as an only child.

◇ PRACTICE 13. Phrasal verbs: three-word. (Group G)

Directions: Complete each sentence with **two** particles.

1. When I cross a busy street, I'm careful. I *look* ___out___ ___for___ cars and trucks.

2. Some friends visited me last night. I hadn't expected them. They just *dropped* _____ _____ me.

3. When I put my name on a list for a class, I *sign* _____ _____ it.

4. If I like people and enjoy their company, that means that I *get* _____ _____ them.

5. My cousin never does anything useful. He just *fools* _____ _____ his friends all day, wasting time.

6. When somebody uses the last spoonful of sugar in the kitchen, we don't have any more sugar. That means we have *run* _____ _____ sugar and need to go to the market.

7. I'm glad when I finish my homework. When I *get* _____ _____ my homework, I can go out and play tennis or do whatever else I feel like doing.

8. In some places, it's important to be careful about pickpockets. There are places where tourists have to *watch* _____ _____ pickpockets.

9. If you return from a trip, that means you *get* _____ _____ a trip.

10. Sometimes students have to quit school because they need to get a job, fail their courses, or lose interest in their education. There are various reasons why students *drop* _____ _____ school.

11. Maria was born and raised in Brazil. In other words, she *grew* _____ _____ Brazil.

◇ **PRACTICE 14. Phrasal verbs: three-word. (Group G)**
Directions: Complete each sentence with the correct word from the list.

assignment	✓gymnastics class	paint	snakes
cord	Hawaii	rocks	their neighbors

1. Martin signed up for a __gymnastics class__ . It starts next week.

2. The Hansens get along well with _____ . They even take vacations together.

3. I can't finish the living room walls because I've run out of _____ .

4. The highway sign said to watch out for _____ . They roll down the hills and sometimes hit cars.

5. As soon as I get through with this _____ , we can go to lunch. I have just one more problem to figure out.

6. Don't fool around with that _____ . You might get an electric shock.

7. You look very rested and relaxed. When did you get back from _____ ?

8. Look out for _____ on the path. They're not poisonous, but they might startle you.

◇ **PRACTICE 15. Phrasal verbs: three-word. (Group H)**
Directions: Complete each sentence with **two** particles.

1. Before we consider buying a home in this area, we'd like to *find* __out__ more __about__ the schools.

2. The mountain climbers *set* _____ _____ the summit at dawn and reached it by lunchtime.

3. A: Marty is 43 tomorrow, and she's decided to *go* _____ _____ school.

   B: Good for her! It's never too late.

4. A: What do teenagers like to do around here for fun?

   B: Some like to *hang* _____ _____ friends at the mall, but I wouldn't recommend it. The management doesn't approve.

5. A: Please *keep* Susie _____ _____ the dog.

   B: Is she afraid?

   A: No, that's the problem. She'll try to kiss him.

6. A: I'm going grocery shopping. Do you want to *come* _____ _____ me?

   B: No, thanks. I've got too much to do. But wait a minute. I *cut* some coupons _____ _____ the paper for you. Let me get them.

7. A: Let's invite the Tangs to *come* _____ _____ our beach house on Saturday.

   B: Good idea. I'll call them now.

8. A: We're going out for pizza at Little Italy. Do you want to come along?

   B: Sure. I wasn't going to do anything except *sit* _____ _____ my cat tonight!

9. A: Let's *go* _____ _____ Brian's tonight.

   B: Shall we call first or surprise him?

10. A: Why don't we *get* _____ _____ Eriko next week?

    B: Great! We can talk to her about our new plans for the company.

◇ **PRACTICE 16. Phrasal verbs: three-word. (Group H)**
Directions: Complete the sentences with words from the list that will give the same meanings as the <u>underlined</u> words.

along with	back to	out for	over to
around	✓ out about	out of	together with

1. I'd like to <u>get information</u> about the company before I apply for a job there.

   I'd like to find ____*out about*____ the company before I apply for a job there.

2. The two brothers <u>left for</u> the lake before sunrise. They wanted to be the first ones there.

   The two brothers set _____ the lake before sunrise. They wanted to be the first ones to arrive.

3. After Maria had her first child, she took a year off before she <u>returned to</u> work.

   After Maria had her first child, she took a year off before she went _____ work.

4. Jimmy really needs to find a job. He spends his days <u>sitting</u> at home <u>doing nothing</u>.

   Jimmy really needs to find a job. He spends his days sitting _____ at home.

5. Mark won't be home for dinner. He plans to <u>join</u> his co-workers for a party.

   Mark won't be home for dinner. He plans to get _____ his co-workers for a party.

6. Who wants to <u>accompany</u> me to the doctor's?

   Who will go _____ me to my doctor's appointment?

7. The dog was growling, so the dog catcher <u>approached</u> him very carefully.

   The dog was growling, so the dog catcher went _____ him very carefully.

8. Here's the article I told you about. I <u>removed</u> it from this morning's paper.

   I cut it _____ this morning's paper.

◇ **PRACTICE 17. Review: phrasal verbs. (Appendix 1)**
   Directions: Choose the correct particle.

1. Professor Brown always *calls* _____ the students who sit in the back of the class to answer.
   (A.) on   B. off   C. out   D. back

2. Tommy takes other children's toys and doesn't want to *give* them _____ .
   A. away   B. back   C. in   D. to

3. Laurie needs to *wake* her roommate _____ every morning because she sleeps through her alarm.
   A. in   B. on   C. up   D. over

4. Bobby, let's take a few minutes and *pick* _____ the toys in your room. They're all over the floor.
   A. over   B. on   C. up   D. away

5. Not enough people *signed up* _____ the gardening class, so it had to be canceled.
   A. for   B. in   C. into   D. with

6. This cold has lasted too long. I feel like I'll never *get* _____ it.
   A. with   B. over   C. away   D. back

7. Aren't you going to *try* _____ these shoes before you buy them?
   A. in   B. on   C. up   D. of

8. *Keep away* _____ the stove! It's still hot.
   A. off   B. from   C. out   D. of

Phrasal Verbs **319**

9. We'll feel more confident about the success of our new business after we *pay* _____ our loan.
   A. back   B. up   C. in   D. together

10. Look how nice Jenny's bedroom looks! She spent all morning *cleaning* it _____ .
    A. over   B. back   C. up   D. away

11. Steven had problems early in his career, but he seems to have *worked* them _____ .
    A. up   B. over   C. off   D. out

12. *Watch out* _____ the cat. She might scratch you.
    A. for   B. in   C. on   D. of

13. The fire department recommends keeping a fire extinguisher in your house to *put* _____ fires.
    A. off   B. out   C. back   D. down

14. It took Tim only 20 minutes to *figure* _____ the entire crossword puzzle.
    A. on   B. in   C. up   D. out

15. Although Mrs. Warren had been very wealthy, the size of her estate was quite small when she died. She had *given* _____ most of her money to charities.
    A. away   B. in   C. into   D. from

16. I *cut* your picture *out* _____ the newspaper today. Did you know you were going to be in it?
    A. in   B. off   C. of   D. from

17. Even though Kimberly's been home from the hospital for a week, she doesn't want anyone to *come* _____ *to* her house. She's still quite weak.
    A. over   B. about   C. into   D. from

18. This hike is pretty exhausting. I don't think I can *go* _____ any farther. I need to rest.
    A. out   B. in   C. to   D. on

19. There's a gas station. I'll wash the windows while you *fill* _____ the tank.
    A. on   B. in   C. out   D. up

20. A fight *broke* _____ among students after school. Fortunately, no one was injured.
    A. out   B. down   C. in   D. off

21. Sometimes when I recite a poem, I forget a line. So I go back to the beginning and *start* _____ .
    A. over   B. to   C. with   D. back

22. The school administrators have started new programs to prevent students from *dropping out* _____ high school.
    A. in   B. off   C. of   D. for

23. Mr. Robinson is happy to lend his adult children money as long as they *pay* it _____ .
    A. up   B. back   C. down   D. for

24. My computer printer isn't working. I can't *print* _____ any of my work.
    A. out   B. in   C. over   D. back

APPENDIX 2
Preposition Combinations

◇ **PRACTICE 1. Preposition combinations. (Group A)**
   Directions: Complete the sentences with prepositions.

1. My eight-year-old son Mark is afraid ____of____ thunder and lightning.

2. My mother really likes my friend Ahmed because he is always polite _____ her.

3. Fifty miles is equal _____ eighty kilometers.

4. A: How do I get to your house?

   B: Are you familiar _____ the red barn on Coles Road? My house is just past that and

   on the left.

   A: Oh, sure. I know where it is.

5. It's so hot! I'm thirsty _____ a big glass of ice water.

6. My boss was nice _____ me after I made that mistake, but I could tell she wasn't pleased.

7. Mr. Watts is often angry _____ some silly little thing that isn't important.

8. A: Harry, try some of this pasta. It's delicious.

   B: No, thanks. My plate is already full _____ food.

9. Four council members were absent _____ the meeting last night.

10. A: Why are you friendly with Mr. Parsons? He's always so mean to everybody.

    B: He's always been very kind _____ me, so I have no reason to treat him otherwise.

11. My sister is very angry _____ me. She won't even speak to me.

12. Is everybody ready _____ dinner? Let's eat before the food gets cold.

13. Ben's wife got a promotion at work. He is really happy _____ her.

◇ **PRACTICE 2. Preposition combinations. (Group A)**
Directions: Create a sentence by matching each phrase in Column A with a phrase in Column B. Use each phrase only once.

Column A
1. Our dog is afraid ___B___
2. The class is curious _____
3. Mr. White is angry _____
4. Several nurses have been absent _____
5. After gardening all day, Helen was thirsty _____
6. The workers are angry _____
7. The baseball coach was happy _____
8. The kitchen cupboard is full _____
9. I'm not ready _____
10. It's important to be kind _____

Column B
A. about his team's win.
✓B. of cats.
C. for a glass of lemonade.
D. for the start of school.
E. from work due to illness.
F. about the snake in the cage.
G. to everyone.
H. of canned foods.
I. about their low pay.
J. at his dog for chewing his slippers.

◇ **PRACTICE 3. Preposition combinations. (Group B)**
Directions: Complete the sentences with prepositions.

1. What are you laughing ___at___ ?

2. I can't stop staring _____ Tom's necktie. The colors are wild!

3. A: I don't believe _____ flying saucers. Do you?
   B: I don't know. I think anything is possible.

4. Ted is going to help me _____ my homework tonight.

5. Do you mind if I apply _____ your job after you quit?

6. Kyong is excited about going back home to see her family. She leaves _____ Korea next Monday.

7. I admire Carmen _____ her courage and honesty in admitting that mistake.

8. A: Where did you get that new car?
   B: I borrowed it _____ my neighbor.

9. A: What are you two arguing _____ ?
   B: Modern art.

10. A: Where will you go to school next year?
    B: Well, I applied _____ admission at five different universities, but I'm worried that none of them will accept me.

11. I hate to argue _____ my older sister. I hardly ever win.

12. I'll introduce you _____ my cousins when they come to my wedding next week.

13. Ivan discussed his calculus problems _____ his college advisor.

◇ PRACTICE 4. Preposition combinations. (Group B)
Directions: Choose the correct preposition.

1. You're shivering. Would you like to borrow a jacket _____ me?
   A. from   B. for   C. with

2. I'm applying _____ a new management position in my company.
   A. to   B. in   C. for

3. It's unfortunate that the Bakers are always arguing _____ something.
   A. with   B. about   C. at

4. Russ believes _____ his ability to succeed under difficult conditions.
   A. in   B. on   C. at

5. Poor Mr. Miller. No one laughed _____ his story even though it was supposed to be funny.
   A. over   B. at   C. from

6. It's rather amazing. Gail and Brian plan to get married soon, but they were just introduced _____ each other a month ago.
   A. to   B. with   C. at

7. Please wake me up at 5:00 A.M. tomorrow. I need to leave _____ work early.
   A. from   B. to   C. for

8. People say they admire me _____ my truthfulness, but sometimes I wonder if I may be too honest.
   A. about   B. with   C. for

9. It's very difficult to discuss serious matters _____ Mark. He always tries to make jokes.
   A. with   B. about   C. at

10. I'm trying not to stare _____ that man, but his toupee keeps falling off.
    A. at   B. with   C. to

◇ PRACTICE 5. Preposition combinations. (Group C)
Directions: Complete the sentences with prepositions.

1. A: Why are you friendly __with/to__ George? I thought you didn't like him.

   B: I'm not crazy _____ his attitude, but I'm his supervisor, so I have to encourage him to do better work.

2. A: Do you think it's bad that I drink so much coffee every day?

   B: I believe too much of almost anything is bad _____ you.

3. I don't know why they fired me. It certainly isn't clear _____ me.

4. A: Dad, I got ninety-five percent on my algebra exam!

   B: I'm proud _____ you. I knew you could do it.

5. A: You seem to be interested _____ aerobic exercise and jogging.

   B: I think regular physical exercise is good _____ everyone.

6. That sweater is very similar _____ mine. Did you buy it at the mall?

7. A: You were up awfully late last night.

   B: I couldn't sleep. I was hungry _____ something sweet, but I couldn't find anything in the kitchen.

8. I have no doubt that I'm doing the right thing. I'm sure _____ it.

9. George Gershwin, an American composer, is most famous _____ his *Rhapsody in Blue*, an orchestral piece that combines jazz with classical music.

10. A: Why is Gary avoiding you? Is he angry about something?

    B: I don't know. I'm not aware _____ anything I did that would upset him.

11. A: Who is responsible _____ this dog? We don't allow dogs in this office!

    B: He belongs to the boss's wife.

    A: Oh.

12. My car is a lot like yours, but different _____ Margaret's.

13. Don't be nervous _____ your job interview. Just be yourself.

14. Teachers need to be patient _____ their students.

15. Ken carelessly dropped the football before he could score, so his team lost. He was very sad _____ that.

◇ **PRACTICE 6. Review: preposition combinations. (Groups A and C)**
Directions: Complete the sentences with prepositions.

1. Dr. Nelson, a heart specialist, is . . .

   a. proud _____ her work.

   b. famous _____ her medical expertise.

   c. sure _____ her skills.

   d. familiar _____ the latest techniques.

   e. patient _____ her patients.

   f. aware _____ the stresses of her job.

g. interested _____ her patients' lives.

h. nice _____ her patients' families.

2. Her patient, Mrs. Green, is . . .

   a. sad _____ her illness.

   b. nervous _____ an upcoming surgery.

   c. aware _____ her chances for survival.

   d. full _____ hope.

   e. not afraid _____ dying.

   f. curious _____ alternative medicines.

   g. ready _____ unexpected side-effects.

   h. hungry _____ a home-cooked meal.

◇ PRACTICE 7. Preposition combinations. (Group D)
Directions: Complete the sentences with prepositions.

1. How much did you pay __*for*__ that beautiful table?

2. A: Did you talk _____ the manager _____ returning that dress?

   B: No. She didn't arrive _____ the store while I was there. I waited _____ her for a half an hour and then left.

3. I listened _____ you very carefully, but I didn't understand anything you said.

4. When I graduated _____ college, my mother and father told everyone we knew that I had graduated.

5. A: We don't have all day! How long is it going to take for someone to wait _____ us? I'm hungry.

   B: We just got here. Be patient. Do you have to complain _____ everything?

6. When did you arrive _____ Mexico City?

7. A: This sauce is delicious!

   B: Well, it consists _____ tomatoes, garlic, olive oil, and lemon juice all blended together.

8. There were ten people at the meeting and ten different opinions. No one agreed _____ anyone else _____ the best way to solve the club's financial problems.

9. I have to complain _____ the manager. Both the food and the service are terrible.

10. We've invited only family members _____ our wedding. I hope our friends aren't offended.

11. The soccer coaches disagree _____ one another _____ the best way to get their team mentally prepared for a game.

◇ PRACTICE 8. Preposition combinations. (Groups B and D)
   Directions: Complete the sentences with the verb in parentheses and the correct preposition.

   1. Margo **got to** the airport early so she wouldn't miss her flight.

      (arrive) Margo _____ arrived at _____ the airport early so she wouldn't miss her flight.

   2. The store manager had time to **help** a few customers.

      (wait) The store manager had time to _____ a few customers.

   3. Sigrid **asked me to go** to the symphony with her.

      (invite) Sigrid _____ me _____ the symphony.

   4. Water **is made of** hydrogen and oxygen.

      (consist) Water _____ hydrogen and oxygen.

   5. Sara **stood at the bus stop** for 20 minutes before the bus came.

      (wait) Sara _____ the bus for 20 minutes.

   6. The restaurant owner **discussed** the management changes with her staff.

      (talk) The restaurant owner _____ the management changes with
      her staff.

   7. Joseph **is going to** Athens for graduate work in archeology.

      (leave) Joseph _____ Athens for graduate work in archeology.

   8. Why is that man **continuing to look at** me?

      (stare) Why _____ that man _____ me?

   9. Barb **assisted** her friend **with** her finances.

      (help) Barb _____ her friend _____ her finances.

   10. I **checked** ten books **out of** the library. I'll return them next week.

      (borrow) I _____ ten books _____ the library.

◇ PRACTICE 9. Preposition combinations. (Group E)
   Directions: Complete the sentences with prepositions.

   1. Molly is always looking __ for __ her keys. She seems so disorganized.

   2. Something's the matter _____ Dan. He's crying.

   3. Do whatever you want. It doesn't matter _____ me.

   4. Look _____ those clouds. It's going to rain.

   5. Are you looking forward _____ your trip to Mexico?

   6. A: Does this watch belong _____ you?

      B: Yes. Where did you find it? I searched _____ it everywhere.

7. I woke up frightened after I dreamed _____ falling off the roof of a building.

8. Tomorrow I'm going to ask my father _____ a ride to school.

9. Tomorrow I'm going to ask my father _____ his work. I don't know much
   _____ his new job.

10. Please empty that bowl of fruit and separate the fresh apples _____ the old apples.

11. Mr. Sanchez looks a lot _____ a famous movie actor I've seen.

12. My brother Ben warned me _____ taking a shortcut through the back streets. I got
    lost and was late for a job interview.

◇ PRACTICE 10. Preposition combinations. (Group E)
   Directions: Create sentences by matching each phrase in Column A with a phrase in Column B.
   Use each phrase only once.

Column A

1. The sheriff is searching __G__
2. The baby keeps looking _____
3. Once again, Rita is looking _____
4. In this picture, Paula looks _____
5. The Browns are looking forward _____
6. Before you do the wash, you need to
   separate the darks _____
7. Sometimes Joey is afraid to sleep. He often
   dreams _____
8. Something's the matter _____
9. The sign on the highway warned
   drivers _____
10. Do you know much _____

Column B

A. about monsters and dragons.

B. to their 20th wedding anniversary.

C. for her glasses. She always misplaces
   them.

D. about housing prices in this area?

E. about high winds on the bridge.

F. with this car. It's making strange noises.

✓G. for the escaped prisoner.

H. from the whites.

I. at the TV screen. The picture is fuzzy.

J. like her maternal grandmother. The
   resemblance is very strong.

◇ PRACTICE 11. Preposition combinations. (Group F)
   Directions: Complete the sentences with prepositions.

1. Please don't argue. I insist ___on___ lending you the money for your vacation.

2. That thin coat you're wearing won't protect you _____ the bitter, cold wind.

3. A: What's the matter? Don't you approve _____ my behavior?

   B: No, I don't. I think you're rude.

4. A: Can I depend _____ you to pick up my mother at the airport tomorrow?

   B: Of course you can!

5. A: The police arrested a thief in my uncle's store yesterday.

   B: What's going to happen _____ him? Will he go to jail?

6. My friend Ken apologized _____ me _____ forgetting to pick me up in his car after the movie last night. I forgave him _____ leaving me outside the theater in the rain, but I'm not going to rely _____ him for transportation in the future.

7. A: Thank you _____ helping me move to my new apartment last weekend.
   B: You're welcome.

8. It isn't fair to compare Mr. Wong _____ Ms. Chang. They're both good teachers, but they have different teaching methods.

9. I've had a bad cold for a week and just can't get rid _____ it.

10. Excuse me _____ interrupting you, but I have a call on the other line. Could I get back to you in a second?

11. A: I need to be excused _____ the office meeting tomorrow morning.
    B: I was going to announce your promotion at the meeting. Can you change your plans?
    A: I'd love to. It's a dental appointment.

12. People don't die _____ embarrassment, but sometimes they wish they could.

13. I'm sorry. The office staff is very busy right now. It will be a half hour before someone can take care _____ your request.

◇ PRACTICE 12. Preposition combinations. (Group F)
Directions: Write "C" beside the correct sentences. Write "X" beside those that are incorrect. In some cases, both may be correct.

1. a. __C__ John needs to be excused from the meeting.

   b. __C__ John excused his associate for the accounting error.

2. a. __C__ Do you approve of your government's international policies?

   b. __X__ Do you approve on the new seat-belt law?

3. a. _____ I apologized for the car accident.

   b. _____ I apologized to Mary's parents.

4. a. _____ Why did you get rid over your truck? It was in great condition.

   b. _____ I got rid of several boxes of old magazines.

5. a. _____ Pierre died of a heart attack.

   b. _____ Pierre's father also died from heart problems.

6. a. _____ It's not a good idea to compare one student to another.

   b. _____ I wish my parents wouldn't compare me with my brother.

7. a. _____ We can rely on Lesley to keep a secret.

   b. _____ There are several people whom my elderly parents rely in for assistance.

8. a. _____ You can relax. I took care about your problem.

   b. _____ The nurses take wonderful care of their patients at Valley Hospital.

◇ **PRACTICE 13. Preposition combinations. (Group G)**
Directions: Complete the sentences with prepositions.

1. Please try to concentrate ___on___ my explanation. I can't repeat it.

2. I spoke _____ my brother _____ your problem, and he said that there was nothing he could do to help you.

3. All right, children, here is your math problem: add ten _____ twelve, subtract two _____ that total; divide ten _____ that answer; and multiply the result _____ five. What is the final answer?*

4. I feel pretty good about my final examination in English. I'm hoping _____ a good grade.

5. A: Did you hear _____ the plans to build a new hotel in the middle of town? It's wonderful!

   B: Yes, I heard, but I disagree _____ you. I think it's terrible! It means the town will be full of tourists all the time.

6. A: Have you heard _____ your friend in Thailand recently?

   B: Yes. She's having a difficult time. She's not accustomed _____ hot weather.

7. A: I must tell you _____ a crazy thing that happened last night. Have you heard?

   B: What? What happened?

   A: A hundred monkeys escaped _____ the zoo.

   B: You've got to be kidding! How did that happen?

8. A: Do you ever wonder _____ the future of our natural environment?

   B: Yes, especially when I read about the deforestation of the rainforests.

9. A: Is Carol hiding _____ me? Is she afraid of me?

   B: No, but since she turned two years old, she loves to play hide-and-seek. She hides _____ everyone now.

———————

Answer: 10

10. A: Can I tell you _____ the new preschool later? Someone's at the door.

B: Sure.

◇ PRACTICE 14. Preposition combinations. (Group G)
Directions: Complete the sentences with the verb in parentheses and the correct preposition.

1. The skiers **wanted** snow for the holiday weekend, but it rained instead.

   (hope) The skiers _____ hoped for _____ snow for the holiday weekend.

2. Jenny often **thinks about** people she went to high school with. She's curious about what happened to them.

   (wonder) Jenny often _____ people she went to high school with.

3. I **cut** the pie **into** eight equal pieces.

   (divide) I _____ the pie _____ eight equal pieces.

4. Could you **put** another egg **in** the mixture? It's a little dry.

   (add) Could you _____ another egg _____ the mixture? It's a little dry.

5. An artist **focuses on** the way light strikes his subject.

   (concentrate) An artist _____ the way light strikes his subject.

6. The prisoners **got away from** their guards and ran into the woods.

   (escape) The prisoners _____ their guards and ran into the woods.

7. I **am used to** humid weather in the summer.

   (accustom) I _____ humid weather in the summer.

8. Ben **got the news about** his father's death from his secretary.

   (hear) Ben _____ the news _____ his father's death from his secretary.

◇ **PRACTICE 15. Review: preposition combinations. (Appendix 2)**
Directions: Circle the correct preposition in each sentence. In some cases, both prepositions are correct.

1. The taxi driver apologized (to,) for Ann for the accident.

2. My mother died (from, of) cancer.

3. Jack was excused *from, for* school for several days so he could travel with his father.

4. Mary always compares her country *with, to* this country.

5. Susie dreamed *of, about* winning the lottery.

6. The mountain climbers were warned *of, about* the avalanche danger.

7. Maria needed ten dollars immediately. She asked her sister *about, for* some money.

8. Beth looks *like, for* her sister. They could almost be twins.

9. Dennis tried talking *to, about* Roman, but the noise in the restaurant was so loud that neither he nor Roman could hear each other.

10. This dish tastes like it has meat in it, but it consists only *in, of* vegetables.

11. Mary and Joe argue *about, with* everything. They always disagree *with, about* each other.

12. Are you sure *of, about* your data?

13. Our dentist is very patient *to, with* children.

14. Professor Case always seems angry *at, with* his students, but maybe he's upset about something else.

15. We discussed our house plans *with, about* several architects.

16. The apartment owner spoke *to, with* several tenants about a possible rent increase.

17. We heard *about, from* the plane crash on the radio.

18. If you multiply any number *from, by* zero, the answer is always zero.

19. Shhh! I'm concentrating *in, on* my homework.

◇ **PRACTICE 16. Review: preposition combinations. (Appendix 2)**
Directions: Choose the correct preposition.

1. What time do you need to be ready _____ work?
   A. at   B. about   C. on   (D.) for

2. One pound is equal _____ 2.2 kilos.
   A. for   B. to   C. in   D. on

3. Too many vitamins may be bad _____ your health.
   A. in   B. about   C. for   D. with

4. That box looks very heavy. Can I help you _____ it?
   A. with   B. in   C. about   D. on

5. Our cat got rid _____ all the mice in our basement.
   A. about   B. of   C. in   D. off

6. Everyone admires Mr. Kim _____ his generosity with his time and money.
   A. for   B. from   C. with   D. about

7. I need to hide this chocolate _____ the children or they will eat it in one day.
   A. with   B. from   C. to   D. at

8. Billy, stop that! It's not polite to stare _____ people.
   A. to   B. at   C. in   D. on

9. Angela has applied _____ several jobs in the airline industry, but she hasn't gotten an interview yet.
   A. to   B. with   C. of   D. for

10. This car can't belong _____ Mike. It's too nice!
    A. about   B. with   C. to   D. at

11. Monica loves vegetables, but she's not crazy _____ fruit.
    A. over   B. of   C. at   D. about

12. Jack paid _____ my dinner.
    A. with   B. for   C. on   D. in

13. I tried to tell Jessica _____ my trip, but she didn't seem interested. I wonder if she was jealous.
    A. to   B. about   C. with   D. off

14. We're really happy _____ Professor James. He just received an award for excellence in teaching.
    A. for   B. to   C. over   D. in

15. People say I shouldn't care what other students think, but their opinions matter _____ me.
    A. to   B. for   C. with   D. on

16. Annie eats vegetables only if they are separated _____ the other foods on her plate.
    A. between   B. from   C. with   D. to

17. Kristi forgave her twin sister _____ taking her cell phone without asking.
    A. about   B. from   C. for   D. with

18. Doctors say that even ten minutes of exercise a day is good _____ you.
    A. at   B. for   C. with   D. about

19. I'm sorry. Your explanation still isn't clear _____ me.
    A. about   B. with   C. to   D. in

20. My sister complained _____ the manager.
    A. to   B. with   C. at   D. for

21. She complained _____ the slow service in the restaurant.
    A. for   B. about   C. over   D. by

22. What happened _____ your hand? It's swollen.
    A. on   B. to   C. in   D. about

23. The problem with your answer is that you multiplied six _____ eight instead of subtracting it.
    A. by   B. from   C. to   D. over

24. Paul is so smart. He graduated _____ the university in just three years.
    A. of   B. at   C. from   D. to

Index

To the student: To make it easy to correct your answers, remove this answer key along the perforations and make a separate answer key booklet for yourself.

Chapter 8: CONNECTING IDEAS

◇ **PRACTICE 1, p. 152.**

1. The farmer has a <u>cow</u>, a <u>goat</u>, and a black <u>horse</u>.
   (noun + noun + noun)
2. Danny is a <u>bright</u> and <u>happy</u> child.
   (adj. + adj.)
3. I <u>picked</u> up the telephone and <u>dialed</u> Steve's number.
   (verb + verb)
4. The cook <u>washed</u> the vegetables and <u>put</u> them in boiling water.
   (verb + verb)
5. My feet were <u>cold</u> and <u>wet</u>.
   (adj. + adj.)
6. Anita is <u>responsible</u>, <u>considerate</u>, and <u>trustworthy</u>.
   (adj. + adj. + adj.)
7. The three largest land animals are the <u>elephant</u>, the <u>rhinoceros</u>, and the <u>hippopotamus</u>.
   (noun + noun + noun)
8. A hippopotamus <u>rests</u> in water during the day and <u>feeds</u> on land at night.
   (verb + verb)

◇ **PRACTICE 2, p. 153.**

1. *(no commas)*
2. I opened the door, walked into the room, and sat down at my desk.
3. *(no commas)*
4. Their flag is green, black, and yellow.
5. *(no commas)*
6. Tom made a sandwich, poured a glass of juice, and sat down to eat his lunch.
7. Ms. Parker is intelligent, friendly, and kind.
8. *(no commas)*
9. Did you bring copies of the annual report for Sue, Dan, Joe, and Mary?
10. *(no commas)*
11. Can you watch television, listen to the radio, and read the newspaper at the same time?
12. *(no commas)*
13. Doctors save lives, relieve suffering, and cure diseases.
14. The restaurant served a five-course dinner: soup, fish, entrée, salad, and dessert.
15. *(no commas)*
16. An invitation should include your name, address, the date, the time, the purpose of the party, and any special activities such as swimming or dancing.

◇ **PRACTICE 3, p. 153.**

1. Birds fly, and fish swim.
   (S V, S V)
2. Birds fly. Fish swim.
   (S V. S V)
3. Dogs bark. Lions roar.
   (S V. S V)
4. Dogs bark, and lions roar.
   (S V, S V)
5. A week has seven days. A year has 365 days.
   (S V. S V)
6. A week has seven days, and a year has 365 days.
   (S V, S V)
7. Ahmed raised his hand, and the teacher pointed at him.
   (S V, S V)
8. Ahmed raised his hand. The teacher pointed at him.
   (S V. S V)

◇ **PRACTICE 4, p. 154.**

1. I	6. C
2. C	7. C
3. C	8. C
4. I	9. I
5. I	

◇ **PRACTICE 5, p. 154.**

1. I talked to Amy for a long time, but she didn't listen.
2. *(no change)*
3. *(no change)*
4. *(no change)*
5. Please call Jane, Ted, or Anna.
6. Please call Jane, Ted, and Anna.
7. I waved at my friend, but she didn't see me.
8. I waved at my friend, and she waved back.
9. *(no change)*
10. *(no change)*
11. My test was short and easy, but Ali's test was hard.

◇ **PRACTICE 6, p. 155.**

1. C	5. B
2. B	6. C
3. A	7. A
4. C	8. C

◇ PRACTICE 7, p. 155.

1. *(no change)*
2. I washed the dishes, and my son dried them.
3. I called their house, but no one answered the phone.
4. *(no change)*
5. I bought some apples, peaches, and bananas.
6. I was hungry, so I ate an apple.
7. *(no change)*
8. *(no change)*
9. My daughter is affectionate, shy, independent, and smart.
10. It started to rain, so we went inside and watched television.

◇ PRACTICE 8, p. 156.

1. . . . Every air traffic controller worldwide uses English, so it is important for Gina to become fluent in the language.
2. Gina has decided to take some intensive English courses at a private language institute, but she isn't sure which one to attend. There are many schools available, and they offer many different kinds of classes.
3. Gina has also heard of air traffic control schools that include English as part of their coursework, but she needs to have a fairly high level of English to attend.
4. Gina needs to decide soon, or the classes will be full . . . .

◇ PRACTICE 9, p. 156.

1. There are over 100,000 kinds of flies. They live throughout the world.
2. I like to get mail from my friends and family. Mail is important to me.
3. We are all connected by our humanity. We need to help each other. We can all live in peace.
4. There was a bad flood in Hong Kong. The streets became raging streams. Luckily no one died in the flood.
5. People have used needles since prehistoric times. The first buttons appeared almost two thousand years ago. Zippers are a relatively recent invention. The zipper was invented in 1890.

◇ PRACTICE 10, p. 157.

1. James has a cold. He needs to rest and drink plenty of fluids, so he should go to bed and drink water, fruit juices, or soda pop. He needs to sleep a lot, so he shouldn't drink fluids with caffeine, such as tea or coffee.
2. My friend and I were tired, so we went home early. We wanted to stay until the end of the game, but it got too late for us. Both of us had to get up early in the morning and go to our jobs.
3. The normal pulse for an adult is between 60 and 80 beats per minute, but exercise, nervousness, excitement, and a fever will all make a pulse beat faster. The normal pulse for a child is around 80 to 90.

4. Many famous explorers throughout history set out on their hazardous journeys in search of gold, silver, jewels, or other treasures, but some explorers wanted only to discover information about their world.
5. Edward Fox was a park ranger for thirty-five years. During that time, he was hit by lightning eight times. The lightning never killed him, but it severely burned his skin and damaged his hearing.
6. The Indian Ocean is bordered on four sides by the continents of Africa, Asia, Australia, and Antarctica. Some of the important ports are Aden, Bombay, Calcutta, and Rangoon.
7. The Indian Ocean has many fish and shellfish, but it has less commercial fishing than the Atlantic or the Pacific. The climate of the Indian Ocean is tropical, so fish spoil quickly out of the water. It is difficult and expensive for commercial fishing boats to keep fish fresh.

◇ PRACTICE 11, p. 157.

1. did	10. are	19. does
2. does	11. will	20. don't
3. didn't	12. am	21. can't
4. do	13. won't	22. don't
5. does	14. will	23. is
6. doesn't	15. can	24. does
7. wasn't	16. has	25. did
8. is	17. did	26. is
9. isn't	18. would	27. isn't

◇ PRACTICE 12, p. 158.

1. does Tom . . . does too
2. does Brian . . . Brian doesn't
3. was I . . . I was
4. is Oregon . . . Oregon is
5. did Jean . . . Jean did
6. did Jason . . . Jason didn't
7. can Rick . . . Rick can't
8. does Laura . . . Laura does
9. does Alice . . . Alice doesn't
10. are porpoises . . . porpoises are
11. have I . . . I haven't
12. does my brother . . . my brother does
13. will Erin . . . Erin won't

◇ PRACTICE 13, p. 160.

PART I.

1. can't either	7. couldn't either
2. does too	8. did too
3. doesn't either	9. can't either
4. is too	10. does too
5. wasn't either	11. would too
6. didn't either	

PART II.

12. so is	18. neither is
13. neither do	19. so does
14. neither did	20. so is
15. so are	21. neither have
16. so do	22. so did
17. so is	23. neither did

◇ PRACTICE 14, p. 161.

1. Mr. Tanaka was late for work <u>because [he] [missed] the bus</u>. (s = he, v = missed)

2. I closed the door <u>because the [room] [was] cold</u>. (s = room, v = was)

3. <u>Because [I] [lost] my umbrella</u>, I got wet on the way home. (s = I, v = lost)

4. Joe didn't bring his book to class <u>because [he] [couldn't find] it</u>. (s = he, v = couldn't find)

5. The teacher couldn't hear the question <u>because the [class] [was] so noisy</u>. (s = class, v = was)

6. <u>Because the [ice cream] [was beginning] to melt</u>, I put it back in the freezer. (s = ice cream, v = was beginning)

◇ PRACTICE 15, p. 161.

1. I opened the window because the room was hot. **W**e felt more comfortable then.
2. Because his coffee was cold, Jack didn't finish it. **H**e left it on the table and walked away.
3. Because the weather was bad, we canceled our trip into the city. **W**e stayed home and watched TV.
4. Debbie is a cheerleader. **S**he woke up in the morning with a sore throat because she had cheered loudly at the basketball game.
5. Francisco is an intelligent and ambitious young man. **B**ecause he hopes to get a good job late in life, he is working hard to get a good education now.

◇ PRACTICE 16, p. 161.

1. *lose weight*—Eric went on a diet because he wanted to lose weight.
2. *didn't have money*—The family couldn't buy food because they didn't have money.
3. *have several children*—Our neighbors are very busy because they have several children.
4. *be tired*—Because I am tired, I am going to bed.
5. *exercise every day*—Because Susan exercises every day, she is in great shape.
6. *have a high fever*—Because Jennifer has a high fever, she is going to the doctor.

◇ PRACTICE 17, p. 162.

1. a. He was hungry, **so** he ate a sandwich.
   b. **Because** he was hungry, he ate a sandwich.
   c. He ate a sandwich **because** he was hungry.
2. a. **Because** my sister was tired, she went to bed.
   b. My sister went to bed **because** she was tired.
   c. My sister was tired, **so** she went to bed.
3. a. **Because** human beings have opposable thumbs, they can easily pick things up and hold them.
   b. Human beings have opposable thumbs, **so** they can easily pick things up and hold them.
   c. Human beings can easily pick things up and hold them **because** they have opposable thumbs.
4. a. Schoolchildren can usually identify Italy easily on a world map **because** it is shaped like a boot.
   b. **Because** Italy has the distinctive shape of a boot, schoolchildren can usually identify it easily.
   c. Italy has the distinctive shape of a boot, **so** schoolchildren can usually identify it easily on a map.

◇ PRACTICE 18, p. 163.

1. like
2. don't like
3. is
4. stayed
5. didn't change
6. didn't pass
7. ate
8. were

◇ PRACTICE 19, p. 164.

1. B
2. A
3. A
4. B
5. A
6. A
7. B
8. B
9. A
10. A
11. B
12. A

◇ PRACTICE 20, p. 165.

1. because
2. even though
3. even though
4. Even though
5. Because
6. Because
7. Even though
8. even though
9. because
10. even though
11. because . . . Even though . . . because

◇ PRACTICE 21, p. 166.

1. C
2. C
3. B
4. B
5. C
6. C
7. B
8. A
9. A
10. B
11. C
12. A
13. C

◇ PRACTICE 22, p. 168.

1. I don't drink coffee, and my roommate **doesn't** either.
2. The flight was overbooked, so I had to fly on another airline. OR The flight was overbooked. I had to fly on another airline.
3. Many people use computers for e-mail, the Internet, and word processing.
4. The room was stuffy and hot, but I didn't close the window.
5. The baby woke up crying **because** her diaper was wet.
6. Even **though** my father works two jobs, he always has time to play soccer or baseball on weekends with his family.
7. I saw a bad accident, and my sister **did** too.
8. Oscar always pays his bills on time, but his brother **doesn't**.
9. **Even though** my mother is afraid of heights, I took her up to the observation deck at the top of the building.
10. Janey doesn't like to get up early, and Joe **doesn't** either. OR Janey doesn't like to get up early, and **neither does** Joe.
11. Although it was raining quite hard, ~~but~~ we decided to go for a bike ride. OR ~~Although~~ It was raining quite hard, but we decided to go for a bike ride.
12. My mother and my father/ ~~They~~ immigrated to this country 30 years ago.
13. **Because** Maya is very intelligent, her parents want to put her in an advanced program at school.

Chapter 9: COMPARISONS

◇ PRACTICE 1, p. 169.

1. (just) as busy as Jason (is)
2. (nearly) as busy as Jason (is)
3. (nearly) as tired as Susan (was)
4. (nearly) as tired as Susan (was)
5. (just) as large as/as big as Po's (is)
6. (nearly) as big as Anna's (is)

◇ PRACTICE 2, p. 169.

1. aren't as noisy as
2. is as lazy as
3. aren't as strong as
4. is as tall as
5. isn't as comfortable as
6. isn't as big as
7. was as nervous as
8. isn't as fresh and clean as
9. am not as ambitious as
10. aren't as interesting as

◇ PRACTICE 3, p. 170.

PART I.
1. not nearly as
2. almost as / not quite as
3. not nearly as
4. just as

PART II.
5. just as
6. not nearly as
7. almost as / not quite as
8. not nearly as

PART III.
9. just as
10. not nearly as
11. almost as / not quite as

PART IV.
12. just as
13. almost as
14. just as
15. not nearly as
16. almost as / not quite as

◇ PRACTICE 4, p. 172.

1. E
2. C
3. D
4. G
5. B
6. H
7. F
8. A

◇ PRACTICE 5, p. 172.

PART I.
1. as snow
2. as ice
3. as a picture
4. as a bat
5. as a bone
6. as a pillow
7. as a wink
8. as a mouse
9. as a bird
10. as pie

PART II.
11. cold as ice
12. quick as a wink
13. blind as a bat
14. white as snow
15. quiet as a mouse
16. pretty as a picture
17. easy as pie
18. free as a bird
19. soft as a pillow
20. dry as a bone

◇ PRACTICE 6, p. 174.

1. stronger . . . the strongest
2. more important . . . the most important
3. softer . . . the softest
4. lazier . . . the laziest
5. more wonderful . . . the most wonderful
6. calmer . . . the calmest

7. tamer . . . the tamest
8. dimmer . . . the dimmest
9. more convenient . . . the most convenient
10. more clever/cleverer . . . the most clever/the cleverest
11. better . . . the best
12. worse . . . the worst
13. farther . . . the farthest
14. slower . . . the slowest
15. more slowly . . . the most slowly

◇ PRACTICE 7, p. 174.

1. colder than
2. older than
3. more expensive than
4. larger
5. hotter than
6. slower than
7. creamier than
8. worse than
9. faster than
10. more important
11. quicker than
12. heavier
13. safer than
14. more difficult than

◇ PRACTICE 8, p. 175.

1. colder
2. more generous
3. more slowly
4. more comfortable
5. friendlier/more friendly
6. more softly
7. softer
8. more careful
9. prettier
10. lazier

◇ PRACTICE 9, p. 176.

1. the worst
2. worse
3. the best
4. better
5. the worst
6. worse
7. the worst
8. better

◇ PRACTICE 10, p. 176.

1. A, B
2. B
3. A, B
4. B
5. B
6. B

◇ PRACTICE 11, p. 177.

1. more slowly (ADV)
2. slower (ADJ)
3. more serious (ADJ)
4. more seriously (ADV)
5. more politely (ADV)
6. more polite (ADJ)
7. more careful (ADJ)
8. more carefully (ADV)
9. more clearly (ADV)
10. clearer (ADJ)

◇ PRACTICE 12, p. 177.

1. I did
2. she is
3. I do
4. she did
5. I was
6. he will
7. he does
8. he has
9. she did
10. he can

◇ PRACTICE 13, p. 178.

	formal	*informal*
1.	I am	me
2.	he is	him
3.	I am	me
4.	she is	her
5.	I am	me
6.	I am	me

◇ PRACTICE 14, p. 179.

1. A
2. B, C, D
3. A
4. B, C, D
5. B, C, D
6. A
7. B, C, D
8. A
9. B, C, D

◇ PRACTICE 15, p. 179.

1. *(no change possible using **less**)*
2. I visit my brother less often than I visit my sister.
3. *(no change possible using **less**)*
4. Sam is less generous than his brother.
5. I'm less eager to go to the circus than the children are.
6. A notebook is less expensive than a textbook.
7. *(no change possible using **less**)*
8. Some people think that life in a city is less peaceful than life in a small town.
9. *(no change possible using **less**)*
10. I travel to Europe on business less frequently than I used to.

◇ PRACTICE 16, p. 180.

1. Sam enjoys football more than his best friend **does**.
2. OK
3. The coach helped Anna more than Nancy **did**. OR The coach helped Anna more than she/he **helped** Nancy.
5. Sara likes tennis more than her husband **does**.
5. OK
6. OK
7. Charles knows Judy better than Kevin **does**. OR Charles knows Judy better than he **knows** Kevin.

◇ PRACTICE 17, p. 180.

1. more newspapers (NOUN)
2. more homework (NOUN)
3. more snow (NOUN)
4. more friends (NOUN)
5. more pleasant/pleasanter (ADJ)
6. more easily (ADV)
7. more books (NOUN)
8. more carefully (ADV)
9. louder (ADJ)

◇ PRACTICE 18, p. 181.

1. better and better
2. bigger and bigger
3. colder and colder
4. louder and louder
5. angrier and angrier/more and more angry
6. longer and longer
7. more and more expensive
8. more and more tired
9. friendlier and friendlier/more and more friendly
10. faster and faster

◇ PRACTICE 19, p. 181.

1. The more . . . the stronger
2. The softer . . . the easier
3. the older . . . the wiser
4. The simpler . . . the more relaxed
5. The longer . . . the more tired
6. The harder . . . the more

◇ PRACTICE 20, p. 182.

1. more he talked, the more bored I became
2. older you are, the more you understand
3. more I thought about it, the more confused I became
4. more polluted the air, the greater the chances of developing respiratory diseases
5. faster he talked, the more confused I became
6. more the fans clapped and cheered, the more shots the basketball team made

◇ PRACTICE 21, p. 183.

1. the most familiar
2. the longest necks
3. the largest ears
4. the largest eyes
5. the most intelligent . . . the most intelligent

◇ PRACTICE 22, p. 183.

PART I.
1. the most difficult . . . ever
2. the friendliest . . . of
3. the most embarrassing . . . in
4. the wisest . . . ever
5. the best . . . in
6. the most artistic of
7. the hottest . . . in
8. the warmest . . . of
9. the brightest . . . ever
10. the highest . . . in
11. the most knowledgeable . . . of
12. the most important . . . in

PART II.
13. the least ambitious of
14. the least expensive . . . ever
15. the least populated . . . in
16. the least amount . . . ever

◇ PRACTICE 23, p. 184.

PART I.
1. A pencil . . . a telephone
2. A diamond ring . . . a paper clip
3. A cup of coffee . . . a can of coffee beans
4. Radios and CD players . . . big screen TVs
5. A compact car . . . a house
6. Footballs, soccer balls, and basketballs . . . ping-pong balls

PART II.
7. Angel Falls . . . than Niagara Falls
8. Giessbach Falls . . . as Cuquenán Falls
9. Angel Falls . . . of all
10. Niagara Falls . . . as Angel Falls
11. Giessbach Falls . . . as Cuquenán Falls

PART III.
12. Air . . . than iron
13. Iron . . . than wood
14. iron . . . of all
15. Air . . . as water
16. air . . . of all
17. Water . . . as air
18. Water and iron . . . than wood

◇ **PRACTICE 24, p. 186.**

1. a   4. a   7. a
2. b   5. a   8. b
3. b   6. b

◇ **PRACTICE 25, p. 186.**

1. the funniest . . . funnier
2. sadder . . . the saddest
3. the best . . . better book
4. more exhausting . . . the most exhausting
5. happier . . . the happiest
6. more entertaining . . . the most entertaining
7. harder . . . the hardest
8. hotter . . . the hottest

◇ **PRACTICE 26, p. 187.**

1. more intelligent than . . . the smartest . . . in
2. the most popular . . . in
3. smaller than
4. More potatoes . . . than
5. the closest . . . faster than
6. the largest . . . in . . . the smallest . . . of
7. more important than . . . less important than
8. more information
9. kinder . . . more generous
10. more honest . . . than
11. the worst
12. the safest
13. faster . . . than
14. bigger than
15. more extensive . . . than

◇ **PRACTICE 27, p. 188.**

1. safer . . . than
2. the largest . . . in
3. more strength than
4. better
5. shortest
6. thinner . . . juicier
7. more comfortable . . . than
8. the most difficult of
9. the worst . . . in
10. harder than
11. lowest
12. the most complex . . . in
13. the funniest of
14. More people . . . than
15. less expensive . . . than

◇ **PRACTICE 28, p. 189.**

1. alike   5. like   9. like
2. like   6. like   10. alike
3. alike   7. alike
4. alike   8. like

◇ **PRACTICE 29, p. 190.**

1. from   7. to
2. to   8. as
3. as   9. to
4. from   10. from
5. as   11. as
6. to   12. from

◇ **PRACTICE 30, p. 190.**

PART I.

1. A is like D.
2. A and D are alike.
3. C is similar to A and D.
4. B is different from A, C, and D.

PART II.

5. similar to
6. the same as
7. different
8. the same as
9. different from

◇ **PRACTICE 31, p. 191.**

1. like
2. like
3. alike
4. A: alike
   B: alike/the same . . . the same . . . the same
5. like
6. A: like
   B: similar to
7. alike . . . alike . . . different
8. the same . . . the same . . . different

◇ **PRACTICE 32, p. 192.**

1. My brother is older **than** me.
2. A sea is ~~more~~ deeper than a lake.
3. A donkey isn't as big **as** a horse.
4. Ellen is **the** happiest person I've ever met.
5. When I feel embarrassed, my face gets **redder** and **redder**.
6. One of **the** largest **animals** in the world is the hippopotamus.
7. The traffic on the highway is **worse** ~~from~~ than it was a few months ago.
8. Jack is the same **age as** Jerry.
9. Peas are similar **to** beans, but they have several differences.
10. Last winter was pretty mild. This winter is cold and rainy. It's much **rainier** than last winter.
11. Mrs. Peters, the substitute teacher, is **friendlier** than the regular instructor.
12. Although alligators and crocodiles are similar, alligators are **not as big as** crocodiles. OR alligators are **smaller** than crocodiles.
13. Mohammed and Tarek come from different countries, but they became friends easily because they speak **the** same language, Arabic.
14. Mothers of young children are **busier** than mothers of teenagers.
15. We'd like to go sailing, but the wind is not as strong today **as** it was yesterday.
16. We asked for a non-smoking room, but the air and furniture in our hotel room smelled **like** cigarette smoke.

Chapter 10: THE PASSIVE

◇ **PRACTICE 1, p. 193.**

	verb	*active/passive*
1.	grow	active
2.	is grown	passive
3.	wrote	active
4.	was written	passive
5.	explained	active
6.	was explained	passive
7.	are designed	passive
8.	design	active

◇ PRACTICE 2, p. 193.

1. is delivered
2. has been eaten
3. was written
4. is going to be fixed
5. will be taught
6. is going to be brought
7. was won
8. will be treated
9. have been planted
10. are caught

◇ PRACTICE 3, p. 194.

1. brought	10. left	19. spent
2. built	11. lost	20. taken
3. bought	12. made	21. taught
4. eaten	13. found	22. gone
5. planned	14. played	23. visited
6. given	15. read	24. worn
7. grown	16. saved	25. written
8. hit	17. sent	26. done
9. hurt	18. spoken	

◇ PRACTICE 4, p. 194.

1. was eaten	7. will be played
2. is spoken	8. can be taught
3. are written	9. are going to be taken
4. was hurt	10. have been grown
5. is going to be visited	11. is worn
6. has been read	12. will be built

◇ PRACTICE 5, p. 195.

1. a	4. b
2. b	5. b
3. b	6. a

◇ PRACTICE 6, p. 196.

PART I.
1. are collected
2. are written
3. is grown
4. are eaten
5. am paid
6. is understood

PART II.
7. were collected
8. was built
9. was written
10. were destroyed

PART III.
11. have been visited
12. has been spoken
13. have been read
14. has been worn

PART IV.
15. will be discovered
16. will be visited
17. will be saved

PART V
18. is going to be hurt
19. are going to be offered
20. is going to be elected

◇ PRACTICE 7, p. 197.

1. The government collects taxes.
2. Big fish eat small fish.
3. Everyone understands the meaning of a smile.
4. Leo Tolstoy wrote *War and Peace*.
5. The dog chased the cat.
6. XYZ Inc. is going to buy ABC Corporation.
7. Millions of tourists have visited the pyramids in Egypt.
8. Scientists in the twenty-first century will discover new information about the universe.

◇ PRACTICE 8, p. 197.

1. Mr. Rice signed the letter.
2. Did Mr. Foster sign the letter?
3. Ms. Owens sent the fax.
4. Did Mr. Chu send the other fax?
5. Will Mr. Berg meet Adam at the airport?
6. Has Mrs. Jordan invited you to the reception?
7. Mr. Lee has invited me to the reception.
8. Is the teacher going to collect the homework?

◇ PRACTICE 9, p. 198.

	verb	*object*
1.	TRANSITIVE	a letter
2.	INTRANSITIVE	*(none)*
3.	INTRANSITIVE	*(none)*
4.	INTRANSITIVE	*(none)*
5.	TRANSITIVE	the ball
6.	INTRANSITIVE	*(none)*
7.	INTRANSITIVE	*(none)*
8.	TRANSITIVE	my car
9.	TRANSITIVE	the book
10.	INTRANSITIVE	*(none)*

◇ PRACTICE 10, p. 198.

	object	*passive sentence*
1.	me	I was awakened by a noise.
2.	*(no change)*	
3.	the mistake	The mistake was discovered by Alice.
4.	*(no change)*	
5.	*(no change)*	
6.	the chair	The chair was fixed by Anita.
7.	*(no change)*	
8.	*(no change)*	
9.	*(no change)*	
10.	*(no change)*	
11.	a quiz	A quiz was announced by the teacher.
12.	*(no change)*	
13.	*(no change)*	
14.	*(no change)*	

◇ PRACTICE 11, p. 199.

Passive (checked) sentences: 2, 4, 6, 9

◇ PRACTICE 12, p. 199.

	passive verb	*action performed by*
1.	are used	unknown
2.	was opened	Shelley
3.	will be translated	unknown
4.	was stolen	unknown
5.	were taken	a professional photographer
6.	is going to be built	unknown
7.	has been rented	a young family
8.	has been rented	unknown

◇ PRACTICE 13, p. 200.

Unnecessary by-*phrases:* 1, 3, 6, 8

◇ PRACTICE 14, p. 200.

1. The soccer game has been canceled.
2. The meeting has been canceled by the president.

3. Beer and wine are served at that restaurant.
4. I was confused in class yesterday.
5. I was confused by the teacher's directions.
6. The dishes haven't been washed yet.
7. They should be washed soon.
8. Was this sweater washed in hot water?
9. Wool sweaters should not be washed in hot water.
10. I was invited to the party by Luis.
11. Have you been invited to the party?

◇ **PRACTICE 15, p. 201.**
1. Sometimes keys are hidden under cars.
2. Cats hide under cars.
3. Students are taught by teachers.
4. Students study a lot.
5. Cereal is often eaten at breakfast.
6. Cats eat cat food.
7. Mice are eaten by cats.
8. Songs are sung to children by their mothers.
9. Children sing songs in school.
10. Thai food is cooked in Thai restaurants.
11. Chefs cook in restaurants.

◇ **PRACTICE 16, p. 201.**
1. are considering . . . is being considered
2. are watching . . . are being watched
3. are painting . . . is being painted
4. is fixing . . . is being fixed
5. was fixing . . . was being fixed
6. are meeting . . . is being met
7. were moving . . . was being moved
8. were singing . . . was being sung
9. are discovering . . . are still being discovered

◇ **PRACTICE 17, p. 202.**
1. is being played
2. was being cleaned
3. is being built
4. is being read
5. were being watched
6. was being flown

◇ **PRACTICE 18, p. 203.**
1. b   4. a
2. b   5. b
3. b

◇ **PRACTICE 19, p. 203.**

	I/C	corrections
1.	I	It ~~was~~ happened many years ago.
2.	C	*(none)*
3.	I	I **went** to school yesterday.
4.	I	Two firefighters **were** injured while they were fighting the fire.
5.	I	Sara ~~was~~ accidentally **broke** the window.
6.	I	Kara **ate** a snack when she got home from school.
7.	C	*(none)*
8.	I	I ~~am~~ agree with you.
9.	I	The little boy **fell** down while he was running in the park.
10.	I	The swimmer ~~was~~ died from a shark attack.
11.	C	*(none)*
12.	I	I ~~was~~ slept for nine hours last night.

◇ **PRACTICE 20, p. 204.**
1. Class might be canceled.
2. Medicine can be prescribed by a doctor.
3. This report must be signed by Mr. Hook.
4. A new post office may be built on First Street.
5. Stamps have to be placed in the upper right-hand corner of an envelope.
6. That fence ought to be painted.
7. The assignment must be done by all of the students.

◇ **PRACTICE 21, p. 204.**
1. shouldn't be put off
2. must be written
3. can be taught
4. could be killed
5. ought to be divided
6. must be sold
7. will not be known
8. has to be torn down . . . can be built

◇ **PRACTICE 22, p. 205.**
1. has to be returned
2. should be returned
3. must be sent
4. could be sent
5. should be sent
6. can be put away
7. may be thrown away
8. might be picked up
9. will be cleaned up

◇ **PRACTICE 23, p. 205.**

	active/passive	verb
1.	ACTIVE	have used
2.	PASSIVE	have been used
3.	PASSIVE	are used
4.	ACTIVE	show
5.	PASSIVE	is shown
6.	PASSIVE	were made
7.	PASSIVE	were worn
8.	ACTIVE	became
9.	ACTIVE	wear
10.	PASSIVE	are sold
11.	PASSIVE	are made and sold
12.	PASSIVE	is being sold
13.	PASSIVE	can be bought
14.	ACTIVE	Do own
15.	PASSIVE	was made

◇ **PRACTICE 24, p. 206.**
1. is being repaired
2. was being repaired
3. repaired
4. is made
5. should not carry
6. ought to be kept
7. are sent
8. has already been hired
9. must be used . . . can produce
10. are manufactured
11. can be used . . . can be recycled . . . should not be thrown away
12. must be protected
13. can be found

◇ **PRACTICE 25, p. 207.**
1. are loved . . . brings . . . are often used . . . can be found
2. exist . . . are found . . . have
3. are carried . . . carries . . . were introduced
4. are appreciated . . . is made . . . is gathered . . . are eaten
5. are made . . . do not come . . . are made
6. may be planted . . . grown . . . survive

◇ PRACTICE 26, p. 207.

PART I.

1. to
2. about
3. from
4. of
5. with
6. of
7. with
8. in
9. about
10. with

PART II.

11. in
12. with
13. of
14. to
15. to
16. with
17. from

PART III.

18. of
19. in
20. with
21. for

◇ PRACTICE 27, p. 208.

1. The little girl is **excited about** her coming birthday party.
2. Mr. and Mrs. Rose **are devoted to** each other.
3. . . . I **am** lost.
4. The students are **bored with** their chemistry project.
5. . . . **are composed of** recycled products.
6. . . . He **is** hurt.
7. How well are you **prepared for** the driver's license test?
8. Mary has been **engaged to** Paul for five years.

◇ PRACTICE 28, p. 209.

1. interesting
2. interested
3. exciting
4. excited
5. fascinated
6. fascinating
7. bored . . . confused
8. boring . . . confusing
9. interesting
10. fascinating . . . surprising

◇ PRACTICE 29, p. 209.

1. boring
2. interested
3. confused
4. exciting
5. confused
6. interesting
7. surprising
8. bored
9. boring
10. fascinating
11. fascinated
12. fascinating
13. embarrassing
14. shocking . . . shocked
15. exciting . . . excited

◇ PRACTICE 30, p. 211.

1. confusing
2. frustrated
3. confusing
4. embarrassed
5. embarrassing
6. interested
7. interesting
8. exhausting . . . tired
9. frightening
10. frightened

◇ PRACTICE 31, p. 211.

Incorrect sentences:

1. c
2. a
3. b
4. a
5. c

◇ PRACTICE 32, p. 212.

1. sick
2. lost
3. dizzy
4. bored
5. hungry
6. late
7. rich
8. arrested
9. dressed
10. wet
11. invited
12. stolen

◇ PRACTICE 33, p. 213.

1. Get
2. got
3. am getting
4. to get
5. got
6. getting . . . to get
7. 's/is getting
8. Get
9. got
10. got
11. 'm/am getting
12. got
13. 's/is getting
14. get
15. 'm/am getting
16. get
17. 'm/am getting
18. getting

◇ PRACTICE 34, p. 214.

1. B, C
2. A
3. B, C
4. A
5. B, C
6. A
7. A
8. B, C

◇ PRACTICE 35, p. 214.

1. Ø
2. is
3. are . . . am
4. Ø
5. is
6. Ø
7. Ø
8. Ø

◇ PRACTICE 36, p. 215.

1. used to get
2. is used to working
3. used to attend
4. used to work
5. is used to teaching
6. am used to eating

◇ PRACTICE 37, p. 215.

1. I was supposed to return this book to the library.
2. We are supposed to read Chapter 9 before class tomorrow.
3. I was supposed to go to a party last night, but I stayed home.
4. We are supposed to do Exercise 10 for homework.
5. . . . is supposed to rain tomorrow.
6. . . . am supposed to take one pill every six hours.
7. I am supposed to dust the furniture and (to) vacuum the carpet.

◇ PRACTICE 38, p. 216.

1. are supposed to be
2. were supposed to sweep/clean
3. was supposed to send
4. are supposed to give
5. are supposed to clean
6. am . . . supposed to register
7. was supposed to cook
8. are supposed to take off

◇ PRACTICE 39, p. 217.

1. The moving boxes **were** packed by Pierre.
2. My uncle ~~was~~ died in the war.
3. Miami **is** located in Florida.
4. *(no change)*
5. Mr. Rivera **is** interested in finding a new career.
6. Did you tell everyone the **shocking** news?
7. After ten years, I **am** finally used to this wet and rainy climate.
8. The newspaper **is supposed** to come every morning before eight.
9. The Millers have been **married to** each other for 60 years.

10. I ~am~ **used** to drink coffee with cream, but now I drink it black.
11. What ~was~ **happened** at the party last night?
12. Several people almost **got killed** when the fireworks exploded over them.
13. A new parking garage **is being built** for our office.
14. I have been living in England for several years, so I **am accustomed to** driving on the left side of the road.

Chapter 11: COUNT/NONCOUNT NOUNS AND ARTICLES

◇ PRACTICE 1, p. 218.

1. **a** game
2. **an** office
3. **a** car
4. **a** friend
5. **a** mountain
6. **a** rock
7. **an** army
8. **an** egg
9. **an** island
10. **an** ocean
11. **an** umbrella
12. **a** university
13. **a** horse
14. **an** hour
15. **a** star
16. **an** eye
17. **a** new car
18. **an** old car
19. **a** used car
20. **an** uncle
21. **a** house
22. **an** honest mistake
23. **a** hospital
24. **a** hand
25. **an** ant
26. **a** neighbor

◇ PRACTICE 2, p. 218.

These do not complete the sentences:

1. b
   d
   e
   h
2. c
   f
3. c
   e
4. d
   f
   h
   g
   h
5. a
   c
   f
   h
6. d
   g

◇ PRACTICE 3, p. 219.

	one	some
1.	words	words
2.	Ø	vocabulary
3.	Ø	slang
4.	Ø	homework
5.	assignment	assignments
6.	Ø	grammar
7.	dress	dresses
8.	Ø	clothes
9.	Ø	clothing
10.	parent	parents
11.	family	families
12.	Ø	knowledge
13.	Ø	information
14.	fact	facts
15.	Ø	luck
16.	Ø	garbage

◇ PRACTICE 4, p. 220.

1. bread, corn, peas, rice, sandwiches
2. apple trees, grass, lakes, mountains, plants, scenery
3. bracelets, jewels, jewelry, rings
4. equipment, hardware, machines, machinery, tools

◇ PRACTICE 5, p. 220.

1. **one** chair
2. **much** furniture
3. **many** vegetables
4. **much** clothing
5. **one** vegetable
6. **many** clothes
7. **much** fruit
8. **many** facts
9. **much** grammar
10. **one** word
11. **many** idioms
12. **much** vocabulary
13. **many** cars
14. **many** games
15. **much** water
16. **one** parent
17. **much** sand
18. **many** professors
19. **much** dust
20. **much** money
21. **much** stuff
22. **one** thing
23. **many** things
24. **much** English
25. **much** toast

◇ PRACTICE 6, p. 221.

1. is . . . snow
2. is . . . weather
3. Sunshine is
4. knowledge
5. fun
6. factories . . . pollution
7. pride . . . children
8. people . . . intelligence
9. peace
10. hospitality
11. beef . . . was
12. is . . . fog

◇ PRACTICE 7, p. 222.

1. many apples
2. much fruit
3. much mail
4. many letters
5. much English
6. much slang
7. many words are
8. much coffee
9. many sandwiches
10. much sugar
11. many courses
12. much homework
13. isn't much news
14. many articles are
15. much fun
16. many stars are
17. isn't much sunshine
18. Is . . . much pollution
19. much luck
20. are many kinds
21. is . . . much violence
22. much makeup
23. many cars
24. Is . . . much traffic

◇ PRACTICE 8, p. 223.

1. many letter**s** are
2. much mail (/)
3. many **men** have
4. many famil**ies** are
5. many sentenc**es** are
6. much chalk (/) is
7. much English (/)
8. much . . . literature (/)
9. many . . . word**s**
10. much gasoline (/)
    much petrol (/)
11. much homework (/)
12. many grandchild**ren**
13. many pag**es** are
14. many librar**ies** are
15. many glass**es**
16. much fun (/)
17. much education (/)
18. much soap (/)
19. many island**s** are
20. many people (/)
21. many zero**es**/zero**s** are

◇ PRACTICE 9, p. 224.

*Circled words are in **boldface**:*

1. **a** flower
2. **some/many** flowers
3. **a** coin
4. **some/much** money
5. **some/many** coins
6. **some/much** salt
7. **an** error
8. **a** mistake
9. **an** honest mistake
10. **some/many** mistakes
11. **a** dream
12. **an** interesting dream
13. **some/many** questions
14. **some/much** soap
15. **a** bar of soap
16. **some/much** beauty
17. **a** cup of tea
18. **an** unsafe place
19. **some/much** fruit
20. **some/many** pieces of fruit

◇ **PRACTICE 10, p. 224.**

1. a little music (/)
2. a few songs
3. a little help (/)
4. a little English (/)
5. a few . . . apples
6. a little honey (/)
7. a little advice (/)
8. a few suggestions
9. a few questions
10. a few people (/)
11. a few . . . minutes
12. a little light (/)
13. a little homework (/)
14. a little . . . grammar (/)
15. a few flowers
16. a little progress (/)

◇ **PRACTICE 11, p. 225.**

1. Kim has applied to **a** university in England.
2. . . . gave her **some** jewelry and a **poem** he **had written**.
3. The politician wanted specific **suggestions** for her speech on the economy.
4. Some of the **homework** for my English class was easy, but many of the **assignments** were unclear.
5. Diane has been to Rome several **times** recently. She always has **a** wonderful time.
6. Many parents need **advice** about raising children.
7. The boys played together in the **sand** and **dirt** for hours.
8. A person doesn't need **much** equipment to play baseball: just **a** ball and a bat.
9. **Much** happiness can come from enjoying the simple **things** in life.

◇ **PRACTICE 12, p. 225.**

1. Plants are the oldest living things on earth. (2)
2. Scientists divide living things into two groups: plants and animals. Generally speaking, plants stay in one place, but animals move around. (7)
3. Flowers, grass, and trees grow every place where people live. Plants also grow in deserts, in oceans, on mountaintops, and in polar regions. (7)
4. Plants are useful to people. We eat them. We use them for clothing. We build houses from them. Plants are also important to our health. We get many kinds of beneficial drugs from plants. In addition, plants provide beauty and enjoyment to all our lives. (7)
5. Crops are plants that people grow for food. Nature can ruin crops. Bad weather—such as too much rain or too little rain—can destroy fields of corn or wheat. Natural disasters such as floods and storms have caused farmers many problems since people first began to grow their own food. (9)
6. Food is a necessity for all living things. All animals and plants need to eat. Most plants take what they need through their roots and their leaves. The majority of insects live solely on plants. Many birds have a diet of worms and insects. Reptiles eat small animals, eggs, and insects. (15)

◇ **PRACTICE 13, p. 226.**

1. cup
2. pounds
3. bowl, cup
4. glass, bottle, quart
5. piece
6. gallons
7. bottle, gallon, quart
8. piece
9. bottle, glass
10. pieces
11. bowl, cup, piece, pound, kilo
12. sheets
13. loaf
14. spoonful
15. tube
16. bar, piece
17. piece
18. piece
19. pieces
20. pieces

◇ **PRACTICE 14, p. 227.**

1. jar
2. bottle, box
3. box, bottle
4. jar, bag, can/tin
5. can/tin
6. bag, box
7. jar
8. bottle
9. box, bag
10. can/tin

◇ **PRACTICE 15, p. 227.**

1. many suitcases
2. much suntan oil
3. many pairs of sandals
4. many tubes of toothpaste
5. many kilos of luggage
6. much money

◇ **PRACTICE 16, p. 228.**

1. **a** letter
2. **some** mail
3. **some** equipment
4. **a** tool
5. **some** food
6. **an** apple
7. **some** old clothing
8. **an** old shirt
9. **some** advice
10. **a** suggestion
11. **an** interesting story
12. **some** interesting news
13. **a** poem
14. **some** poetry
15. **a** song
16. **some** Indian music
17. **a** new word
18. **some** new slang

◇ **PRACTICE 17, p. 228.**

singular / *plural*

1. **a** bird — I saw some birds.
2. **some** corn — Ø *(none possible)*
3. **some** tea — Ø *(none possible)*
4. **a** flower — I picked some flowers.
5. **some** water — Ø *(none possible)*
6. **a** horse — I fed grass to some horses.
7. **some** jewelry — Ø *(none possible)*
8. **some** honey — Ø *(none possible)*
9. **a** new shirt — Tom bought some new shirts.
10. **some** soap — Ø *(none possible)*

◇ **PRACTICE 18, p. 229.**

1. **A** dog
2. **the** dog
3. **a** desk . . . **a** bed . . . **a** chest of drawers
4. **the** desk . . . **the** top drawer
5. **the** basement
6. **a** basement
7. **a** subject . . . **a** verb
8. **the** subject . . . **the** verb
9. **a** meeting
10. **the** meeting
11. **a** long distance . . . **a** telephone
12. **The** distance . . . **the** sun . . . **the** earth
13. **the** telephone
14. **the** cat
15. A: **a** cat
    B: **a** dog
16. **a** poem
17. A: **the** lecture
    B: **The** speaker . . . **an** interesting talk
18. A: **a** cup of coffee
    B: **the** cafe . . . **the** corner
19. **a** quiet street
20. A: **the** restaurant
    B: **the** street
21. A: **a** job
    B: **a** restaurant

◇ **PRACTICE 19, p. 230.**

1. Ø **D**ogs
2. **the** dogs
3. Ø **F**ruit
4. **The** fruit
5. **the** milk . . . **the** refrigerator . . . **the** table
6. Ø **M**ilk
7. Ø wine

8. **the** wine
9. Ø meat
10. **The** meat
11. **the** potatoes
12. Ø P̸otatoes . . . Ø vegetables
13. Ø F̸rogs . . . Ø small animals . . . Ø tails . . . Ø T̸urtles . . . Ø trails . . . Ø hard shells
14. **The** frogs . . . **The** turtles
15. **the** weather

16. Ø C̸opper
17. Ø candles . . . Ø light . . . Ø electricity
18. Ø books . . . Ø textbooks . . . Ø workbooks . . . Ø dictionaries . . . Ø encyclopedias . . . Ø entertainment . . . Ø novels . . . Ø poetry
19. **The** books

◇ PRACTICE 20, p. 231.
1. **some** coffee . . . **some** milk . . . **The** coffee . . . **The** milk
2. **some** soup . . . **a** sandwich . . . **The** soup . . . **the** sandwich
3. **some** clothes . . . **a** suit . . . **a** shirt . . . **a** tie . . . **The** suit . . . **The** shirt . . . **the** tie
4. A: **an** accident . . . **A** man . . . **a** Volkswagen . . . **a** bus
   B: **the** accident
   A: **The** man . . . **the** Volkswagen . . . **the** bus
5. **a** man . . . **a** woman . . . **an** argument . . . **The** man . . . **the** woman . . . **the** woman . . . **the** man . . . **the** argument
6. **some** birds . . . **a** tree . . . **a** cat . . . **the** tree . . . **The** birds . . . **the** cat . . . **the** cat . . . **the** birds

◇ PRACTICE 21, p. 233.
1. **a** man
2. **a** truck
3. **a** covered bridge
4. **The** bridge
5. **a** small river
6. **the** man
7. **the** man
8. **the** top
9. **the** bridge
10. **the** bridge
11. **a** solution
12. **the** solution
13. **the** truck
14. **the** bridge
15. **the** river
16. **a** great idea
17. **the** man
18. **the** tires
19. **the** river

◇ PRACTICE 22, p. 234.
1. B: **An** egg
   A: **the** egg
2. Ø E̸ggs
3. **a** scientific fact . . . Ø steam . . . Ø water
4. Ø G̸as
5. **The** gas
6. Ø N̸ewspapers . . . **an** important source . . . Ø information
7. **The** sun . . . **a** star . . . **the** sun . . . Ø heat . . . Ø light . . . Ø energy
8. Ø D̸ucks
9. Ø P̸izza . . . . Ø cheese . . . Ø tomatoes . . . Ø P̸izza . . . Ø Italian
10. A: **the** pizza
    B: **the** big piece . . . **the** small one
11. Ø G̸old . . . **an** excellent conductor . . . Ø electricity . . . **a** spaceship
12. **the** kitchen . . . **a** sandwich
13. A: **the** plumber . . . **The** sink
    B: **the** water supply . . . **the** house . . . **the** leak
14. **the** man . . . **the** president
15. **a** president

16. B: **a** blouse . . . Ø jewelry
    A: **the** blouse
17. **the** floor . . . **the** corner . . . **the** sofa
18. Ø furniture . . . **a** sofa . . . **an** easy chair
19. Ø F̸urniture
20. **A** vegetarian . . . Ø meat
21. **the** continents . . . **the** world
22. **an** easy exam . . . **the** right answers . . . **the** questions . . . **the** exam
23. **a** job interview . . . Ø nice clothes
24. **a** mouse . . . Ø R̸ats . . . Ø long, skinny tails
25. Ø wood . . . Ø coal . . . Ø heat . . . Ø gas . . . Ø oil . . . Ø electricity
26. **an** interesting experience . . . **A** man . . . **a** blue suit . . . **a** bouquet . . . Ø flowers . . . **the** man . . . **the** flowers . . . **the** door
27. Ø I̸ce cream
28. Ø steamed rice . . . Ø fish . . . Ø vegetables . . . **The** rice . . . **The** fish . . . **The** vegetables
29. **an** exceptionally talented person
30. A: **the** letter
    B: **A** strong wind . . . **the** floor . . . **the** dog . . . **the** scraps . . . **the** wastebasket
31. A: **the** tape player
    B: **the** shelves
    A: **the** batteries
32. Ø C̸halk . . . **a** necessity
33. **An** efficient transportation system . . . **an** essential part

◇ PRACTICE 23, p. 236.
1. Ø Paris
2. **The** Atlantic Ocean . . . **the** Pacific
3. Ø Dr. James
4. Ø Mt. Rainier . . . **the** Cascade Mountain Range
5. **The** Nile . . . Ø Africa
6. Ø Toronto . . . Ø Montreal
7. Ø Mt. Kilimanjaro . . . Ø Kenya
8. Ø New Zealand
9. **The** Himalayas . . . Ø Pakistan . . . Ø India . . . Ø Tibet . . . Ø Nepal
10. Ø President Davis
11. Ø Ho Chi Minh City . . . Ø Vietnam . . . Ø Saigon
12. **The** Andes Mountains

◇ PRACTICE 24, p. 237.
1. **the** Dead Sea
2. **the** Amazon River
3. Shanghai
4. **the** Sahara Desert
5. **the** Thames River
6. Europe
7. **the** Alps
8. Lake Tanganyika
9. North America
10. **the** Indian Ocean
11. **the** Netherlands
12. North America
13. Tibet
14. **The** Urals
15. Lagos
16. **the** United Arab Emirates

◇ PRACTICE 25, p. 238.
1. I'm taking **B**iology 101 this semester.
2. I'm taking history, biology, **E**nglish, and calculus this semester.
3. Some lab classes meet on **S**aturday.
4. Marta lives on a busy street. Marta lives at 2358 **O**live **S**treet.
5. We went to **C**anada last summer. **W**e went to **M**ontreal in **J**uly.
6. My roommate likes **V**ietnamese food, and **I** like **T**hai food.

7. The religion of **S**audi **A**rabia is **I**slam.
8. Shelia works for the **X**erox **C**orporation. **I**t is a very large corporation.
9. Pedro is from **L**atin **A**merica.
10. My uncle lives in **S**t. **L**ouis. I'm going to visit **U**ncle **B**ill next spring.
11. We went to a park. **W**e went to **W**aterfall **P**ark.
12. Are you going to the **U**niversity of **O**regon or **O**regon **S**tate **U**niversity?
13. Alice goes to a university in **O**regon.
14. The next assignment in literature class is to read *The Adventures of **T**om **S**awyer.*
15. ... In **F**rance, they call it "**B**astille **D**ay."

◇ PRACTICE 26, p. 238.
1. Do you know **R**obert **J**ones?
2. *(no change)*
3. I like **U**ncle **J**oe and **A**unt **S**ara.
4. *(no change)*
5. **S**usan **W**. **M**iller is a professor.
6. I am in **P**rof. **M**iller's class.
7. The weather is cold in **J**anuary.
8. *(no change)*
9. I have three classes on **M**onday.
10. I would like to visit **L**os **A**ngeles.
11. It's the largest city in **C**alifornia.
12. *(no change)*
13. There are fifty states in the **U**nited **S**tates of **A**merica.
14. *(no change)*
15. Today we can fly across the **A**tlantic **O**cean in hours.
16. *(no change)*
17. Mark lives on **M**arket **S**treet near **W**ashington **H**igh **S**chool.
18. *(no change)*
19. Our family stayed at the **H**ilton **H**otel in **B**angkok.
20. Yoko is **J**apanese, but she can also speak **G**erman.

◇ PRACTICE 27, p. 239.
1. The mail carrier brought only one **letter** today.
2. Mr. Dale gave his class **a** long history assignment for the weekend.
3. Tariq speaks several **languages**, including Arabic and Spanish.
4. Dr. **Kim** gives all her patients a toothbrush (OR **toothbrushes**) and toothpaste at their dental appointments.
5. I usually have **a** glass **of** water with my lunch.
6. A helpful policeman gave us ~~an~~ information about the city.
7. This cookie recipe calls for two **cups** of **nuts**.
8. **Many vegetables** are believed to have cancer-fighting ingredients.
9. Only applicants with the necessary experiences̸ should apply for the computer position.
10. When Vicki likes a movie, she sees it several time**s**.
11. A popular children's story is *Snow White **and the** Seven Dwarfs*.
12. Is it possible to stop all violences̸ in the world?

Chapter 12: RELATIVE CLAUSES

◇ PRACTICE 1, p. 240.
1. who helped me move the refrigerator
   1: I thanked
   2: He helped

2. who was wearing a gray suit
   1: A woman asked
   2: She was wearing
3. who aided the rebels
   1: The woman put
   2: She aided
4. who was wearing a blue coat
   1: I saw
   2: He was wearing
5. who broke the vase
   1: The girl apologized
   2: She broke

◇ PRACTICE 2, p. 241.
1. The woman who answered the phone was polite.
2. The man who sang at the concert has a good voice.
3. We enjoyed the actors who played the leading roles.
4. The girl who fell down the stairs is hurt.
5. I read about the soccer player who was injured in the game yesterday.

◇ PRACTICE 3, p. 241.
1. The people who live next to me are nice.
   They live next to me.
2. The people whom Kate visited yesterday were French.
   Kate visited them yesterday.
3. The people whom I saw at the park were having a picnic.
   I saw them.
4. The students who go to this school are friendly.
   They go to this school.
5. The woman whom you met last week lives in Mexico.
   You met her last week.

◇ PRACTICE 4, p. 242.
1. The woman whom Jack met was polite.
2. I like the woman who manages my uncle's store.
3. The singer whom we heard at the concert was wonderful.
4. The people who came to dinner brought a small gift.
5. What is the name of the woman whom Tom invited to the dance?

◇ PRACTICE 5, p. 242.

1. who	6. who(m)	11. who(m)
2. who(m)	7. who	12. who(m)
3. who	8. who	13. who
4. who(m)	9. who	14. who(m)
5. who	10. who	15. who

◇ PRACTICE 6, p. 243.

1. O ~~that~~	6. S
2. S	7. S
3. S	8. O ~~that~~
4. O ~~who~~	9. S
5. S	10. O ~~that~~

◇ **PRACTICE 7, p. 243.**

1. That man ~~that~~ I saw was wearing a black hat.
2. *(no change)*
3. The fruit ~~that~~ I bought today . . . .
4. . . . a person ~~that~~ I will never forget.
5. *(no change)*
6. The girl that sits in front of Richard has long black hair ~~that~~ she wears . . . .
7. *(no change)*
8. *(no change)*

◇ **PRACTICE 8, p. 244.**

1. who/that
2. who(m)/that/∅
3. who(m)/that/∅
4. who/that
5. who/that
6. who(m)/that/∅

◇ **PRACTICE 9, p. 245.**

1. C   5. B
2. A   6. A
3. C   7. C
4. C   8. C

◇ **PRACTICE 10, p. 245.**

1. who/that designs buildings.
2. who/that doesn't eat meat.
3. which/that forms when water boils.
4. which/that has a hard shell and can live in water or on land.
5. who/that leaves society and lives completely alone.
6. which/that grows in hot climates and produces large bunches of yellow fruit.
7. which/that can be shaped and hardened to form many useful things.
8. which/that cannot be understood or explained.

◇ **PRACTICE 11, p. 246.**

1. O ~~which~~   6. S
2. S   7. O ~~which~~
3. O ~~that~~   8. S
4. O ~~which~~   9. S
5. S   10. O ~~that~~

◇ **PRACTICE 12, p. 246.**

1. which/that/∅   4. which/that
2. which/that   5. which/that/∅
3. which/that/∅   6. which/that

◇ **PRACTICE 13, p. 247.**

Incorrect (crossed out) pronouns:
1. them   4. him
2. it   5. her
3. them   6. him

◇ **PRACTICE 14, p. 247.**

1. A, C, D   8. C, D
2. A, D   9. A, C, D
3. C, D, E   10. C, D, E
4. A, C, D   11. A, C, D
5. A, D   12. A, C, D
6. C, D   13. C, D
7. C, D, E

◇ **PRACTICE 15, p. 248.**

1. students . . . are   6. student . . . is
2. people . . . are   7. people . . . live
3. compound . . . consists   8. person . . . makes
4. students . . . speak   9. artists . . . make
5. people . . . know

◇ **PRACTICE 16, p. 249.**

1. that . . . for   3. that . . . in
   which . . . for   which . . . in
   ∅ . . . for   ∅ . . . in
   for which . . . ∅   in which . . . ∅
2. that . . . to   4. that . . . with
   which . . . to   who(m) . . . with
   ∅ . . . to   ∅ . . . with
   to which . . . ∅   with whom . . . ∅

◇ **PRACTICE 17, p. 250.**

1. that . . . to   4. who(m) . . . for
   who(m) . . . to   that . . . for
   ∅ . . . to   ∅ . . . for
   to whom . . . ∅   for whom . . . ∅
2. that . . . with   5. that . . . for
   which . . . with   which . . . for
   ∅ . . . with   ∅ . . . for
   with which . . . ∅   for which . . . ∅
3. who(m) . . . about   6. that . . . in
   that . . . about   which . . . in
   ∅ . . . about   ∅ . . . in
   about whom . . . ∅   in which . . . ∅

◇ **PRACTICE 18, p. 250.**

Adjective clauses:
1. we listened **to** at Sara's apartment
2. I accidentally broke ∅
3. we were waiting **for**
4. I always enjoy talking **to** about politics
5. I had just written ∅
6. I've been interested **in** for a long time
7. I talked **to** at the reception
8. I want to visit ∅ next year
9. I was looking **at**
10. I wanted ∅
11. we were listening **to** at Jim's yesterday
12. I'm not familiar **with**
13. I was carrying ∅
14. I can always rely **on** for support and help
15. our fourteen-year-old is responsible **for**
16. I was reading ∅
17. I bought ∅
18. ∅ which I enjoy studying the most
19. I waved **at**
20. **for** whom Alex was waiting

◇ **PRACTICE 19, p. 251.**

1. <u>whose daughter is a pilot</u>
   1: I know a man.
   2: His daughter is a pilot.
2. <u>whose husband is out of work</u>
   1: The woman found a job.
   2: Her husband is out of work.
3. <u>whose wallet I found</u>
   1: The man gave me a reward.
   2: I found his wallet.

◇ **PRACTICE 20, p. 251.**

1. The firefighters are very brave. <u>Their</u> department has won many awards.
   → The firefighters whose department has won many awards are very brave.

2. I talked to the boy. <u>His</u> kite was caught in a tree.
   → I talked to the boy whose kite was caught in a tree.

3. The family is staying in a motel. <u>Their</u> house burned down.
   → The family whose house burned down is staying in a motel.

4. I watched a little girl. <u>Her</u> dog was chasing a ball in the park.
   → I watched a little girl whose dog was chasing a ball in the park.

5. The reporter won an award. <u>Her</u> articles explained global warming.
   → The reporter whose articles explained global warming won an award.

6. I know a man. <u>His</u> daughter entered college at the age of fourteen.
   → I know a man whose daughter entered college at the age of fourteen.

7. We observed a language teacher. <u>Her</u> teaching methods included role-playing.
   → We observed a language teacher whose teaching methods included role-playing.

8. The teachers are very popular. <u>Their</u> methods include role-playing.
   → The teachers whose methods include role-playing are very popular.

◇ **PRACTICE 21, p. 252.**

True (checked) answers:

1. a, c   5. a
2. c   6. a, c
3. b, c   7. b
4. c

◇ **PRACTICE 22, p. 253.**

1. which/that is used to carry boats with goods and/or passengers
2. whose children were doing poorly in her class
3. Ted bought for his wife on their anniversary
4. whose views I share
5. which/that had backbones
6. which/that disrupted the global climate and caused mass extinctions of animal life

◇ **PRACTICE 23, p. 253.**

1. who/that
2. who/that . . . whom
3. who/that . . . which/that . . . which/that
4. who/that
5. which/that/Ø
6. whose
7. which/that
8. who(m)/that/Ø
9. whose
10. which/that
11. who/that
12. who(m)/that/Ø

◇ **PRACTICE 24, p. 254.**

1. A movie that **looks** interesting opens tomorrow.
2. My family lived in a house which ~~it~~ was built in 1900.
3. The little boy **who** was lost asked for directions.
4. I don't know people **whose** ~~their~~ lives are carefree.
5. It is important to help people who **have** no money.
6. At the airport, I was waiting for friends **who(m)/that/Ø** I hadn't seen ~~them~~ for a long time.
7. The woman **who/that lives** next door likes to . . . .
8. My teacher has two cats **whose** ~~their~~ names are Ping and Pong.
9. A beautiful garden ~~that~~ separates my house from the street.
10. I asked the children who **were** sitting on the bench to help us.
11. The school that my children attend ~~it~~ is very good academically.
12. I enjoyed the songs which we sang ~~them~~.
13. One of the places that I like to visit **is** Central Park.
14. The movie we saw ~~it~~ last evening was very exciting.
15. I sent the parents **whose son** I hiked with a picture of us on Mt. Fuji.
16. Do you know the man who **works** in that office?
17. A mother **whose** daughter is in my class often brings cookies for the children.
18. The CD player **which/that/Ø** I bought can hold several CDs at once.
19. The bed which I sleep **in** is very comfortable. OR The bed **in** which I sleep is very comfortable.
20. . . . problems which I have had ~~them~~ since I came here.

Chapter 13: GERUNDS AND INFINITIVES

◇ **PRACTICE 1, p. 256.**

1. moving   7. reviewing
2. living   8. running
3. taking   9. driving
4. buying   10. retiring
5. giving   11. getting married
6. doing   12. working

◇ **PRACTICE 2, p. 256.**

1. went dancing   6. go sightseeing
2. is going to go hiking 7. go camping
3. went shopping   8. go sailing
4. go swimming   9. go skiing
5. goes fishing   10. went skydiving

◇ **PRACTICE 3, p. 257.**

1. INF   to wait   5. INF   to call
2. GER   walking   6. GER   quitting
3. INF   to help   7. INF   to work
4. GER   writing   8. INF   to grow

◇ **PRACTICE 4, p. 258.**

PART I.

1. to work   7. to work
2. working   8. to work
3. to work   9. working
4. working   10. to work
5. to work   11. working
6. to work/working   12. working

13. to leave
14. to leave
15. leaving
16. leaving
17. leaving
18. leaving
19. to leave
20. to leave
21. leaving
22. to leave

PART III.

23. to know
24. to know
25. to know
26. knowing
27. to know
28. to know
29. to know/knowing
30. to know
31. to know
32. to know/knowing

◇ **PRACTICE 5, p. 258.**

1. B
2. A
3. B
4. B
5. A
6. B
7. B
8. B
9. A
10. A
11. A
12. B
13. B
14. B
15. A
16. B
17. B
18. B
19. A
20. B
21. B
22. B
23. B
24. A

◇ **PRACTICE 6, p. 261.**

1. B
2. A, B
3. A, B
4. B
5. A, B
6. A, B
7. A, B
8. B
9. A
10. A, B
11. A, B
12. A, B
13. B
14. A
15. B

◇ **PRACTICE 7, p. 261.**

1. to go
2. to buy
3. looking
4. to go shopping
5. passing
6. to go fishing
7. to cry/crying
8. to go/going
9. to go
10. to have
11. to meet
12. changing
13. camping
14. to arrive
15. writing
16. jogging
17. to call
18. to pass
19. hoping
20. to concentrate . . . to make
21. to go
22. to do/doing
23. to help
24. to learn
25. driving . . . to fly
26. to postpone
27. to be
28. teaching
29. to read/reading
30. to go dancing
31. building
32. to play/playing . . . to be . . . to be
33. to take

◇ **PRACTICE 8, p. 262.**

PART I.

1. of <u>flying</u>
2. for <u>hurting</u>
3. in <u>helping</u>
4. at <u>listening</u>
5. of <u>working</u>
6. about <u>walking</u>
7. of/about <u>owning</u>

PART II.

8. for <u>closing</u>
9. for <u>lending</u>
10. on <u>becoming</u>
11. for <u>taking</u>
12. on <u>eating</u>
13. to <u>finishing</u>
14. from <u>making</u>
15. about . . . <u>having</u>

◇ **PRACTICE 9, p. 263.**

1. for . . . for interrupting
2. in . . . in learning
3. for . . . for helping
4. on . . . on walking
5. for . . . for losing
6. like . . . like going
7. at . . . at drawing
8. in . . . in saving
9. about . . . about falling . . . making
10. about . . . about going
11. to . . . to going
12. of . . . of staying

◇ **PRACTICE 10, p. 264.**

PART I.

1. about asking
2. to ask
3. on asking
4. about asking
5. about asking
6. to ask
7. for asking
8. to ask
9. to ask/asking
10. to ask/asking

PART II.

11. to fix
12. to fix/fixing
13. to fix
14. to fix
15. to fix
16. about fixing
17. to fix/fixing
18. to fix
19. to fix
20. fixing

◇ **PRACTICE 11, p. 265.**

1. writing
2. to install
3. to cash
4. staying
5. to go
6. adopting
7. to take
8. in using
9. to be
10. to lower

◇ **PRACTICE 12, p. 265.**

1. going
2. of driving
3. to park/on parking
4. to watch/watching
5. to cook/cooking
6. baking
7. of going
8. of/about becoming
9. having
10. running
11. for watering
12. for speaking
13. on washing
14. from hitting
15. to be
16. repairing
17. to get
18. to have/on having
19. to taking
20. about seeing

◇ **PRACTICE 13, p. 267.**

1. by holding
2. by reading
3. by reading
4. by watching
5. by running
6. by treating

◇ **PRACTICE 14, p. 268.**

1. I arrived on time by taking a taxi instead of a bus.
2. I put out the fire by pouring water on it.
3. Giraffes can reach the leaves at the tops of trees by stretching their long necks.
4. I fixed the chair by tightening the loose screws.
5. Sylvia was able to buy an expensive stereo system by saving her money for two years.
6. A hippopotamus can cross a river by walking on the bottom of the riverbed.
7. I figured out how to cook the noodles by reading the directions on the package.

8. Pam finished her project on time by working all through the night.
9. You can figure out how old a tree is by counting its rings.

◇ PRACTICE 15, p. 268.

1. with	7. by	13. by
2. by	8. by	14. with
3. with	9. with	15. with
4. by	10. with	16. with
5. by	11. by	
6. with	12. with	

◇ PRACTICE 16, p. 269.

1. a. It is . . . to learn
   b. Learning . . . is
2. a. Eating . . . is
   b. It is . . . to eat
3. a. Driving . . . is
   b. It is . . . to drive
4. a. It is . . . to swim
   b. Swimming . . . is
5. a. Is it . . . to live
   b. Is living
6. a. Is it . . . to complete
   b. Is completing

◇ PRACTICE 17, p. 270.

1. It is difficult for shy people to meet
2. It is interesting for babies to look
3. it is customary for young children to sleep
4. It is necessary for airline pilots to have
5. It is hard for many teenagers to wake up
6. It is important for elderly people to keep
7. It is boring for people to listen
8. It is necessary for students to have
9. It is impossible for scientists to know
10. It is important for parents to teach
11. It is easy for people to be
12. It is dangerous for small children to cross

◇ PRACTICE 18, p. 271.

PART I.	PART II.
1. for	8. to
2. to	9. to
3. to	10. for
4. for	11. for
5. to	12. to
6. to	13. to
7. for	14. for
	15. to

◇ PRACTICE 19, p. 271.

1. to	5. for	9. to
2. for	6. to	10. for
3. for	7. to	11. for
4. to	8. for	

◇ PRACTICE 20, p. 271.

1. turned on the TV (in order) to watch the news.
2. goes to the laundromat (in order) to wash his clothes.
3. runs (in order) to get to class on time.
4. open the bedroom windows (in order) to let in some fresh air.
5. writes a letter to his parents (in order) to ask them for some money.
6. have the radio on (in order) to listen to a baseball game.
7. go to the library (in order) to study in peace and quiet.

◇ PRACTICE 21, p. 272.

1. a. enough time to go
   b. too busy to go
2. a. tall enough
   b. too short
3. a. enough money
   b. too poor
4. a. too hot
   b. cool enough
5. a. too sick to eat anything
   b. well enough to eat anything
6. a. isn't old enough to stay home by herself
   b. too young to stay home by herself

◇ PRACTICE 22, p. 273.

1. Ø . . . enough		7. too . . . Ø
2. too . . . Ø		8. Ø . . . enough
3. enough . . . Ø		9. enough . . . Ø
4. too . . . Ø		10. too . . . Ø
5. Ø . . . enough		11. enough . . . Ø
6. Ø . . . enough		12. Ø . . . enough

◇ PRACTICE 23, p. 273.

1. being . . . to be
2. to stay
3. to help
4. to thank
5. going . . . to stay
6. to learn
7. to cause . . . to destroy
8. to recognize . . . to build . . . to knock
9. Predicting . . . to predict . . . reading . . . to act . . . running . . . counting . . . to be able to predict

◇ PRACTICE 24, p. 274.

1. studying
2. jotting
3. to be
4. B: flying
   A: crashing
5. A: arguing . . . to disagree . . . be
   B: raising . . . to yell
   A: to get
6. A: to sneak . . . paying
   B: doing
   A: trying to sneak . . . to have . . . to like . . . liking . . . to do
7. to build
8. to do . . . to do . . . to do . . . to do
9. A: doing
   B: going shopping
   A: going . . . pretending to be . . . buying
   B: to do
   A: to get . . . to buy . . . to have
   B: Pretending to be . . . buying

10. B: putting . . . forgetting to send
    A: to get . . . not remembering
11. interrupting
12. to taste . . . to make

◇ PRACTICE 25, p. 276.

1. I decided not **to buy** a new car.
2. The Johnsons are considering **selling** their antique store.
3. Sam finally finished **building** his vacation home in the mountains.
4. My wife and I go ~~to~~ dancing at the community center every Saturday night.
5. Suddenly, it began **to rain/raining** and the wind started to blow.
6. The baby is afraid **to be/of being** away from her mother for any length of time.
7. I am excited **about starting** college this September.
8. You can send your application **by fax**.
9. My country is **very** beautiful. OR My country is ~~too~~ beautiful.
10. **It is** exciting **to drive** a sports car.
11. My grandparents enjoy ~~to~~ traveling across the country in a motor home.
12. Elena made this sweater **by hand**.
13. Swimming ~~it~~ is one of the sports we can participate in at school.
14. That was very good, but I'm too full **to eat** any more.
15. My mother-in-law went to a tourist shop **to buy** a disposable camera.
16. Instead **of getting** her degree in four years, Michelle decided **to travel** abroad first.
17. **Swimming** with a group of people is more enjoyable than **swimming** alone.
18. **It is** interesting **to meet/meeting** new people.
19. **It is** hard **for** me to stay up past 9:00.
20. The professor thanked his students **for doing** well on the test.

Chapter 14: NOUN CLAUSES

◇ PRACTICE 1, p. 278.

1. I don't know <u>where Jack bought his boots</u>. NOUN CLAUSE
2. Where did Jack buy his boots**?** QUESTION
3. I don't understand <u>why Ann left</u>. NOUN CLAUSE
4. Why did Ann leave**?** QUESTION
5. I don't know <u>where your book is</u>. NOUN CLAUSE
6. Where is your book**?** QUESTION
7. When did Bob come**?** QUESTION
8. I don't know <u>when Bob came</u>. NOUN CLAUSE
9. What does "calm" mean**?** QUESTION
10. Tarik knows <u>what "calm" means</u>. NOUN CLAUSE
11. I don't know <u>how long the earth has existed</u>. NOUN CLAUSE
12. How long has the earth existed**?** QUESTION

◇ PRACTICE 2, p. 278.

Noun clauses:

1. where [Patty] [went] last night
2. where [Joe's parents] [live]
3. where [Joe] [lives]
4. what time [the movie] [begins]
5. where [Brazil] [is]
6. what [Estefan] [said]
7. when [the packages] [will arrive]
8. how far [it] [is] to the post office
9. [who] [knocked] on the door
10. [what] [happened] at the party last night

◇ PRACTICE 3, p. 279.

question	*noun clause*
1. Why did Tim leave?	why Tim left
2. Where did he go?	where he went
3. Where does he live?	where he lives
4. Where is he now?	where he is now
5. What time will he return?	what time he will return
6. How far is it to his house?	how far it is to his house
7. Who lives next door to him?	who lives next door to him
8. What happened to him?	what happened to him

◇ PRACTICE 4, p. 279.

question	*noun clause*
1. did Marcos leave?	when Marcos left?
2. did he say?	what he said.
3. is the post office?	where the post office is?
4. is it?	what time it is?
5. did David arrive?	when David arrived.
6. is Anna from?	what country Anna is from.
7. was Kathy	why Kathy was
8. lives	who lives
9. did Eric invite	who(m) Eric invited
10. borrowed	who borrowed
11. are the restrooms located?	where the restrooms are located?

◇ PRACTICE 5, p. 281.

1. who(m) Helen talked to?
2. who lives in that apartment?
3. what he said.
4. what kind of car Pat has.
5. how old their children are.
6. why you said that.
7. where I can catch the bus?
8. who(m) Sara talked to.
9. how long Ted has been living here?
10. what this word means?

◇ PRACTICE 6, p. 281.

1. A: were you
   A: you were
2. A: did Tom go
   B: you said
   A: Tom went
3. A: is a bumblebee . . .
   a bumblebee is
4. A: did Oscar borrow
   B: Oscar borrowed
5. A: Mr. Gow's office is . . .
   is Mr. Gow's office
6. A: did she come
   B: she came
   A: was she
   B: she was

18 ANSWER KEY Chapter 14

Noun clauses:

$$\text{S} \qquad \text{V}$$

1. who [that man] [is]
2. [who] [called]
3. who [those people] [are]
4. who [that person] [is]
5. [who] [lives] next door to me
6. who [my teacher] [will be] next semester
7. [who] [will teach] us next semester
8. what [a lizard] [is]
9. [what] [happened] in class yesterday
10. whose hat [this] [is]
11. [whose hat] [is] on the table

◇ **PRACTICE 8, p. 282.**

1. / . . . is
2. is . . . /
3. / . . . is
4. is . . . /
5. / . . . is
6. / . . . is
7. is . . . /
8. / . . . is
9. / . . . is
10. is . . . /

◇ **PRACTICE 9, p. 283.**

1. who she is.
2. who they are.
3. whose book that is.
4. whose glasses those are?
5. what a wrench is?
6. who that woman is.
7. what a clause is?
8. what is in that drawer.
9. who is in that room.
10. what is on TV tonight.
11. what a carrot is?
12. who I am.

◇ **PRACTICE 10, p. 283.**

1. whose car that is
2. whose car is in front of Sam's house
3. who the best students are
4. what time dinner is
5. who's next in line
6. whose purse this is
7. what the main ideas of the story are
8. whose shoes those are under the chair
9. what causes tornadoes

◇ **PRACTICE 11, p. 284.**

1. if (whether) Tom is coming
2. if (whether) Jin has finished medical school yet
3. if (whether) Daniel has any time off soon
4. if (whether) the flight is on time
5. if (whether) there is enough gas in the car
6. if (whether) Yuki is married
7. if (whether) the Petersons are going to move
8. if (whether) Khaled changed jobs

◇ **PRACTICE 12, p. 285.**

1. if I'm going to need
2. if chicken is
3. if the new teaching position includes
4. if there will be a movie
5. if Greg has to come
6. if penguins ever get
7. if you can drive
8. if Nasser has already left

◇ **PRACTICE 13, p. 285.**

1. if (whether) Karen is
2. where Karen went?
3. how Pat is feeling
4. if (whether) Pat is feeling
5. if (whether) the bus stops
6. where the bus stops.
7. why Elena is absent
8. if (whether) Elena is going to be absent
9. if (whether) I should buy
10. which book I should buy.
11. if (whether) we are going to have
12. if (whether) there is

◇ **PRACTICE 14, p. 286.**

1. rains
2. gets
3. like
4. runs
5. run
6. takes
7. enjoy
8. seems

◇ **PRACTICE 15, p. 287.**

1. I'm sorry that
2. I predict that
3. I'm surprised that
4. Are you certain that
5. Did you notice that
6. John is pleased that
7. Anna was convinced that
8. It's a fact that
9. A: Guido is delighted that
   B: I'm surprised that
10. A: How do you know that
    I'm still worried that
11. A: Mrs. Lane hopes that
    B: I don't think that
    A: I wish that
12. A: Do you think that
    B: Everyone knows that
    A: I'm not sure that that's true.

◇ **PRACTICE 16, p. 288.**

1. (that) I will have a peanut butter sandwich.
2. (that) I should study tonight
3. (that) flying in an airplane is safer than riding in a car.
4. (that) I'll get married someday.
5. (that) a huge monster was chasing me.
6. (that) John "Cat Man" Smith stole Mrs. Adams' jewelry.
7. (that) people are pretty much the same everywhere.
8. (that) high school students in the United States don't study as hard as the students in my country do.
9. (that) he always twirls his mustache when he's nervous?
10. (that) all people are equal.

11. (that) more than half of the people in the world go hungry every day?
12. (that) plastic trash kills thousands of marine animals every year?

◇ PRACTICE 17, p. 289.
1. I feel (don't feel) that smoking in public places should be prohibited.
2. I regret (don't regret) that I'm living in this country.
3. I would like to know (wouldn't like to know) when I will die.
4. I doubt (don't doubt) that there will be peace in the world soon.
5. I remember (can't remember) what I was like as a child.
6. I wonder (don't wonder) why the world exists.
7. I am afraid (am not afraid) that someone may make unwise decisions about my future.
8. I know (don't know) what I want to do with my life.

◇ PRACTICE 18, p. 290.
1. The Jensens are pleased that their granddaughter graduated from the university. They are pleased that she was offered a good job.
2. Po is lucky that the smoke alarm in his apartment rang. He is lucky that he woke up and discovered that his apartment building was on fire.
3. Ming Soo was surprised that she didn't fail the math exam. She was surprised that she got one of the highest grades in the class.
4. Karen is sorry that she lent her cousin Mark some money. She is sorry that she can't afford to buy her children new shoes.

◇ PRACTICE 19, p. 290.
1. that Alice has a car
2. that the library is open
3. that Ann speaks Spanish
4. that Alex passed his French course
5. that Mr. Kozari is going to be at the meeting
6. that the photos are ready to be picked up at the photo shop

◇ PRACTICE 20, p. 291.
1. Alex said, "Do you smell smoke?"
2. "Something is burning," he said.
3. He said, "Do you smell smoke? Something is burning."
4. "Do you smell smoke?" he said. "Something is burning."
5. Rachel said, "The game starts at seven."
6. "The game starts at seven. We should leave here at six," she said.
7. She said, "The game starts at seven. We should leave here at six. Can you be ready to leave then?"

◇ PRACTICE 21, p. 291.
1. Mrs. Hill said, "My children used to take the bus to school."
2. She said, "We moved closer to the school."
3. "Now my children can walk to school," Mrs. Hill said.
4. "Do you live near the school?" she asked.

5. "Yes, we live two blocks away," I replied.
6. "How long have you lived here?" Mrs. Hill wanted to know.
7. I said, "We've lived here for five years. How long have you lived here?"
8. "We've lived here for two years," Mrs. Hill said. "How do you like living here?"
9. "It's a nice community," I said. "It's a good place to raise children."

◇ PRACTICE 22, p. 292.
"Why weren't you in class yesterday?" Mr. Garcia asked me.
"I had to stay home and take care of my pet bird," I said. "He wasn't feeling well."
"What? Did you miss class because of your pet bird?" Mr. Garcia demanded to know.
I replied, "Yes, sir. That's correct. I couldn't leave him alone. He looked so miserable."
"Now I've heard every excuse in the world," Mr. Garcia said. Then he threw his arms in the air and walked away.

◇ PRACTICE 23, p. 293.
One day my friend Laura and I were sitting in her apartment. We were having a cup of tea together and talking about the terrible earthquake that had just occurred in Iran. Laura asked me, "Have you ever been in an earthquake?"
"Yes, I have," I replied.
"Was it a big earthquake?" she asked.
"I've been in several earthquakes, and they've all been small ones," I answered. "Have you ever been in an earthquake?"
"There was an earthquake in my village five years ago," Laura said. "I was in my house. Suddenly the ground started shaking. I grabbed my little brother and ran outside. Everything was moving. I was scared to death. And then suddenly it was over."
"I'm glad you and your brother weren't hurt," I said.
"Yes, we were very lucky. Has everyone in the world felt an earthquake sometime in their lives?" Laura wondered. "Do earthquakes occur everywhere on the earth?"
"Those are interesting questions," I said, "but I don't know the answers."

◇ PRACTICE 24, p. 293.
1. he . . . his
2. his . . . them
3. she . . . her
4. him . . . them
5. they . . . me . . . they
6. she . . . her
7. they . . . my
8. he . . . us . . . he . . . his

◇ PRACTICE 25, p. 294.

	formal	informal
1.	would meet	will meet
2.	was going to be	is going to be
3.	had	has
4.	needed	needs
5.	had flown	has flown
6.	were planning	are planning
7.	didn't want	doesn't want
8.	could babysit	can babysit

◇ PRACTICE 26, p. 295.

1. (that) you didn't have
2. (that) you hadn't found
3. (that) the Smiths hadn't canceled
4. (that) it wouldn't rain
5. (that) the Whites hadn't gotten
6. (that) Mei didn't exercise
7. (that) your computer wasn't working
8. (that) Ali was coming

◇ PRACTICE 27, p. 296.

1. how old I was
2. if/whether he was going to be
3. if/whether she had
4. if/whether he had changed his
5. how long I had been
6. if/whether she could speak
7. if/whether he would be in his office
8. why she was laughing
9. if/whether I had ever considered

◇ PRACTICE 28, p. 296.

1. "Have you ever gone skydiving?"
2. "Will you be at the meeting?"
3. "Are you going to quit your job?"
4. "Where is your car?"
5. "What did you do after class yesterday?"
6. "Do you know Italian?"
7. "Can you guess what I have in my pocket?"
8. "Why aren't you working at your desk?"

◇ PRACTICE 29, p. 297.

1. where I was from.
2. how I liked it here.
3. how long I would stay.
4. why I had come here.
5. if/whether I had met many people.
6. what I was going to study.
7. if/whether the local people were friendly to me.
8. if/whether I liked the weather here.
9. how I had chosen this school.

◇ PRACTICE 30, p. 298.

1. he was going to call me
2. (that) he had to talk . . . her
3. (that) she could meet me
4. (that) she had written him
5. (that) I needed his
6. she would see him
7. (that) he was going to meet . . . me
8. what he was doing
9. (that) he was sure he had met me

◇ PRACTICE 31, p. 299.

1. told
2. said
3. asked
4. told
5. said
6. told . . . said
7. asked . . . asked . . . said
8. told . . . told
9. told
10. asked . . . said . . . asked . . . told

◇ PRACTICE 32, p. 299.

1. asked me where I lived.
2. asked me if/whether I lived
3. told him / replied / said that I had
4. told me / said that he was looking
5. told me / said that he didn't like living
6. asked him if / whether he wanted to move in with me.
7. asked me where my apartment was.
8. replied / told him / said that I lived
9. told me / said that he couldn't move
10. told me / said that he would cancel his
11. asked me if/whether that was okay.
12. told him / replied / said that I was looking forward to having him

◇ PRACTICE 33, p. 300.

Correct (checked) answers:
1. The teacher asked if I was finished.
   The teacher asked, "Are you finished?"
2. Aki said he was finished.
   Aki said that he was finished.
   Aki replied that he was finished.
   Aki answered that he was finished.
3. Ann told Tom she needed more time.
   Ann said she needed more time.
4. Donna answered that she was ready.
   Donna answered, "I am ready."
5. Mr. Wong wanted to know if Ted was coming.
   Mr. Wong wondered if Ted was coming.
   Mr. Wong wondered, "Is Ted coming?"

◇ PRACTICE 34, p. 300.

1. (that) he had forgotten
2. where his bicycle was . . . told me/said (that) he had sold
3. (that) we would miss
4. if/whether she could swim
5. if/whether she wanted . . . (that) she couldn't . . . had to study
6. (that) she had broken
7. was . . . (that) he wasn't . . . (that) he had gone
8. if/whether I would be . . . (that) I would be
9. if/whether he had . . . been . . . (that) he had been
10. where his cane was . . . (that) I didn't know . . . if/whether he needed . . . (that) he wanted to walk . . . (that) I would find it

◇ PRACTICE 35, p. 302.

The husband asked where the children were. His wife replied/said (that) they had already left for school.

The father said that they had forgotten to take their books with them. The mother wondered how they could be so irresponsible. She asked the father what they were going to do.

The father told her not to worry. He said (that) he would take the books with him and drop them off at the school on his way to work. The mother told him (that) that was okay and said goodbye. She told him to have a good day.

The children asked their mother where their schoolbooks were. They said (that) they had left them on the kitchen table. They said (that) they couldn't go to school without their books.

◇ PRACTICE 36, p. 303.

1. . . . May I ask ~~if~~ how old **you are**?
2. I wonder, **"Did** Rashed pick up something for dinner?"
3. I'm unsure what **Lawrence does** for a living.
4. Fernando said, **"The** best time for me to meet would be Thursday morning."
5. Eriko **asked** me **if** I **was** coming to the graduation party. I **told** her that I wasn't.
   OR I said ~~her~~ I wasn't.
6. I hope ~~so~~ that I will do well on my final exams.
7. Antonio asked his mother what she **wanted** for her birthday**.**
8. I'm not sure if the price **includes** sales tax.
9. My mother **asked** me, **"How** many hours **did you spend** on your homework?"
10. Pedro asked **if/whether** that **was** okay.
    Pedro asked**, "Is** that okay?"
11. Mika told **me** she **was** going to stay home today.
12. I'd like to know how ~~do~~ you do that.
13. My parents knew what Sam and I **did**. OR . . . **know** what Sam and I do.
14. Beth said she had **been** working hard all week, but now **she** had some time off.
15. **It is** a fact that life always changes.

Appendix 1: PHRASAL VERBS

◇ PRACTICE 1, p. 305.

1. on
2. up
3. down . . . up
4. off
5. B: on
   A: off
6. away/out
7. A: down
   B: up
8. out . . . out
9. off . . . on
10. A: up
    B: off

◇ PRACTICE 2, p. 306.

Correct (circled) completions:
1. her socks
2. the TV, the stove
3. his new shoes
4. a story, a fairy tale, an excuse
5. some rotten food, an old shirt
6. a doctor's appointment, a meeting, a trip
7. a puzzle, a math problem, a riddle
8. a report, some late homework
9. a message, a phone number
10. a box, a sack of mail
11. my coat, my wedding ring
12. the light, the computer, the car engine

◇ PRACTICE 3, p. 307.

1. out of
2. on
3. off
4. over
5. into
6. into
7. from
8. in
9. on

◇ PRACTICE 4, p. 308.

1. B
2. C
3. A
4. G
5. F
6. D
7. E

◇ PRACTICE 5, p. 308.

1. back
2. down/off
3. out
4. away
5. on
6. up . . . off
7. back
8. up
9. A: out
   B: up
   A: off
   B: back
10. back

◇ PRACTICE 6, p. 309.

1. out . . . out
2. on . . . X
3. into . . . X
4. into . . . X
5. up . . . up
6. away . . . away
7. down . . . X
8. X . . . up
9. away . . . X
10. up . . . up
11. off . . . X
12. from . . . X

◇ PRACTICE 7, p. 310.

1. over
2. out
3. in
4. out
5. out
6. down
7. around
8. out
9. up
10. out
11. out
12. up
13. over

◇ PRACTICE 8, p. 311.

1. a. off
   b. on
   c. down
   d. back
   e. out
   f. away
2. a. in
   b. out
3. a. over
   b. off
   c. on
   d. into
   e. out of
4. a. out
   b. up
   c. down
5. a. into
   b. up
   c. over
6. a. up
   b. off
   c. back
7. a. down
   b. back
   c. up
   d. over
8. a. in
   b. out
   c. up

◇ PRACTICE 9, p. 312.

1. on
2. up
3. out
4. out
5. out
6. A: out
   B: over
7. A: off
   B: over
8. back
9. up
10. on
11. A: up
    B: up

◇ PRACTICE 10, p. 313.

1. lay . . . off
2. take . . . back
3. take . . . out
4. blow . . . out
5. give . . . away
6. cheer . . . up
7. clean . . . up
8. worked . . . out
9. think . . . over
10. bring . . . up

◇ PRACTICE 11, p. 314.

1. off
2. out
3. up
4. up
5. over
6. up
7. in . . . down
8. out
9. down
10. down
11. up
12. up
13. up
14. up
15. out of
16. out
17. on
18. up
19. back
20. up
21. up

◇ PRACTICE 12, p. 316.

1.	a. up	2.	a. up
	b. up		b. up
	c. up		c. up
	d. out		d. up
	e. out		e. up
	f. out of		f. up

◇ PRACTICE 13, p. 316.

1.	out for	7.	through with
2.	in on	8.	out for
3.	up for	9.	back from
4.	along with	10.	out of
5.	around with	11.	up in
6.	out of		

◇ PRACTICE 14, p. 317.

1.	gymnastics class	5.	assignment
2.	their neighbors	6.	cord
3.	paint	7.	Hawaii
4.	rocks	8.	snakes

◇ PRACTICE 15, p. 317.

1.	out . . . about	6.	A: along with
2.	out for		B: out of
3.	back to	7.	over to
4.	out with	8.	around with
5.	away from	9.	over to
		10.	together with

◇ PRACTICE 16, p. 318.

1.	out about	5.	together with
2.	out for	6.	along with
3.	back to	7.	over to
4.	around	8.	out of

◇ PRACTICE 17, p. 319.

1. A	7. B	13. B	19. D
2. B	8. B	14. D	20. A
3. C	9. A	15. A	21. A
4. C	10. C	16. C	22. C
5. A	11. D	17. A	23. B
6. B	12. A	18. D	24. A

Appendix 2: PREPOSITION COMBINATIONS

◇ PRACTICE 1, p. 321.

1. of	6. to	11. with
2. to	7. about	12. for
3. to	8. of	13. for
4. with	9. from	
5. for	10. to	

◇ PRACTICE 2, p. 322.

1. B	5. C	9. D
2. F	6. I	10. G
3. J	7. A	
4. E	8. H	

◇ PRACTICE 3, p. 322.

1. at	6. for	11. with
2. at	7. for	12. to
3. in	8. from	13. with
4. with	9. about	
5. for	10. for	

◇ PRACTICE 4, p. 323.

1. A	5. B	9. A
2. C	6. A	10. A
3. B	7. C	
4. A	8. C	

◇ PRACTICE 5, p. 323.

1. A: with/to	6. to	13. about
B: about	7. for	14. with
2. for	8. of/about	15. about
3. to	9. for	
4. of	10. of	
5. A: in	11. for	
B: for	12. from	

◇ PRACTICE 6, p. 324.

1.	a. of	2.	a. about
	b. for		b. about
	c. of		c. of
	d. with		d. of
	e. with		e. of
	f. of		f. about
	g. in		g. for
	h. to		h. for

◇ PRACTICE 7, p. 325.

1. for		6. in
2. A: to . . . about		7. of
B: at . . . for		8. with . . . about
3. to		9. to
4. from		10. to
5. A: on		11. with . . . about
B: about		

◇ PRACTICE 8, p. 326.

1. arrived at		6. talked about
2. wait on		7. is leaving for
3. invited . . . to		8. is . . . staring at
4. consists of		9. helped . . . with
5. waited for		10. borrowed . . . from

◇ PRACTICE 9, p. 326.

1. for	6. A: to	10. from
2. with	B: for	11. like
3. to	7. about/of	12. about
4. at	8. for	
5. to	9. about . . . about	

◇ PRACTICE 10, p. 327.

1. G	5. B	9. E
2. I	6. H	10. D
3. C	7. A	
4. J	8. F	

◇ PRACTICE 11, p. 327.

1. on	6. to . . . for . . .	10. for
2. from	for . . . on	11. from
3. of	7. for	12. from/of
4. on	8. to	13. of
5. to	9. of	

◇ PRACTICE 12, p. 328.

1. a. C	4. a. X	7. a. C
b. C	b. C	b. X
2. a. C	5. a. C	8. a. X
b. X	b. C	b. C
3. a. C	6. a. C	
b. C	b. C	

◇ PRACTICE 13, p. 329.

1. on	7. about . . . from
2. to . . . about	8. about
3. to . . . from . . . by . . . by	9. A: from
4. for	B: from
5. A: about	10. about
B: with	
6. A: from	
B: to	

◇ PRACTICE 14, p. 330.

1. hoped for	5. concentrates on
2. wonders about	6. escaped from
3. divided . . . into	7. am accustomed to
4. add . . . to	8. heard . . . about

◇ PRACTICE 15, p. 331.

Correct (circled) prepositions:

1. to	8. like	15. with
2. from/of	9. to	16. to/with
3. from	10. of	17. about
4. with/to	11. about . . . with	18. by
5. of/about	12. of/about	19. on
6. of/about	13. with	
7. for	14. at/with	

◇ PRACTICE 16, p. 331.

1. D	7. B	13. B	19. C
2. B	8. B	14. A	20. A
3. C	9. D	15. A	21. B
4. A	10. C	16. B	22. B
5. B	11. D	17. C	23. A
6. A	12. B	18. B	24. C